SATURNALIA

MITYANA,
UGANDA

KAMPALA,
UGANDA

KIGALI,
RWANDA

ZANZIBAR ISLAND

DAR ES SALAAM,
TANZANIA

LUSAKA,
ZAMBIA

VICTORIA FALLS,
ZIMBABWE

GABORONE,
BOTSWANA

JOHANNESBURG,
SOUTH AFRICA

CAPE TOWN,
SOUTH AFRICA

SATURNALIA

*Traveling from Cape Town
to Kampala in Search of
an African Utopia*

JUSTIN
CHAPMAN

THIS IS A GENUINE BARNACLE BOOK

A Barnacle Book | Rare Bird Books
453 South Spring Street, Suite 531
Los Angeles, CA 90013
abarnaclebook.com
rarebirdbooks.com

Set in Goudy Old Style
Printed in the United States
Distributed in the US by Publishers Group West

Thanks to Mary, Adam, Roslyn, and Aaron for these chapter photographs:
"Banana Fiber Futbol" by Mary, "Unnecessary Strife" by Adam, "The Only
American" and "Escape from Guguletu" by Roslyn, "In Zanzibar Rainbows"
by Aaron. A special thanks to Adam for the cover portrait.

Africa map designed by Mercedes Blackehart

Publisher's Cataloging-in-Publication data:

Chapman, Justin.
    Saturnalia : traveling from Cape Town to Kampala in search of an African
utopia / Justin Chapman.
    p. cm.
    ISBN 978-1940207384

1. Chapman, Justin—Travel—Africa. 2. Africa, Central—Description and travel. 3.
Africa, Southern—Description and travel. 4. Heroin abuse. I. Title.

DT12.2 .C53
916/.04/3092—dc23

Dedicated to Galvin and Kelsey.

And to Mercedes for giving me a second chance at life.

"The person who doesn't scatter the morning dew will not comb gray hairs."

—Irish proverb

"Live as much as you can—it's a mistake not to."
—Lambert Strether, *The Ambassadors*

"I always went my own road and on my own legs where I had a mind to go."
—Joseph Conrad, *Heart of Darkness*

"For those who believe in God, most of the big questions are answered. But for those of us who can't readily accept the God formula, the big answers don't remain stone-written. We adjust to new conditions and discoveries. We are pliable. Love need not be a command nor faith a dictum. I am my own god. We are here to unlearn the teachings of the church, state, and our educational system. We are here to drink beer. We are here to kill war. We are here to laugh at the odds and live our lives so well that Death will tremble to take us."
—Charles Bukowski, *LIFE*,
"The Meaning of Life: The Big Picture"

(ALMOST) LOCKED UP ABROAD

"When a man gives up drugs he wants big fires in his life."
—Hunter S. Thompson

DURING MY FIRST COUPLE days in Africa, I was nearly imprisoned in a maximum security mental institution. The kind that a short, twenty-six-year-old white boy like me wouldn't survive in for more than a couple minutes, let alone long enough for some stiff from the American embassy to come save me.

I was already late to have breakfast with two friends I met at Riverlodge Backpackers, the hostel I was staying at in Cape Town, South Africa, which happened to be located on part of a compound that used to be an extension of Valkenburg, a notorious prison and nuthouse. In the nineties, the psychiatric hospital had been consolidated and reduced to nearly half its original size, but it still remained in operation. Riverlodge and a handful of other small businesses occupied the remaining decrepit buildings. It wasn't entirely clear where the institution ended and the tourist mecca began.

Cameron and Synnøve, a strikingly gorgeous blonde couple about my age from Australia and Germany, respectively, had just moved into their new apartment near Observatory Road, on the other side of the compound. It was a long walk around, and though I had been warned many times not to enter what was left of the Valkenburg grounds, I hated being late.

Before the consolidation, the building that Riverlodge occupied and the rooms rented out to travelers like me were used to house the black inmates. Apartheid-era doctors experimented with electroshock therapy on them before performing it on the whites in the other buildings on the compound. If these walls could talk, they would choke on their screams.

Behind Riverlodge and the mental institution sat Ward 20, a still functioning maximum security prison complex full of rapists and murderers. The entire compound was called Oude Molen Eco Village, a square neighborhood block of abandoned structures with broken windows and run-down apartheid-era buildings that had been inhabited for years by a variety of businesses, such as Riverlodge, a community pool, a café, a small convenience shop, a barber, a prop art shop, and its fair share of squatters. Roosters, chickens, horses, dogs, cats, and other animals roamed the walled-up neighborhood freely. Some windows here and there were smashed out, some had bars on them. One building still read Ward 22 on the side, rows of dark windows lining each floor. Barbed wire remained on some walls and fences. A haunting place that was trying to remain invisible while still catering to its various clientele, mostly tourists, and inhabitants.

I knew I was supposed to sign in at the front gate of the Valkenburg compound, where the businesses gave way to the hospital and prison grounds, but I decided to avoid that time-sucking mess and sneak around the back of Ward 20 and walk along the river full of stolen wall safes to a small opening in the wire fence that led to a narrow bridge. I crossed it and walked through the rest of the compound to the Station Road gate, just a couple blocks from where I was to meet Cameron and Synnøve. I asked the three guards there how to get to Observatory Road, and they immediately became alarmed and demanded to know who I was and what I was doing there. Did I check in at the front gate?

"...yyyes..." I lied.

They radioed the front gate and asked, "Did a young man with big black glasses and a light complexion wearing a black shirt and gray pants check in with you?"

"Negative, negative," came the reply.

Shit.

One of the guards said he had to walk me all the way back to the front gate and figure out the story.

"I don't know if you're a patient who has escaped or what," he said.

Fuck, I wish I brought my passport.

"Look, man, friends are waiting for me," I told him. "Is there anywhere I could buy airtime for my phone and let them know I'll be late?"

We stopped in a small shop in the middle of the grounds, but they only had Vodacom airtime, not MTN, which was the service I was using. As I was asking for airtime, however, I pulled everything out of my pockets: camera, phone, wallet, lighter, and cigarettes, making sure the guard could see. What escaped mental patient would have such items in his pockets?

It must have convinced him, because as we walked to the gate he basically gave me a free, guided tour of the compound, a service they would never have provided on request. We passed a ward with a yard that was surrounded by an electrical fence. About thirty patients roamed the open-air yard, one white patient sitting silent and still in the corner, not making eye contact with anyone.

"In this ward the inmates and patients fight each other every single day," the guard told me. "If I get a job inside the ward I couldn't wear a tie like this." He nervously stroked his striped, black and red state-issued silk fastened snugly around his neck. "A patient would grab it and choke me. If a patient attacks a guard, the guard can't fight back or he'll get arrested."

Once someone becomes a psychiatric patient, he explained, they become the property of the state of South Africa. Hitting them is like destroying state property. That label and protection continues to exist even after the patient leaves the hospital, and they know it. They use it to their advantage. They can fuck anyone up and no one can touch them.

The guard decided to tell his boss that I was just trying to visit the Environment Center, whatever the fuck that was, and that I didn't know the procedure. We reached the end of the bridge on the other side of the front gate and he talked to his boss. There was a good amount of arguing in Afrikaans, one of the local languages, which went right over my head. Finally, the guard and I turned around and headed back to the Station Road gate. The female guard there did *not* want to let me leave, and they argued in Afrikaans until the guy quietly said to me, "It's fine. Go."

I wasted no time booking it the fuck out of there, and downed a couple Valium as quickly as possible.

I bought airtime at the nearest store and called Cameron and Synnøve, an hour late. I met up with them at a café and told them the whole story over hot cocoa. We talked and smoked and ate and smoked.

"So what brings you to Africa, Justin?" Synnøve asked. It was a fair question. What is a young, white boy doing on the edge of the Dark Continent by himself, on the verge of thrusting himself into the mire?

Would I tell them the truth? I trusted them. They were among the first few people I had met in Africa, standing outside their tent in Riverlodge's backyard rolling cigarettes. I had befriended them immediately, and we spent many nights drinking and smoking and gabbing about the human condition and world affairs. Cameron, a thirty-year-old air conditioner repairman from Melbourne, and Synnøve, a constant student who was beginning two years at the

University of Cape Town, had met three years before whilst traveling in Cambodia. They had spent the last three years before the time I met them in Cape Town camping in various treacherous countries, such as Iran and Iraq. They weren't your average tourists.

"Well, I'm a journalist," I said, but I didn't tell them that I was also a heroin addict, and that Africa was about the only place in the world I could think of where I could get some respite and distance from a drug that was destroying my life. I told them half-truths. That I was going to write about a nonprofit organization called Art Aids Art that buys beaded artwork from women in a township in Cape Town called Khayelitsha. They sell the art in California and then reinvest the profits back into the township. I told them after that I had a vague and partially formed plan to take buses and trains all the way up to Uganda, picking places to visit along the way. There was a Catholic priest named Father Odo waiting for me in Uganda. He wanted me to teach English at a high school there.

"How do you know him?" Cameron asked, sealing his rolled cigarette with a quick lick. "Are you religious?"

"Not at all. I was raised Catholic, but that's about the furthest thing from who I am now. I know him through my mom. He visits her church every couple of years and fills in as guest pastor."

I told them that I had way too much stuff to drag across Africa with me. Most of it was books I had brought for the students at the high school in Mityana, a small town west of Kampala, the Ugandan capital. Cameron and Synnøve brought me to a post office nearby to see about shipping my excess luggage to Uganda, but the rates were just too expensive and even the post office employee told me the service was too unreliable. It could take three months for my bags to arrive in Uganda, if they did at all.

Cameron and Synnøve finally showed me their apartment, a very cool, cozy place on a quiet street in a quaint neighborhood, walking distance from hell on earth.

THE
ONLY AMERICAN

HAD BEEN TO EIGHTEEN other countries before this trip and I'd never seen so many people consistently chain-smoke like they did in South Africa. While leaning against a fence in one of Riverlodge's yards, I noticed a black South African kid about ten years old yelling a girl's name up to an empty window on the second floor. When he noticed me, he walked over. We were separated by the fence.

"Lemme get a loose," he said, which is slang for cigarette.

"I don't have any," I told him. He was fucking ten.

"I can see your pack right there in your pocket," he said, eyeing my pants.

I looked down and saw how obvious it was. I thought about it for a second, made sure no one else was looking, then handed him the rest of the cigarette I was smoking through the fence and told him to get lost.

"Lekker, man," he said, which means "cool." He went back to calling the girl's name.

. . . .

I WASN'T DOING THE trip sober; that wasn't even a consideration for me at the time. I told myself that as long as I wasn't doing heroin, everything else was fine. I had even brought a big prescription bottle filled with two-milligram Xanax bars—yet another drug that turned me into someone I wasn't—and popped two to four of them every day for the rest of the trip. *My addiction is opiates*, I told myself. *Xanax isn't an opiate, I'll be fine.*

I didn't yet know which route I'd be taking on my three month trip through Africa, what cities or even countries I'd be visiting, how I would get there, or where I'd be staying. Before I left for Africa I worked my ass off to save up money for the trip. Freelance writing gigs, manual labor, anything I could get my hands on. It was much more difficult than it could or should have been because I also had to support my habit. I had saved up just a couple thousand dollars for three months, and once I got back home I'd likely have no money left over. I had to make it last.

I contemplated the distance I had before me as I stared at a map of Africa on the wall next to the locked door that led to the hostel's bar. It was closed, so I went exploring.

Riverlodge Backpackers had an artistic and familiar vibe. All the room doors were painted with lions and sharks and elephants and other common African animals. Art adorned every wall of every corridor, from posters of jazz musicians from the thirties to the fifties, to ancient maps, to horns sticking out of the walls, to colorful cloths, to paintings of African women dancing.

My roommate, Willem, told me about the difference between "black" and "colored" people in South Africa, a distinction I was totally unaware of. He identified as colored, which is a term that comes with heavy meaning in the States. In South Africa, it simply meant someone of mixed ancestry. He looked black to me, but in South Africa blacks and coloreds did not get along. During apartheid coloreds were not considered white enough to avoid racial segregation, and now in the time of the African National Congress, they are not considered black enough to reap the benefits of majority rule. As Willem put it, they have been the real victims in South Africa's long and sordid history.

Most of the other tenants at Riverlodge were Germans who had driven their motorbikes all the way down from Germany. In fact, most of the white people I ended up meeting throughout Africa were German.

Still adjusting to African time during those first few days, I'd go to sleep at 5:30 p.m. and wake up just before midnight. Sitting on one of the many dirty but comfortable couches on Riverlodge's patio, I lit a cigarette and wondered why I wasn't dope sick. It had only been a few days since I'd last used, on the other side of the planet. Heroin withdrawals should have been fucking up my good time, but I felt fine. No vomiting, no shivers and chills up and down my spine, no aches and pains, no wanting to crawl out of my own skin. *What gives?*

Across the road in the dark I heard African voices as they boarded the early morning trains at Pinelands Station, as well as god knows how many roosters, which roamed the property, screeching for hours. It was still dark out. It had been a windy night. I was still trying to find the pace and rhythm of South Africa. I wasn't reeling from opiate withdrawal like I should have been, but the weight of the impending journey ahead of me, the implications of the possible scenarios that could unfold, and the consequences of my decision to explore unknown lands as a result of an unshakable addiction to traveling and dope overwhelmed my thoughts as the city began to stir from its slumber around me. There was no turning back now.

· · · · · · ·

AS OPEN MINDED AND progressive as Riverlodge—and by extension Cape Town and South Africa—first seemed, it was all still segregated. The black South Africans staying at Riverlodge and the white South Africans and Europeans hung out in separate groups. For the most part, I hung out with white people, though not always. Segregation was the natural rhythm of the place, and it was a struggle to overcome it. I hoped and suspected all that would change once I left South Africa. I suspected many things would change once I left South Africa.

I was the only American at Riverlodge, and indeed I had not met any other Americans thus far, though it had only been a few days. Being not only the minority, but the singularity, was not an experience I was used to in Southern California.

That night, my new group of European friends invited me out to the Cape Town Carnival. It was the first time I had taken the Metro train in Cape Town, and it was during hours of the night that everyone had told me to avoid. I never really understood how different a Metro could be from other cities until I rode the one in Cape Town. The trains in Los Angeles, New York, San Francisco, Paris, Munich, London—they're all more or less the same. But not here. For instance, in none of those cities would you see people holding the doors open as the train was moving to yell at people on the platforms, and then decide, "Hey, I'm gonna just jump off right here while the train is picking up speed." Trash floats freely among the very wide, mustard-yellow train cars (the outsides of which have been entirely tagged with graffiti), which rock back and forth. The schedules are unreliable, the ticketing process is confusing, and I could see how it'd be dangerous to travel alone on these fuckers.

We were supposed to get a ticket at the Cape Town Central Station from someone carrying a yellow machine, who we eventually found in the crowd, but he let the six of us (two German guys, Cameron, Synnøve, and myself, as well as a young, black South African who pretended to be with us) through the gate without paying, with the stipulation that we make up for the train fare by buying lots of drinks during Carnival. Seemed like a fair deal.

Cape Town was already a party town, but when Carnival went down, the city exploded. Put that many people together anywhere and the energy is bound to be electric. It wasn't just a parade—it was thundering music, it was outrageous costumes, it was a citywide extravaganza.

The five of us walked for what seemed like an hour into the city center, the smell of cooked meat and vomit lingering everywhere, 'til we found the parade: thousands and thousands of people packing the streets, watching the parade, walking in between speeding cars.

"It's a goddamn miracle that people don't get hit," I said.

"Oh, they do," Synnøve said matter-of-factly.

We watched several rows of dancers, wearing all kinds of headdresses and African fashion costumes, marching through the main street in front of and behind such Rose Parade-esque floats as a giant, spiky flower with a beautiful girl dancing inside, an acrobatic flamingo with a girl doing flips in the middle, and—by far the best—a giant alligator float with another gorgeous girl dancing in its open mouth as more girls carried the rest of the gator float, like a dragon in a Chinese New Year's parade, followed by an amazing drum section that had everybody dancing.

The five of us walked to Long Street, a famous party strip lined up and down for miles with bars and clubs and restaurants.

We found a table in a balcony bar overlooking the party and ordered a round of Black Labels, the local brew.

"Fuck, dude, I think I left my wallet in the toilet," I said to Cameron. I ran back to the dirty, tagged stall but it wasn't there. Luckily I had taken all IDs out and left them in my room safe (a locker) at Riverlodge, and put most bills straight in my pocket.

"Do you need me to cover you?" Cameron asked when I returned.

"No, thanks mate," I said. "I put the cash in my pocket. All I lost was that wallet and about fifty rand."

Fifty rand was about five US dollars.

We watched the street craziness below. The crowd had increased one hundredfold. People were watching from higher balconies as a thick sea of human bodies flowed through the streets. It was an African Mardi Gras. On the boulevard below, cars were zooming up and down Long Street, barely missing stumbling pedestrians. I flinched just watching the close calls.

Synnøve was telling us how Cameron was interested in having a threesome.

"I'm fine with that, but if he gets to have sex with another girl, I should get to also," she said.

"Well, sure, you'd get to have sex with her, too," I said. "I think that would be half the point."

"No, I mean I should get to have sex with another guy."

"Oh."

"What, why isn't that fair?" she asked.

Cameron didn't say anything, just took a sip from his Black Label.

I wanted to say, "I'd sleep with you guys," but I couldn't find the right words.

"You don't want to go down that road," one of the German guys from Riverlodge said to Synnøve. "He'll fuck some other girl, you'll fuck some other guy, you'll start keeping score and resenting each other and it'll just destroy the relationship eventually."

Once we left the balcony bar we walked back to the train, which was free to all passengers heading home from the Carnival. The five of us were the only white people on the train heading back to Pinelands Station at 2:00 a.m., and the train was packed with drunk Carnival-goers. We were so exhausted. Synnøve passed out on Cameron's lap and dropped a handful of coins all over the train car floor, grabbing everyone's attention. The train went silent. I looked around nervously for a second, unsure of what was going to happen next. Would the passengers make a mad dash for the money? After a few moments, a fellow passenger, a young black man with a gray hoodie, picked up the coins and handed every last cent back to Synnøve.

When we finally arrived at Pinelands Station and made our way to get off, every black person on the train (which was everyone—about one hundred people per car, and there were about ten cars to every train) started cheering and hollering and clapping for us and at us. They gave us a standing ovation. I wasn't quite sure why—because we made it drunkenly but safely home from the craziness of Carnival, because we were white—but I played along and cheered and applauded back at them.

POLITICAL AND ECONOMIC PRISONERS

A BOUT FOUR MILES OFF the coast of Cape Town lies Robben Island, Nelson Mandela's "home" for eighteen of the twenty-seven years of his prison sentence. Former South African president Kgalema Motlanthe and current president Jacob Zuma each spent ten years imprisoned on the oval-shaped island before the fall of apartheid.

For thirteen of those long years, Mandela was forced to work in a limestone quarry. The limestone was so bright that it blinded many prisoners, and from that time until his death no one was allowed to take a picture of Mandela with a flash because his tear ducts had dried out.

I had to see the quarry that nearly blinded the Black Pimpernel.

I took the train into the city center to go on the tour of Robben Island, Dutch for "Seal Island." On the train platforms during the day there were yellow-vested security guards everywhere. At night there was one, if that. Every one of them was black. In the evening if they decided to hop on the train, which was rare, it was interesting and somewhat unnerving to watch them pass me by with just a semicurious glance and then use their batons to not-so-lightly tap the seats to wake up napping colored passengers and check their tickets. During the day, depending on the line, the trains were packed to the brim with people. Personal space was not a consideration. As I stood with my hand on a pole for balance, a guy next to me leaned back and pinned my thumb to the pole for about two station stops.

I was usually the only white person on the train. I'd been told so many horror stories—by people who had actually been to Cape Town—that it was hard to know who to trust. I imagined getting mugged in broad daylight, and not just having my few expensive items like my camera and phone stolen from me, but also being beaten for no good reason. Would the other passengers be willing to save me if I were threatened or jumped? It was a common occurrence on the Cape Town Metro, so I was told, though I never saw any evidence of it. Africa was actually turning out to be a hell of a lot less scary than what I had been led to expect and fear.

· · · · · · ·

IT WAS HOT AS fuck, the sun shone brightly and the wind and clouds waited till evening to make an appearance. From Cape Town Station I walked through the city for about fifteen minutes, passing rows of makeshift shops on the sidewalks showing off all kinds of wares from fruit and vegetables, to cell phones, to African crafts like wooden elephants and facemasks. I passed people building the stage in Greenmarket Square for Wednesday night's free community jazz concert leading up to that weekend's renowned International Cape Town Jazz Festival, and people working on old, gigantic ships, until I reached the Victoria & Alfred Waterfront, which was awash with tourists and all the trimmings to go along with them. There was a tall Ferris wheel, fancy banks, expensive restaurants, helicopter tours, great white shark diving; all matters of Cape Town tourism that were absent in most other parts of the city.

I missed the 11:00 a.m. ferry to the island so I bought a ticket for 1:00 p.m. and walked around the waterfront. I found a reasonably priced bar by the water and ordered a Castle Lager, then watched all the faces go by: black South Africans, white Europeans on holiday, different African nationalities, all converging on the city shaped by two great oceans colliding.

• • • • • • •

IT WAS THE FIRST time I had been on this side of Table Mountain, and the first time I could see how long and flat the top of the mountain really is. Originally it was named Hoerikwaggo, coined by the San people.

With thirty minutes to go before the ferry began boarding, I sat on a bench in a half circle overlooking the water, next to a pole with a dozen signs pointing at and reading big city names like San Francisco and Paris and Sydney, along with the distance to said cities. As I watched the action unfolding around me whilst smoking a cigarette, a girl about my age sat down right next to me.

There are benefits and drawbacks to traveling solo: You're free to do anything you want without worrying about someone else's agenda, and at the same time it can get incredibly lonely if you're not careful. The latter point I needed to be particularly careful about. Boredom and loneliness were among the root causes of my addiction. Back then, if I didn't surround myself with people, my idle brain was the devil's playground.

There were plenty of empty benches around, and I was quite near the edge of this bench, so her taking a seat next to me startled me at first. She didn't say anything, just sat inches from me eating chips. I gave her a quick once over, and recognized instantly how cute she was, what with her curly, golden blonde hair. She had curled her hair just to visit Nelson Mandela's prison cell on Robben Island. I asked her where she was from. Her name was Alondra and she was from Germany, of course. We talked for a couple minutes and it seemed promising, as in perhaps a new friend that I could hang out with later.

She was waiting for the same ferry to Robben Island. When she was done eating her chips, however, she abruptly got up and said, "Okay, well, I'll see you later." It hurt more than it should've.

I watched a pirate ship full of tourists pass by and then walked over to the Nelson Mandela Gateway building to wait in line for the ferry. The boat had three levels: the first completely enclosed, the second with an inside and side balconies, and an open air upper level. I made my way up the stairs and as I rounded the last turn Alondra rounded the opposite turn. I was just a couple feet in front of her ready to go up the remaining stairs to the deck. We smiled at each other and a ferry employee informed us that there was only one seat left upstairs. I said, "Oh, okay," and turned to Alondra. "Go ahead," I motioned with my hand.

"Yah?" she asked. I nodded and she walked up the stairs. I eyed her legs as she went up, but at the top of the stairs she quickly turned her head to glance back down at me, catching me in the act.

I walked over to the side balcony, and about thirty seconds later the same employee told me one more seat opened up on the deck. I rushed upstairs, but the seat next to Alondra was already taken. I took the only unoccupied seat.

The rush of energy from standing at the front and top of the boat as it sped out of Table Bay and away from the mainland was exhilarating. The sun was hot and the wind was freezing, blowing my shirt and hair everywhere it could. Women wearing sundresses had to hold their skirts down because of the wind.

I could see the coast wrapping around land for hundreds of miles, with Table Mountain, Lion's Head, and Signal Hill jutting out of the city. Manmade landmarks were also unmistakable, such as the newly built, bowl-shaped stadium. I watched Cape Town spread out and disappear as Robben Island materialized on the other side of the boat.

The island was bigger than I imagined. It reminded me of Alcatraz: a foreboding, haunted island covered in succulents and rocks. As we started to leave the boat, Alondra and I walked down the stairs next to each other. I commented on the view and the boat ride, but she didn't respond, really. I watched her get on a separate tour bus, and I never saw her again.

Our tour guide asked where each passenger was from and then related that country to Robben Island's storied past and/or South Africa's liberation from apartheid. As the only American on board, he picked on me a lot.

We pulled up to a large cannon, which was built during World War II in case of a German or Japanese invasion. Unfortunately, the five cannons on the island weren't finished being built until 1947. The guide said he was assigned to take several dignitaries on Robben Island tours, including Mandela, German chancellor Angela Merkel, Bill Cosby, and Barack Obama when he was a senator getting ready to run for president. As they stopped at the same cannon where we were stopped, our guide said to Senator Obama, "Please, when you go back to America, don't tell Bush that we have weapons of mass destruction." Everyone on the bus laughed, and I could picture Obama's appeasing smile.

We passed a large thicket that was littered with countless bodies from over the centuries next to a leper graveyard. Male lepers were separated from female lepers, but where there's a will—and there is a fucking will, there's a way—and there is a fucking way. Forty-two babies were born of the leper colony, who were all immediately whisked away from their parents and brought to the mainland or abroad, never to see mom and dad again.

The guide, who was the first general secretary of the Western Cape region of Cape Town under Nelson Mandela and the ANC when his particular political party, the Pan-African Congress, was no longer a banned organization, took us to the limestone quarry where Mandela was forced to dig for thirteen years. We weren't allowed to get too close because it was blocked off, but I'm not sure I would've wanted to. It was bright enough from where we stood. I couldn't even imagine spending a decade inside that glaring, blinding hell. The prisoners' labor had gone toward making the roads we were driving on around the island.

We reached the first set of cells, which were large rectangular rooms and housed thirty inmates, including our guide who actually served time there as a political prisoner.

"The unemployment rate is forty-three percent in South Africa," the guide told us. "For every sixth visitor to Robben Island there's one job created. So thank you for coming."

He didn't want to be on Robben Island all the time, retelling and reliving his years of sadness and captivity. It was just a job. *He went from being a political prisoner held captive on Robben Island,* I thought to myself, *to an economic one.*

The resistance leaders were held in the maximum security building, separated in their own cells. When they used concrete during working hours, they would save the brown bags the cement came in and later use them as writing paper. They would pen political literature, which was then passed secretly to the prisoners working in the kitchens and then to the rest of the prisoners. The guide said there were four main activities that the prisoners would do when they were left alone by the guards: political education and analysis; stealing and reading newspapers;

cultural activities like dancing, songs of freedom, stage plays, and standup comedy; and literacy education, because about half of the prison's population was illiterate.

We walked through the maximum security wing and saw Mandela's former cell, a heartbreakingly small, plain space to spend the majority of two decades. If it wasn't the limestone quarry, it was this tiny, concrete box. Our guide had been told by Mandela, when he took him on a tour of the island on one of his fourteen trips back there since his release, that one of the hardest parts of his prison experience was not being able to see children, and that there was no way to explain how disheartening that was for him.

While I didn't doubt him, it was also very disheartening to see so many children still living in abject poverty in a liberated South Africa. The country had clearly come a long way, to be sure. But for millions of black South Africans living in townships, not much had changed at all. Mandela had always been an inspiration to me. He was a larger-than-life figure with a seemingly inhuman capacity for forgiveness and compassion. After nearly three decades in prison, longer than I had been alive when I visited one of his prisons, he negotiated with his captors to bring a peaceful end to apartheid and avoid a civil war that nearly everyone felt was inevitable. I didn't blame him for the dire economic situation most South Africans endured every day. Decades of apartheid left behind institutionalized racism and a systematic superiority/inferiority complex that kept the poor in their place and made upward social mobility nearly impossible. It was too much to overcome, even for someone of his stature and empathy. His successors didn't fare much better. Even during my visit, President Zuma was being heavily criticized for not doing enough to bring people out of poverty. My Riverlodge roommate Willem told me that the ANC would soon fall, and for that he couldn't wait.

HOME IN THE HOOD

THE MOST DEPRESSING AND unfortunate thing about the townships in South Africa was that they still existed.

The morning after Robben Island, I woke up to the incessant Riverlodge roosters at the break of dawn to visit the poor township of Khayelitsha. I hated the damn roosters, but it was just as well because I had to be at St. James Station, at least an hour away, by 8:45 a.m.

I downed a couple Xanax and headed out the door.

I was meeting members of the Altadena, California-based nonprofit organization Art Aids Art at their posh bed-and-breakfast. It's a fantastic group of people that has empowered women in Khayelitsha. I had written several *Pasadena Weekly* cover and feature stories about them and their artists for years. Hugh and Miriam, a married couple who founded Art Aids Art, were always good sources who tipped me off to great stories for the newspaper. They were one of the main reasons why I had bought a plane ticket to Cape Town.

We took two cars for the thirty-minute drive to Khayelitsha, home to 1,000,000 black people living in slums and tin shacks with very little, if any, electricity. On the way there, we passed what used to be the white beach, the colored beach, and the black beach. Now, after apartheid, anyone can go to any beach. Hugh told us about his near death experience on the very road we were traveling, where the sands blow onto the street. He was driving along and lost control of his car. He veered off into oncoming traffic then back towards the sand dunes where his car flipped three or four times. All the black people who witnessed it rushed to his aid, flipping the car over and rescuing him.

"If they had been white, they would've been like, 'What do we do?'" joked Hugh, who's white himself.

Khayelitsha was one of the biggest townships in Cape Town. Most of its residents came from the Eastern Cape, an area that's more veldt than urban. When we arrived, I expected more people to be wandering the streets, and there were a few, but it seemed mostly deserted. Mangy dogs roamed around. No one was letting them inside or giving them any love. Children also meandered about, unsupervised.

There were different styles of housing in the townships. Some were government-built and subsidized with satellite dishes on the roofs, and others were squatter shacks crammed together over winding hills, providing a picturesque view of a tragically beautiful way of life. Every one hundred yards or so by the highway, kids were playing soccer with whatever ball they could find. Township residents were very resourceful, the whole system very organized. They had what they needed to survive, but at the same time they couldn't afford to leave the township. They were trapped, but that created a sense of community I hadn't seen anywhere else in my world travels.

We arrived at enKosi eKuzeni (which means "Home in the Hood"), the multipurpose community center that Art Aids Art built and opened on World AIDS Day a few years before my arrival in the township. The two-story structure, designed by a group of Harvard students, includes an art boutique, tea shop, and bed-and-breakfast intended to draw in tourists to an area previously avoided due to blight and crime.

Here, formerly unemployed women learn skills and grow their businesses. The center promotes education and self-sufficiency, and serves as an oasis for families impacted by HIV/AIDS. The women of enKosi eKuzeni create beautiful handcrafted beadwork, from makeshift radios, to floral patterns, to shoes, to you name it.

Everyone there was so friendly and welcoming. Miriam, always a bundle of joy and love, started handing out condoms from a huge bag to all the women, and that was the real icebreaker. Several of the women were HIV positive. A few were busy cooking lunch for the group. It wafted deliciously throughout the center as I walked around and explored.

When I stepped outside for a smoke, three children ran up to the gate and started giggling and talking to me in Xhosa. They were wearing brightly colored sweatshirts and their teeth were all messed up. I couldn't understand most of what they were saying, but I took pictures of them and they let out the high-pitched squealing laughter of innocent, joyous kids. They motioned that they wanted to see each shot I took, and then laughed hysterically when I showed them, making fun of each other for how they looked in the photos. They were all smiles. Directly behind them sat poorly constructed makeshift shacks, their homes.

Before lunch, one of the women told her story about becoming a *sangoma*, or healer. Leona was a short, dark, portly woman who had to wear all white all the time. Everyone who wanted to listen to her story had to put a shiny coin into her cup. She would use those coins to buy beaded bracelets that signified different levels of achievement in the *sangoma* tradition. She couldn't physically touch anyone, ever, so she had a wand-like branch that she used to shake people's hands. The idea was that she had been chosen out of her living family members by her dead ancestors to be a *sangoma*, and had to leave the Christian church in order to do so.

"Everything I do is dictated through my dreams from my dead ancestors," she said. "They tell me what to do. I do not listen to the advice of living people. My dreams are very specific. I received instructions from my ancestors about where to find the person who would oversee my initiation ritual, in which a chalice of white brandy, a chalice of red brandy, African beer, and snuff had to be consumed. I told my ancestors that I don't drink or use tobacco, but they told me through my dreams that I must. If I resisted this path, life would be even worse than it already is. People I love would die, I would be fired from a job, if I had one, and wouldn't be able to find one, if I didn't, like that. I had no choice in the matter. My dreams told me not only who would administer the ceremony, a woman I had never met before, but also where to find her. I had to walk miles and miles for hours and hours to find this woman in a place I had never been. I found the exact woman the ancestors told me, through my dreams, was the right ritual host."

I stopped myself from rolling my eyes. Nothing I knew about the laws of physics permitted anything close to what she was describing. Nevertheless, the other half of me sat transfixed, hanging on her every word. At the very least, the story was this woman's reality. The more you know, the less you know.

Then, the ceremony. She told us goats had to be slaughtered as a sacrifice, the red and white brandy and African beer and snuff had to be prepared and consumed by her, and there was dancing and singing and music.

Leona said she was still in the process of becoming a *sangoma*. She was not yet allowed to heal others, but she received instructions from her ancestors through her dreams on where to find medicines that would "cure HIV and cancer" and on and on. For instance, she had a dream that instructed her to travel a great distance to find an orb in the middle of a dangerous river. This orb, she was told, would cure a number of diseases. Clearly the claim was false, and dangerously so. Blind faith in unsubstantiated, wishful thinking is always a lose-lose, in my opinion. Still, this woman was utterly convinced. Either she did have these extremely specific, behavior-altering dreams, or something else was going on. I suppose the reasons were irrelevant: she was gripped by this powerful source outside herself, and there was no reasoning with that.

I knew the feeling.

Leona talked about her "partner," a man she said was very understanding. But since she wasn't allowed to make love or even touch anyone, they could only talk and hang out. They never touched each other or kissed and they never shared a bed.

The poor woman. I would go mad with sexual frustration. There are some things I'm just not willing to give up.

There was hope for her yet, however. Once she becomes a *sangoma*, she could remain one for the rest of her life, or, as in the case of another former *sangoma* at the center who told me, after her "purpose" as a *sangoma* is complete, she can ask her ancestors if it is okay to return to the Christian church. The two *sangomas* I spoke with told me they preferred going to church.

Ha, I guess returning to the church means you can fuck again.

After Leona finished her story, lunch was ready. It was delicious and cooked with love in the heart of a township.

I don't know if Leona was one of the women who was HIV positive, but either way it was a possible reason for her supposedly unchosen calling. In a land awash in microscopic death, fabricated meaning tends to overrule common sense. Fear can make you compromise, and pull you out to sea.

CLOSE
CALL

THE PACE AND ENERGY of Africa is so much different than America. Buses and trains don't leave on time, people don't show up when they say they will, everyone has a different opinion about how far away things are or how long it takes to get somewhere, and you're expected to know how things work. The problem with the system in Africa is that there is no system. There is a certain warped method to the madness, but you must speak the local languages and live there a long time to really figure it out. There's a sense of liberation in this vastly different consciousness, but it can also be very frightening and confusing and uncomfortable a lot of the time, to those of us who are accustomed to arbitrary structure.

A writer from Oregon who had made a similar trip through Africa told me before I left, "Prepare to be bored a lot, frightened a little, and hopefully fascinated for most of the time."

Pretty accurate description of what I experienced.

• • • • • • •

THAT NIGHT WILLEM INVITED me to a poetry performance featuring a South African poet, a Dutch poet, and an English poet. The event was in Sybrand Park, Athlone, two stops away from Pinelands Station.

On the train there I was sitting in a car with about thirty people when one young, dorky, black South African wearing a cheap suit and tie boarded the train, along with his posse.

"Good evening everyone, may I please have your attention!" he stated. It wasn't a question, or a request. "I want to tell you about the glory of God!"

He went on and on about the word of God, about Jesus Christ, about depression and worrying about your future and money and corruption, performing a whole sermon right there on the train, belting out in a loud voice how "There is still hope, and that hope is having faith in the Lord." He wasn't asking for money, he just wanted to preach. Most people ignored him; others, like me, watched with curious fascination.

"It's not a religion!" he yelled repeatedly. "It's a relationship with God!"

I got off at the same stop as the young train preacher and his friends. I walked behind them out of the station, eavesdropping on their conversation as they hugged and high fived each other.

"Oh man, that was so exciting!" the preacher exclaimed. The others giddily agreed, gripping their bibles. "What a rush! Ah!"

As it turned out, I had left too late and ended up on the wrong side of the park after dark, carrying my video and digital cameras in my backpack. Not knowing the address, I had left Riverlodge for the fuck of it, for the random adventure. When I got to Athlone, I had to exit on one side and go through a sketchy tunnel that went under the street to the other side. As I walked through the streets not knowing what to look for, I knew that I was out of place. It was too dark. There was no poetry jam going on anywhere near this neighborhood.

"Excuse me, sir," I said to a man walking across the street. "Where is Sybrand Park?"

He pointed down a long, pitch black street, then looked me up and down and shook his head. "It is too dangerous for you to cross the bridge to get over there," he said. "Even here. These guys...they'll see you're white, you know. You should be very careful 'round here."

I made my way back to the Athlone train station, careful to avoid anybody and everybody, and listened to a man a couple blocks away sing a slow, loud, soulful African melody. It was the beautiful performance I had ventured out to hear. I eventually boarded a train heading back to Pinelands. I was alone in a car with one other guy, and when we stopped at Pinelands, I couldn't open any of the doors of the car. Frustrated and frightened, I sat down as the train moved on. I took out my video camera and took a couple of shots, but the situation was too risky to use the camera so blatantly. I got off at the next station, N'dabeni, and walked to the other side of the platform to wait for a train to bring me back to Pinelands. It was almost completely dark, one or two soft lights on the stairs. There was no one around.

I looked up at the stars, and over at the crescent moon and adjacent planet hanging low in the sky. It was late. I didn't know if a train was going to come back in the opposite direction to take me home. I listened to the crickets and electricity from the wires and towers over the tracks and people working in factories directly across those tracks, hoping no one else would join me on the platform.

Finally, a train came. The Cape Town Metro cars were either packed incredibly tight, with people hanging out the train doors or in between cars, or they were empty and dirty and eerie. This one was thankfully the latter.

We stopped at Pinelands and I was able to open the door this time. As I walked down the platform towards the stairs to exit the station, a teenager holding the car doors open looked at me and jumped off the train.

Oh boy. What's all this, then?

He ran in a circle in front of me and tried to jump back on the train while the doors were closing. He looked at me and we smiled at each other as he struggled to squeeze back through the doors, the train picking up speed.

It was time to move on.

"FUCK
THE MAYOR"

MY RESERVATION AT RIVERLODGE was due to expire in a couple days anyway, so I headed into the city to buy an advance ticket for the Shosholoza Meyl train to Johannesburg, my next planned destination. As the Metro pulled into the city center, the clouds poured over Table Mountain like a wall of water was falling down into the valley. At the same time, the setting sun broke through a portion of the clouds, making it look like a red hot volcano about to burst as we arrived in the heart of Cape Town.

I was heading back into the city anyway because of a free community concert that evening, a preview of that weekend's International Cape Town Jazz Festival.

I arrived just in time to buy my train ticket, as they were closing the gate behind me at the Shosholoza Meyl ticket office. The next leg of my trip secured, I walked to Greenmarket Square, a perfect square shape surrounded by tall buildings and laid with small bricks like something you'd see in Europe, and found a table with a view of the stage. Cape Town the city over was like that, an aesthetically pleasing mixture of Europe and California, making it one of my favorite cities in the world.

I ordered a Black Label beer at an outdoor café on the perimeter of the square. Before the concert began, guys wearing and controlling huge puppets that resembled different ages of black men danced into the square, followed by a band playing upbeat jazz. The eldest black puppet looked like he had been a drinker and a smoker all his life. A couple South Africans at the next table joked with me about the puppets' stereotypical appearance. The puppets were as big as two tall humans on top of each other. As an unsuspecting group of girls who hadn't noticed the puppets were walking into the square, one of the puppeteers swung his huge puppet arms around them, scaring the shit out of them. We were all in tears laughing. Random comedy is what makes the world go round.

When the music started, I decided to go into the crowd to dance. I hated dancing. I had always thought I was terrible at it. But *Fuck it, I'm in Africa.*

Maybe it was the Xanax and alcohol talking (as they so often did *for* me and *in spite of* me at the time), but I let myself go and danced, surrounded by black South Africans, many locals who couldn't afford the upcoming weekend's rather pricey Jazz Fest tickets. Before the last act the mayor of Cape Town came out, a small, wispy, old, colored woman who was part of the Democratic Alliance, the ruling ANC's rival political party. I'd say about eighty percent of the crowd loudly and angrily booed her. She said a few words that no one could hear and exited the stage real quick. The head of espAfrica, the event organizer, came out and said, "To all you who are booing...I'm apolitical. The mayor has done a lot to put this free concert on for you..."

The crowd hissed at him so he proceeded to give them the bird. The crowd returned the favor. The energy was getting uglier. Someone threw a shoe at the stage and a fight broke out in the crowd. I recognized my cue to leave. I made my way through the empty streets to the train station, but no trains were heading back to Pinelands that night. I called Cameron and begged him to come pick me up. Thankfully he agreed, otherwise I have no idea how I would have gotten home. I hadn't brought enough cash with me for a cab.

While I waited for him, I wandered the streets looking for a store that sold cigarettes. Everything was closed. The streets were dark and empty. The only people around were hobos. I walked to the median of Adderley Street, almost a highway right in front of the Cape Town train station, to have the last smoke from my pack. As I rounded a small wall, a horrible stench hit my nostrils before I could even see the homeless man who had decided to lay his head down in the middle of the road, this small space on the planet that he had claimed as his own for the night.

Cameron found me and we went back to Riverlodge, where we met up with Synnøve and listened to an older, white South African woman, Irene, tell stories. She lived in the backyard of Riverlodge in a large tent with her autistic son and worked at the backpackers to pay off her rent. She was a large, gentle, intelligent woman, full of outlandish tales. She radiated warmth and love, and she had a sonorous, ashy laugh that enveloped everyone in its path, though I could see the years of strife and struggle strewn across her tired face. She had seen some shit.

As she rolled yet another cigarette, she told us about the local prison and street gangs, the Number Gangs: 26, 27, and 28. If you go to prison in South Africa and are labeled a 27, you are considered a bitch to be used as a come dumpster for the other gang members.

"Your only hope of surviving a life of rape and degradation is to state from the very beginning that you're a *franse*, that you're neutral," she said in her deep, booming voice, marred by having smoked since she was nine years old. "For whatever reason they'll respect that."

Just a few years before, she continued telling us, the gangs hired people to break into houses near Riverlodge and instructed them to steal only wall safes. If it was a safe but wasn't attached to the wall, they left it alone. She didn't explain why. They would then transfer the safe to a meeting location where another person would take it to another meeting location where that person would pry open the safe with a crow bar and pay a kid twenty rand (about two dollars and fifty cents) to dump the empty safe in a reservoir that still existed on the compound.

"I was there, I watched the police raid the area one day to recover the safes," Irene said. "Police divers jumped in the water and brought out hundreds of safes. Most were empty, but the police found one that was still shut and cracked it open. They stole everything inside: gold, diamonds, you name it. When the police commander arrived, the other officers said that all the safes they pulled from the reservoir were empty. Crooked bastards."

This was the same river in the Valkenburg compound that I walked along to avoid going through the front gate, the day I was mistaken for an escaped mental patient.

"To this day, there are still some unopened safes in that reservoir," Irene continued. "Yeah, this place is pretty fucked up. You know, there have been people who hung themselves, right here in Oude Molen Eco Village. A couple of rapists, pedophiles, and murderers have also escaped from the next door maximum security prison, Ward 20. Some of them are still on the loose. Hell, back in the nineties, there were even people who drove into the compound to shoot up heroin."

My ears perked up.

"In the morning we'd find the junkies dead in their cars, needles still stuck in their arms."

I still hadn't told a soul I had been a heroin addict back home. They didn't realize I had come to Africa to get away from that shit. And yet there it was, happening just feet from my room, on the other side of the world.

ESCAPE
FROM GUGULETU

I HAD NOTHING TO DO one day, so while trying to escape the dangers of boredom I asked Willem to suggest something cheap and close by. He said I should check out Mzoly's, which he described as a place with a chill vibe in a township called Guguletu, where people looked after each other and *braaied* (barbequed—pronounced "bride"). I pictured fifteen to twenty people. Turned out to be thousands. As it so happened, a friend from Riverlodge, an outgoing girl named Roslyn, was going that day as well. The thirty-four-year-old was born in Zimbabwe but lived in London with her seventeen-year-old daughter, though she didn't even look old enough to have kids.

I made a deal with one of the backpackers at Riverlodge to drive us to Guguletu for fifty rand, about five bucks.

When we got there, it turned out to be yet another dirty, poor township, and we were greeted by two drunken guys fighting on a street corner. They were so drunk they could barely land any punches. A crowd watched them and laughed, until someone finally broke them up. The backpacker from Riverlodge let us out of the car, because when we got close to the legendary Mzoly's, the streets were so packed with people that not even motorcycles could get through. There were thousands and thousands of people everywhere, block after block, walking around and sitting in their cars or on chairs in the street next to coolers full of alcohol. It was more or less an enormous street party. The energy was rowdy and rambunctious.

We found a bar next to Mzoly's, an open-air lounge where people brought meat to be cooked, and pushed our way through to get some beer. Everywhere we went, we had to shove our way through. Imagine a sea of black faces, sprinkled with a few beautiful white girls (who were certainly not there to meet a short white guy like me). I did my best to look nonchalant, like I did this all the time, like I belonged there.

Roslyn and I met up with a middle-aged, balding man from the townships named Edgar who she had met at the free community concert at Greenmarket Square. He took us to the spot where his friends had a cooler and chairs on the sidewalk. We sat and talked and they gave me Jameson and Bells.

"This is a wild scene, man," I said to Edgar.

"Yep," he nodded. "This is black people chillin'."

We talked politics and the changing face of race relations in South Africa.

"The real change," he said, "is coming from the young people. Everywhere you look you can see young interracial couples and friends."

"Well, it seems this country is still in a transitional period," I said. "Not everybody gets along."

Edgar nodded and changed the subject.

We were sitting in front of the house of an old woman who had "adopted" Edgar and his friends and allowed them to set up there every Sunday. Several kids were running around her front yard and in her house. The old woman let us use her outhouse for a few coins.

"Hoekom is jy nie getroud nie?" she asked me.

I looked at Edgar.

"She's speaking in Afrikaans," he said. "She asked you why you're not married."

"Oh, because I can't afford a woman," I replied, which I certainly believed at the time.

Edgar translated for her and she laughed.

"Leuenaar!" she said.

"She called you a liar."

"No, it's true, it's true," I said.

The truth is that I was a drug addict and couldn't find a woman willing to put up with my bullshit.

We were having a great time until the sun went down. Once it got dark, the energy changed in an instant. I was still having fun, dancing with big African ladies with gaps in their teeth who wanted to take pictures with me. The original idea was that Roslyn and I were going to get a ride with Edgar and his friends back to Pinelands. However, once Edgar realized that Roslyn was not the kind of girl who was down to just up and fuck him, he and his friends said their car was full and tried to ditch us. I don't know how he came to that conclusion. Maybe he made a move on her that I didn't catch and she rebuffed him. One of his friends said he would help us find a cab and ride with us to Riverlodge. He slyly handed me a one-hundred-rand bill and whispered, "Just in case."

He helped us find two residents of Guguletu who said that no cabs came into the area, but that they knew someone who could drive us to a store just outside of town where we could catch a cab. They spoke to each other in Afrikaans, and Roslyn heard them say to Edgar's friend, "I knew you weren't going to stay with them the whole time."

I got the sense that a hidden conversation was going on, that these men were determining our fate. They would disappear and then come back with new information for us. I wondered if my presence was a liability or burden, or the only thing preventing them from raping Roslyn. Were they really prepared to murder a white tourist just to get their nut off?

They told us to wait in a *shebeen*, or unlicensed bar. We took one look at the unlit, sketchy tavern and said, "No fucking way."

I could tell Roslyn was panicking, and that's when I fully realized the shitty situation we had found ourselves in. All the nervous undercurrents came rushing to the surface. Edgar and his friends kept disappearing and reappearing. It was like they were keeping an eye on us, waiting til the remaining street party stragglers left.

Neither of us had airtime on our phones, so during one interval when Edgar and his friends disappeared, Roslyn borrowed some random dude's phone and called a cab driver she knew. At first the driver said he was in the city and that it was too far to come get us. Our options were running out.

"Call him again," I said.

Roslyn called the cabbie again, a last ditch effort before all hope was lost. If he didn't come get us, where the fuck were we supposed to go? I guess this time he could hear the desperation in her voice. He told us to wait in a small, unpaved petrol station a few blocks out of the main party neighborhood. We headed in that direction and Edgar and his friends joined us again. *Fuck.*

We didn't tell them where we were going. Just wandering. They walked with us.

Within twenty minutes the cab driver pulled into the station. Roslyn recognized him and bolted for the car.

"Hey!" Edgar yelled.

I was about ten feet in front of him. He looked at me and I turned and ran as fast as my little legs could carry me. The cabbie hit the gas and I jumped through the open back door as he sped out of the station.

I looked out the back window. Edgar and his friends were chasing the cab in the middle of the street, a stampede of rage. I gave the entire one hundred rand that Edgar's friend had handed me to the cab driver.

GET
DOWN

SLEPT ALL THE NEXT day, a slumber of relief. Roslyn and I didn't discuss what happened the night before in Guguletu. We didn't have to.

That night was the International Cape Town Jazz Festival, and she was the only other person I knew who had tickets. We went to the enormous convention center, where the Jazz Fest was held, together. I was glad to have a beautiful female companion, let alone any companion, on this journey.

She bought us tall cups of beer and whiskey, which we mixed together, and we visited the different stages. We saw Zamajobe, a South African singer; Steve Dyer, who put on a beautiful jazz performance where every instrumental song told an intricately woven story; Dave Koz with Patti Austin, an upbeat and surprisingly wonderful performance that finished with a cover of a Rolling Stones song; Alfredo Rodriguez, the only Cuban musician I'd ever heard or seen live; Atmosphere, the highlight of the night (a white rapper who I wasn't the biggest fan of, but several of my best friends were, and they would never hear the end of how I got to see him perform in South Africa); and Zakes Bantwini, a local favorite.

For the first few acts, we just sat and watched. They were low-key performances. During the Cuban set, Roslyn grabbed my hand and pulled me onto the dance floor.

"Okay, but I'm no good," I told her, resisting a little.

"Bullshit," she said.

I bopped back and forth, enjoying the beat. She laughed at me.

"Told you." But I kept going.

Maybe it was the alcohol, but by the time Atmosphere came on I was dancing with Roslyn without a shred of self-consciousness, an unusual occurrence for me. I grabbed her close and we threw our bodies around, letting the rhythm and the beat control our movements from within. It was a dance of relief. The fucking place was poppin'. Interesting how your inhibitions dissipate without notice when you're surrounded by the energy of another culture.

. . . .

ON MY WAY TO a family friend's house the next day, I didn't feel like paying the train fare. There was a woman at the ticket window at Pinelands Station, but she didn't notice me, so I just walked through and hopped on the train. *What's the point of buying a ticket if no one's going to check?*

I rode the train for an hour all the way down to Fish Hoek, an upscale neighborhood on the beach. The total opposite of the townships I had been spending time in. When I got off I had to go through a checkpoint and show my train ticket, which I didn't have. The officer was going to charge me something like ten times the price of the ticket.

"Look lady, there was no one at the ticket window at Pinelands Station, so I couldn't buy a ticket," I lied.

She called my bluff and phoned the station.

I stood there waiting and cursing myself as the phone rang. Of course the one time I said, "Fuck it," I actually needed a ticket to get out. I did not want to have to call Thelma, the family friend I was meeting who was waiting in the station parking lot, to bail me out. The ticket taker held the phone to her ear as it rang and rang and rang, until she finally hung up and let me through scot-free. I'm a lucky bastard.

Thelma was waiting for me outside the station. I had never met her before. She was a middle-aged, native, white South African who, along with her husband, had a mansion on the hillside and a wine cellar built into the mountain. She had been reading my blog about my African adventure thus far, which unnerved me a little. I wrote as if no one but me was reading.

I didn't tell her about my near-citation experience.

Our first stop was the beach. Kids were playing soccer, twentysomethings were playing rugby, beautiful blondes were sunbathing on their stomachs with their tops off, and the hot sun was shining bright. I went for a cool, refreshing swim in the Atlantic Ocean, close to where it meets the Indian Ocean. I heard the bay was full of great white sharks, and the water was crystal clear. So clear I would be able to see one coming, but by then it would still be too late.

"Are you going to go in?" I asked Thelma when I joined her on the shore.

"No, I can go anytime," she replied.

I motioned towards a group of black and white children playing in the water as I toweled off.

"Amazing, isn't it?"

"The country's changing," she nodded in agreement. "I remember when this used to be a whites-only beach."

She took me for a drive around the peninsula. We passed the famous Cape of Good Hope and stopped at an African bazaar on the side of the road. Thelma waited in the car while I perused their wares, which were animal statues advertised as native African creations.

"My husband thinks all the products come from China," she told me before I got out. I left my wallet in the car.

The men manning the tables hounded me to make a purchase. I kept saying I didn't have any money.

"What about your mother?" they asked, pointing to Thelma, waiting patiently in her car down the street.

When I got back in the car, Thelma said, "So, you managed to ward them off?"

"They're just trying to make a living like everyone else," I shrugged. "But no, I didn't buy anything. I'm on a budget."

On our drive we saw spectacular ocean and mountain views and baboons crossing the street and humping on the side of the road.

"Cheeky bastards!" Thelma exclaimed, accelerating away before I could snap a photo.

We stopped at an ostrich farm and two of the strange creatures came right up to me, their beaks inches from my face, looking into my eyes. They were much bigger than I expected, their white, hairy necks jabbing their inquisitive faces at me. Thelma and I passed Misty Mountains and Chapman's Peak, then drove through the small colored and black towns where the upscale Fish Hoek and Simon's Town got most of their cheap labor. I was a little embarrassed to be riding around in a BMW in Africa. I left America to get away from opulence.

I told Thelma about my love of traveling. Back in America, I shared, most people live in their own bubble and never venture out to see what the world is really like.

"Well, my husband and I definitely live in our own bubble," she replied to my surprise, "but we know that. It's certainly by design."

We arrived at Thelma's three-story home on the mountainside with the most exquisite view of the colorful bay. I met her husband and their friends, who handed me a beer and braaied us up a delicious meal as baboons yelped in the hills above. The sun set and the moon rose and the colors across the bay and hills changed every few moments, a painting slowly transforming before our eyes until it was swallowed up by darkness.

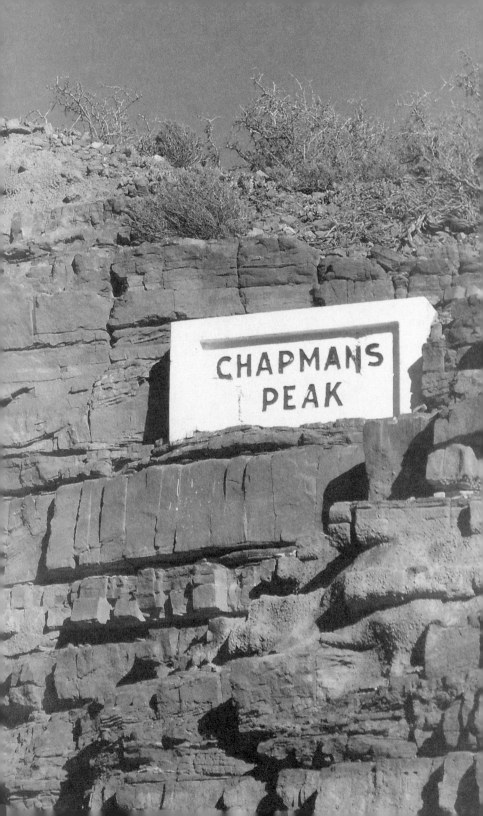

A MAP-TURNED-TO-LANDSCAPE

O N MY LAST FULL day in Cape Town, I woke up in Thelma's television room to a beautiful sunrise overlooking False Bay in Fish Hoek Valley. I realized I had left my bottle of Xanax at Riverlodge. Fuck. Could I even make it through the day?

Thelma prepared breakfast for the two of us and asked me about my relationship with God.

Oh, shit, I thought, put on the spot. *Here we go.*

"Is He your friend?" she asked, sitting across from me at the table holding a cup of coffee.

I didn't even know where to begin answering that question. I don't believe God exists, so how could he be my friend? Of course, the only reason she asked in the first place is because my blog implied that he was not. You don't ask a priest if Jesus is his BFF.

I tried to the best of my ability not to offend.

"Hmm, how do I explain my relationship with God? Well, first off, I don't see God as a human form, or a male for that matter. I have come to see it more as an energy that is unexplainable and incomprehensible to the human mind."

I told her I was raised Catholic but became an atheist in sixth grade, which lasted all the way through high school and then some. Over the previous few years I'd come to the conclusion that I couldn't say one way or the other if God exists or not, and I really didn't think anyone else could, either.

"So I suppose, for lack of a better term, I'm an agnostic," I continued, "because I can't be sure and because I've been *way* too fortunate and lucky throughout my life to disregard the notion that I have a purpose here, or that some force or other is looking after me. I guess that's the best way I can put it."

"That's a good way to put it," she said, surprising me again.

"I've always had a problem with organized religion, though," I continued, feeling braver. "I hate the idea of people telling other people that *this* is the way you *have* to behave in order to be 'right with God.'"

"Well," she replied, "just don't let other people distort or ruin the way you feel about God."

"I have definitely done that," I acknowledged.

"We all do."

She felt satisfied with the conversation, but I wasn't sure I did. Religion is, in my view, one of the most destructive forces to humankind. It was tragic to me that so much of Africa was awash in spiritual bullshit.

. . . .

THELMA DROPPED ME OFF at the cable car station entrance to Table Mountain and said goodbye. I was going to hike the top of Table Mountain. I thanked her for her generosity and hospitality. Through her I got to see a totally different side of Africa, and though I disagreed with her on the nature of life, she treated me with respect, brought me to the beach, drove me around the Cape, fed me, got me drunk, let me sleep in her hillside quarters overlooking a ridiculously gorgeous bay, and fed me again. Looking back, having to answer a couple questions about God was a small price to pay.

On the way to Table Mountain we passed through Chapman's Peak on Chapman's Peak Highway, a road carved into the cliffside of the mountain with overhead, arching rock tunnels and encompassing views. I felt a sense of pride seeing my last name etched into the side of a mountain on the southernmost tip of the Dark Continent.

There was a long queue to take the cable car up to the top of the mountain, but it moved fairly quickly. The cable car fit sixty-five people at a time, though it certainly didn't seem like it. The cable car itself spun internally so as we were pulled up the sheer cliff drop to the top, everyone inside got a 360-degree view of Cape Town sprawling out to one side and the Atlantic Ocean sprawling even further to the other side.

Most visitors stayed fairly close to the cable car entrance, which did have some amazing views, but I wanted to hike the entire length of the top of the Table. The more adventurous didn't even use the cable car; they hiked up the very steep and long path to get to the top. I saw several people complete the grueling hike, though they were too exhausted to give a shit about the view by the time they reached the top.

I was happy with the route I decided to take; I walked a total of about four or five miles, from one end of the Table top to the other and back again. I headed for MacClean's Peak, the highest point of Table Mountain.

I saw several species of animals during my hike. Apparently, lions used to inhabit this skyscraping stretch of earth until man drove them off. The top is not as flat as it seems from the streets of

Cape Town. I took one route along the Indian Ocean side, which was dry and arid. There were drought-resistant plants, rocks, moss, and small ponds in the holes of the cracked, rocky ground. Once I reached MacClean's Peak there was a big pile of rocks with a pole sticking up out of it. I climbed to the top of it and had a panoramic view around this mighty mountain. It was a breathtaking sight to behold. The rock formations were so intricate, the rivets and handles and steep, sheer cliff drops having formed over 600,000,000 years under the sea and weathered by wind and rain.

I ate my brown bag lunch at MacClean's Peak and took in the scenery. I could see Robben Island, which looked surprisingly flat and insignificant. I could see huge tanker ships, the V&A Waterfront, Cape Flats, Pinelands, Khayelitsha, Guguletu, Mitchell's Plain, St. James, Fish Hoek, the Cape of Good Hope, a few big fires off in the distance throwing plumes of black smoke into the sky, the whole city, and South Africa as far as the next set of towering mountains would let me. From all the way up here, I could see the horizon at the end of the ocean, giving me a perspective on the shape of the earth I'd never experienced before. That's how high I was.

The hike back on the Atlantic Ocean side was even more beautiful, if that was even possible. There were many narrow walkways made of cylindrical wooden planks and bars that stretched for hundreds of winding feet, followed by longer stretches of rocky paths. From up there, I really got a different, clearer frame of reference of the round shape of the earth, and how fragile we all are. The vertical and horizontal depth of natural and manmade monuments, a map-turned-to-landscape, this ball we live on, so big and so small, simultaneously. We're just hanging here in space, where everywhere is the middle of nowhere, and everyone is the middle of no one.

When I first arrived there were no clouds in sight. Just as I was leaving, a huge storm was forming out on the oceans, which looked like a giant tsunami of a wave rolling in towards Cape Town. The infamous, view-snuffing "Tablecloth" cloud cluster swept over Table Mountain as I swiftly made my way back to the cable car.

Thelma's husband picked me up at the bottom of the mountain and dropped me off at Cape Town Station. I took the train back to Riverlodge and immediately grabbed a beer at the bar with Cameron and Synnøve, who still loved hanging around Riverlodge even though they had their own apartment. I felt more at home at Riverlodge, back in my comfort zone. It wasn't the townships and it wasn't a mansion on a hillside. It was a happy in-between. Right where I belonged. I had no qualms about venturing out into the extremes, but I always wanted a comfortable, familiar place to sleep at night. A place where I wasn't suffering and wasn't contributing to the suffering of others.

But it was time for me to leave Cape Town and venture outward—this was only my first stop on a vast, aimless journey across Africa, after all.

THE AFRICAN
DARJEELING LIMITED

TRAVELING IS ALWAYS SAYING goodbye to people.

My train was departing midmorning, so I ate a quick breakfast with Cameron, Synnøve, Irene, and Roslyn at Riverlodge.

"Where are you off to next, Justin?" Roslyn asked.

"Johannesburg."

"Be careful there, mate," Cameron said. "That place is no joke."

"Yeah, I know, but that place is only one of my worries. I'm mostly worried about Zimbabwe. And knowing my luck, when I get to Uganda I'll run into fucking Joseph Kony."

Kony, the leader of the Lord's Resistance Army which had been kidnapped children in northern Uganda and turning them into child soldiers for nearly two decades, was all over the news at that time.

"If you do, don't mention my name," Cameron said. "Seriously, be careful. I don't want to see you on the news as that creep's hostage."

After breakfast, I went through my stuff to see what I could discard or give away to make my load a little lighter: not much. Mostly clothes, which I gave to Irene, who I knew would put them to good use. I had taken a couple pieces from her loaf of bread in the pantry without asking, so I figured I owed her.

She had told me a story a couple days before that at one time a lot of food was being stolen from the fridge, so Riverlodge's owner put strong laxative in a chocolate cake. When some tenant started throwing up and shitting left and right, they identified the food thief and kicked him out.

I said goodbye to my hodge-podge of unlikely friends, all of whom I had grown quite close to in less than two weeks.

"Bon voyage!" I said to Cameron and Synnøve, who were about to leave on a trip to Kruger National Park in their new car. I envied their life.

"Merci! Be safe!" Synnøve said, giving me a hug goodbye.

Traveling is perpetual farewells and meaningful connections cut too short. You meet people who contribute so much to your adventure wherever you happen to be visiting, as well as to your experience of life itself, then get sucked away into the eternal void of time and distance, never to be heard from again, never to contribute to the extent they truly could have, which is immeasurable. How curious and ultimately dispiriting the circumstances surrounding traveling and meeting friends, experiencing things you would never experience with anyone you interact with on a regular basis back home, and then having to depart abruptly, probably never to see or speak to them again.

Take the lessons you can get as they happen, and forge on. Life is hurrying up.

· · · · · · ·

As I was walking to my room to gather my shit, I passed a drop-dead gorgeous blonde Brit sauntering through the hallway in her bikini. *Good lord.*

"Good morning," she said, smiling at me.

As she passed, I turned and watched her ass as she walked down the hallway. Hers was the perfection of tried-and-true beauty, the kind of confidence that one could strut through that hostel with while leaving very little to the imagination, like she owned the fucking place—and she did. She made everyone she glanced at feel special, and brightened all of our days. *Jesus put her on this earth to prove to us that he loves us.* A lovely visual send-off.

I dragged my heavy bags full of books for unknown students in some village in Uganda across the street to Pinelands Station. It took every ounce of my energy to pull those fucking bags up and down the stairs several times, missing a couple trains each time. Furious and exhausted, I finally got on the right train. Sitting on my bags in one of the cars, a local silently handed me pieces of candy.

I got to Cape Town Station and waited on the platform for the Shosholoza Meyl train to arrive. It was going to be a twenty-eight-hour trip. The name Shosholoza (pronounced "show-shuh-LOH-zuh") comes from the title of a popular South African song about workers on a train and moving forward, and Meyl (pronounced "may") means long distance train.

When the train did arrive, I had to board the third-class section and shove my way through a frantic, scrambling crowd of people to find a seat. Fortunately, I sat next to a very nice, skinny, twenty-seven-year-old black South African named David, who was training to become a firefighter. I was starving and thought I only had thirty-five rand (about three bucks) for the entire twenty-eight-hour trip, so David kindly offered me bread, French fries, juice, and a piece of KFC chicken—the first piece of meat besides fish I'd eaten in almost a decade. I knew from the beginning that I would have to eat meat in Africa eventually, and with only thirty-five rand for a trip that would last more than a full day, I just couldn't refuse the generous offer.

The train was packed, with people sitting on the floor and standing in the small smoking sections in between cars. Everyone in my car had been drinking since 10:00 a.m. or earlier and was singing and dancing nonstop—and I mean pounding the windows and walls and stomping and clapping and really belting it out. David said they were all Christian songs, and that they never repeated a single song for the hours upon hours that they carried on like that, turning the train into their own cathedral full of a jubilant and thoroughly drunk congregation. It was exciting and vibrant and made them happy, and I enjoyed every slap on the wall, every beautiful, fat African woman dancing, every unique note from their soulful vocal chords. But by five in the morning the next day, it got a little tiresome, to say the very least.

· · · · · · ·

WE EXITED THE CITY and passed townships, and empty fields, and farms, and train stops, and mountains, and abandoned buildings.

Luckily, whilst desperately digging through my backpack, I found 300 rand (about thirty bucks) I had tucked away in my money belt earlier for safekeeping. I decided to buy beer and dinner for David and myself in the dining car. How I forgot that I had stored away the money there is beyond me. *Oh right, it was probably the Xanax I was swallowing on a daily basis.*

There we were: A black South African and a white American sharing a meal together as the train rolled along. We passed the time by listening to music on my laptop, each using one of my earphones. He bobbed his head in rhythm to Bob Marley and Modest Mouse like he'd never heard them before.

"I am so glad I met you, Justin," he told me. "I cannot wait to tell my friends."

All around us the passengers permeated the train with utter craziness. Police and security walked by every now and then, but they did nothing to stop the throngs of drunk men fighting each other, screaming at the top of their lungs almost as consistently as the singing and dancing women, accidentally kicking beer cans down the aisle as they stumbled by.

I smoked in the filthy bathrooms, walked up and down the train, ate in the dining car, and sat and watched the veldts of South Africa fly by out the windows. After a full twenty-eight hours on the train, I was grateful to arrive in the sprawling, filthy, crime-ridden city of Johannesburg.

JOBURG

A SHITHOLE OF A CITY and one I never want or need to see
again.

Johannesburg is a large, sprawling metropolis, trash
everywhere, throngs of people flooding the streets and selling
their wares and creating a violent pulse that no one needs to
experience. That's not to say I had a bad time—far from it. In
fact, it was basically a four-day party. I quickly made friends with
three guys who were staying at the same backpackers as me,
Sleek Hostel. They identified as colored and lived in a township
in Cape Town. Mitchell's Plain to be exact, near Mzoly's in
Guguletu. I told them about my close call there, how Roslyn and
I almost got stranded.

"Promise me you will never do anything like that again!" Paul,
one of the colored guys, told me. "You're very lucky to be alive."

These guys, who said they were former gangsters but now
had wives and children, took me under their wing immediately.
Every day we'd wake up and start drinking and smoking and
braaiing and listening to music through my laptop. They didn't
care for most of my music, not even the reggae. They preferred
hip-hop, though they did enjoy UB40. "Red Red Wine" came

on and joy filled their faces. We'd do this until late at night, then wake up and start all over again. If we needed to sober up, we'd just jump into Sleek Hostel's freezing-cold pool.

Paul taught me a specific handshake that varied across Africa but was distinct from handshakes in America. You start by shaking the person's hand, then you swing your fingers slightly towards the other person to interlock thumbs, then you slide your hand back and catch each other's fingers as you snap thumbs over the clasped fingers as if you were thumb wrestling. The further north I traveled, the quicker the handshake became. In Uganda, it consisted of a regular handshake followed by thumb-snapping.

The gangsters-turned-family-men were electricians, and had traveled from Cape Town to Namibia and Botswana on business. They were resting in Johannesburg for a few days before heading back home. One night we went out with three local black girls they knew who said there was a party nearby.

"We're going to fuck these girls, J," Paul said to me in that way some men talk to each other when women aren't around, with a shit-eating grin on his face. I nodded and shrugged. *Don't you have a wife and kids at home?*

"Okay," is all I said. I was just along for the ride.

We picked up the girls in their utility truck, which sat two people in the cab. The rest of us had to cram into the covered bed, which was full of electrician's tools. There were five of us back there, lying sideways, with sharp instruments sticking into our sides. Very romantic.

Before going to the party, the girls asked the electricians to drive them to a friend's house. As it turned out, they had us driving from one place to another for hours. Each time the girls were meeting someone or picking something up. Eventually we ended up at a bar, which turned out to be owned by the girls' friend, and they suggested that we buy some wine there. The electricians were furious.

"You see what these fucking black girls did, man?" Paul said to me as we drove away. I didn't say anything, just let him rant and vent. "They knew the whole time there was no party. They just got a free ride from us to do all their little errands, and now they want us to buy wine from their friend's bar? See how deceitful they are? Fucking black bitches..."

· · · · · · · ·

THE BACKPACKERS' INTERNET WAS out, so I walked up to an Internet café to book my bus ticket to Gaborone, the capital of Botswana. I planned on staying there one night and then heading into Zimbabwe and up to Victoria Falls. My debit card didn't work online for some reason, so I had to catch a minibus to Park Station in the center of the city, where the Intercape Bus ticket office was located, and buy my ticket in person.

I walked through several blocks that were essentially closed to vehicles because there were so many people walking around and setting up shop in long rows in the middle of the road. The bus ticket was more than I expected, leaving me with only two rand (nineteen cents), not enough even for the cheapest mode of transportation in South Africa, the minibus, which was four times as much as I had, to get back to the backpackers. In what was turning out to be a recurring theme, I had also forgotten my cell phone at the backpackers. Of course, it didn't occur to me that maybe I was being so forgetful because I was taking too much Xanax. *If anything*, I thought, *I'm not taking enough*. I had no choice but to walk all the way back, about ten miles or so, through smelly, dirty downtown Joburg, passing smelly, dirty open-air markets packed with people trying to sell me shit I didn't want and couldn't afford. I ventured out of the downtown area with a vague sense of which direction the backpackers was located. The sooner I started walking that way, the quicker I'd eventually get there. I passed construction sites, parks, the Joburg Zoo, and a very wealthy neighborhood where every mansion and property had electrical fencing to keep the riffraff and ruffians out. Along the way, there were headlines of various newspapers posted to phone poles that read shit like, "Waitress Stabbed in Joburg Eatery."

By the time I got back to the backpackers, I needed a beer and a swim. I found the gangster electricians and told them what happened.

"Justin, why do you keep doing dangerous shit?" Paul asked me. "You should have just called us, man! We would have picked you up."

"I forgot my phone, otherwise I would have," I said.

They just shook their heads.

"That was a dangerous thing to do, my man, walking all the way through this city by yourself like that," said Paul.

"I didn't have any other option," I replied. "Anyways, I didn't have anything of value on me."

"Doesn't matter. In Joburg, strangers looking to rob you will just beat the shit out of you and then find out that you have nothing worth taking, and leave you there. Straight up."

The next day Paul suggested I go to Lion Park, a lion wildlife conservation, instead of the zoo like I had planned, which he said was for kids. I took a minibus to the outskirts of Joburg and walked to the entrance of the Lion Park game reserve. The ticket for a guided tour was more than I thought (225 rand) and I only had 200 rand plus another ten to take the minibus back. I was *not* walking back this time. Luckily a very generous Argentinian woman next to me overheard my dilemma and offered to pay the twenty-five rand difference for me and told the ticket seller that I was with her group. I thanked her profusely. As I walked to the open-air caged bus, I joined a crowd watching a half-naked African dance troupe in traditional garb thrashing their limbs and torsos around in perfect, spiritual time with two bongo drummers.

We drove around the park in caged buses and saw zebras, giraffe, wildebeest, springboks, antelope, several species of birds, wild dogs, cheetahs, and lions, just a few feet away from us. At one point the bus driver joined a big circle of cars and parked the bus. People sat in their idle cars, surrounding a large patch of grass, and waited.

Finally, a pickup drove through with a man standing in its bed, covered by a cage. A pride of white lions chased the truck, running in between all the cars, lunging at the thick hunks of meat that the guy from the back of the caged truck threw out to them.

ZIMBABWE
THE HARD WAY

WHEN I LEFT SOUTH Africa I was planning on heading into the country I was the most nervous about: Zimbabwe. The place had a corrupt president, a tanked economy, a defunct currency, a murderous energy, and racial tension up the wazoo. But fear hadn't stopped me so far. It wasn't like I could go home.

I took a bus from Joburg to Gaborone, and sat next to a polite Serbian gentleman who gave me his Botswana SIM card for my African phone, just in case. In Africa you need a different SIM card each time you enter a new country. I was only staying in Gabs for one night, but you never know.

People seemed to just be giving me shit and helping me out left and right. Before I left the States, when I was doing research to prepare for my trip, I reached out to a writer from Oregon who had made a similar trek twelve years before. He was massively helpful and gave me an idea of what to expect. On his website there was a picture of a kanga (colorful cloth from eastern Africa) with a Swahili slogan that translated to "Money in your underwear, a weapon in your hand." I brought it up to him, mentioning that I was a small guy who looked a lot younger than twenty-six.

"I looked a bit young as well," he wrote. "Had conversations with folks who didn't believe I'd finished high school. The advantage of that is that expats might feel sorry for you and offer to host you. Worked for me."

And that's exactly what happened, time and time again. What little people had, they shared.

At the border I met an American student. She was from Richmond, Virginia, and was studying abroad for a semester at the University of Botswana. As we waited in line in the customs building, I told her what Paul had said about muggers in Joburg beating you up before they even know if you have something to steal, and she told me she had been mugged in Botswana.

"This guy approached me on the street and basically said, 'Okay, this is how it's gonna go. I don't want to hurt you, so give me your laptop and your money.' I told him, 'Fine, but I really need some of this money to get home.' And no joke, he said, 'Okay, let me give you change. How much of this bill do you need?' I was being mugged, but it was like a negotiation!"

In Botswana I basically only got to sleep for a few hours before it was off to the Zimbabwe border early the next morning. I took a minibus to the border. We had to stop periodically to let donkeys and cows move off the highway, I shit you not.

Botswana is a beautiful country, and I wish I could have stayed longer, but I was on a tight schedule and an even tighter budget. I had to keep moving.

At the Zim border, I had to go through customs and immigration. It was a small, square, brick building in a clearing in the jungle. Inside, customs agents sat around, bored as fuck. I had to pay thirty dollars for a visa just to enter the country, which turned out to be on the cheaper side for visas. I paid the money and the agent issued my visa sticker, which took up a whole page in my passport. I walked outside and asked a Zimbabwean standing there how to get to Bulawayo, where I needed to buy my overnight train ticket up to Victoria Falls in the northwestern region of Zimbabwe.

"Well, I have a ride coming and we're going to Bulawayo," said the man, who was wearing a tweed jacket and had a calm energy. "It's probably better to wait with me than go outside the gate and be surrounded by vultures."

He motioned to the swarm of unlicensed, sketchy taxi drivers waiting outside the customs property fence. I decided to stay with him.

He was a professor of sociology at a university in Zim. We talked about the political and economic situation of the country, and how Zim was using US currency because their old currency was useless. At one point, everyone in Zim was a billionaire, and the minimum amount one could withdraw from a bank per day was 1,500,000 Zim dollars. People would bring wheelbarrows full of cash to the market to buy milk. When I talked to him, he told me no one trusted the banks, and everyone was waiting for the unannounced deadline when Zimbabwe would have to stop using US currency.

I have to admit, it was comforting, though also unnerving, to be able to use American currency in the middle of Africa. I didn't have to deal with math, but it also pointed out to me how pervasive American influence and control truly is.

Finally, the van we were waiting for arrived, and we crammed our luggage and ourselves in along with nine other people and their luggage. It was a very tight and uncomfortable fit. There was no room to put on our seatbelts. Third world problems.

After we passed the first gate, a few of us had to get into a taxi to pass the vehicle inspection up the road in a town called Plumtree.

After that we all smooshed ourselves back into the van and began speeding along the road, which was undergoing construction, so cars had to veer into the oncoming lanes in order to get by.

Not five minutes past the border, I was asking the professor his opinion on President Robert Mugabe when a car slammed into us from the right side, just inches from hitting us head on. The car spun for what seemed like ten minutes and one second at the same time. We had been going fifty or sixty miles per hour. I felt the wheels on the left side of the car lift up as we did a 180-degree turn, and I thought for sure the van was going to flip over into the bush. To my surprise, the driver managed to bring the van to a stop. Everyone immediately scrambled out of the vehicle. The windows on the right had shattered in our faces, but it wasn't until I got out that I realized there were tiny shards of glass in the hair on my head, on my face, the hair on my arms, in my shoes, in my pant cuffs, and all over our luggage inside the van. The car that hit us was at least 300 feet down the road, having landed in the bush. About eight or nine people quickly got out of that car, too, one being a mother holding a baby. Both cars were done. The side of the van was completely smashed in.

"Hey! Help me out! Get me out of here!"

In our haste to exit the van we forgot about the guy in the very back, covered from view and prevented from getting out himself by luggage. He was panicking.

It was amazing that no one got hurt, especially the girl who was sitting to my right. She was closest to the point of contact and the right-side window had shattered directly in her face. It was a terrible crash, the worst I'd ever been in, and certainly a near-death experience. Had that car been just a couple inches to its right, the driver would have been killed, and I would have gone flying through the front windshield.

"Welcome to Zimbabwe..." the professor said to me, grinning. "Holy fuck," I said.

After we made sure no one was hurt, the professor flagged down a truck and asked for a ride for him and me to Bulawayo. As the driver of the van was screaming and yelling at the people from the other car (it *was* their fault), the professor and I grabbed our luggage out of the van, glass falling everywhere, and ran for the truck. We hopped into the bed, which already had a couple people in it, and sped away. Still shaken and shocked, we sat mostly in silence for the drive to Bulawayo, grateful to be alive, and watched the small villages and animals and people in the middle of nowhere fly by.

When we got to Bulawayo, I said goodbye to the professor, we two strangers who had experienced something together that we'd never forget as long as we lived. I dragged my heavy bags to the train station where I bought a second-class ticket, and got some beers, and played pool with four young German guys who were taking the same overnight train to Vic Falls.

I wanted to buy a first-class ticket, but they were all sold out. I did not want to repeat the sleepless experience of the Shosholoza Meyl. I felt terrible for the unlucky bastards who were stuck in third class, and recognized how lucky I was that I could afford to ride in a car where I was treated like a human being. I was grateful to have experienced third class, but once was plenty.

The Germans' sleeper cabin was right next to mine, and while I did spend time with the Zimbabwean and Zambian guys in my cabin, I was able to drink and smoke and listen to music and talk and stay up late with the nineteen-year-old German guys next door.

The wood-paneled train was built by the British in 1952. There was no electricity, so it got very dark at night once we left the city of Bulawayo. We had to fetch a candle, which we put in an empty bottle of Black Label beer. There was no toilet paper in any of the restrooms, which was very frustrating. The bottom of the toilet opened up to the tracks below, so everyone's shit and piss and shit-stained toilet paper (if they had brought their own) fell down below the train as we sped along.

My bed's foam mattress had a big hole ripped out of it, so I had to stuff it with a couple shirts and use my jacket as a pillow. The loud, cranky, swaying train made it difficult to get some rest. I was running on empty, so naturally I popped some Xanax. I was running low on the pills, and worried about what would happen when, not if, I ran out. Benzo withdrawals can be nearly as gut-wrenching as opiate withdrawals.

In the morning, I ate breakfast in the dining car, listening to the cook play Bob Marley's "Three Little Birds." I sat in an open door and watched the jungle landscape of Zimbabwe fly by. That part of the country, at least, looked a lot like parts of Jamaica. I could see the connection.

"Don't worry about a thing / 'Cause every little thing gonna be alright..."

The train pulled into Vic Falls, a small but touristy village not too far from the actual Victoria Falls, the massive waterfalls I planned to visit the next day. Each backpackers I stayed at throughout Africa had its own cool style, but Shoestring Backpackers was one of the most unique and artistic. It was shaded by huge trees and surrounded by stone walls with colorful murals. It was basically a jungle art garden, with a pool, and a bar, and a restaurant, and a massage parlor.

I stayed in a room with a blonde girl (just my type) from Amsterdam named Norma, who was in her bikini when I first arrived. I instantly started flirting with her. We talked about the new law in the Netherlands that only allowed citizens to buy marijuana (and no longer foreigners).

"I'm sure there will be some coffee shops still selling to tourists," I said.

"Of course," she replied. "That'll never work. It won't stop them."

Then the four German guys from the train showed up and checked in, and coincidentally ended up in the same room as Norma and me.

"Justin!"

"Hey guys!" I said.

"Let's go get drunk!"

Before we grabbed a beer they left to rent a car and visit Victoria Falls, and I went into town to see if my debit card would work there, which, thankfully, it did. After I left the bank and started heading back, I was swarmed by locals trying to sell me their wares. I bought some old Zim dollars (including the highest and rarest one, a 100,000,000-dollar bill) from before they switched to US dollars. I told the rest of the hagglers to fuck off all the way back to Shoestring.

RIVER
RAIN

PART OF SHOESTRING BACKPACKERS, where the lounge, and pool table, and restaurant, and bar were located, was open to the public. By nightfall, many local white and black Zimbabweans flooded the place. That night, I joined the Germans there for pizza and beer.

The party was hoppin', and we heard that President Mugabe, a corrupt, murdering, dictatotorial piece of shit, was in a hospital in Singapore. We all got very excited, and pondered the idea of being in his country when that fucker croaked.

"We'd be part of history," said Ricardo, one of the blonde Germans. "Like the people who were in Berlin when Hitler died."

I was a little taken aback to hear that come out of a young German.

Ricardo and I went up to a white Zimbabwean to ask for details (it was illegal to talk shit about Mugabe).

"Mugabe has genital cancer," said the white Zim, who was either thirteen or thirty years old—it was hard to tell. He meant prostate cancer. Ricardo and I cracked up at the verbal faux pas.

"What do you think'll happen?" I asked.

"I don't care what's happening with Mugabe," said the ageless white Zim. "Everyone's just waiting for him to die."

"Who will take over if he dies?"

"The prime minister," came the obvious answer. He wasn't as interested in the conversation as Ricardo and I were.

Morgan Tsvangirai, Zimbabwe's prime minister, was a political rival of Mugabe and helped to form the ineffective "unity" government after he won the last election a couple years before, but hadn't received enough votes to beat Mugabe outright (if the election results were to be trusted).

"What would happen tomorrow if Mugabe died tonight?" I asked.

"We'd all be fucked," he said matter-of-factly, and we didn't know if he meant everyone in the country or just white people. "There would be a civil war and the country would go under military rule."

That took the wind out of any notion we had to travel to the capital, Harare, to see what would transpire if that old fucker breathed his last. What a scary adventure that would be, and one I would feel compelled to undertake as a journalist.

Once the bar closed down the Germans and I walked around the corner to another bar, and about ten or fifteen people who were partying at Shoestring followed a few minutes later. We danced and talked to a few locals (a couple of whom were willing to discuss politics—a rarity in these parts). We were incessantly approached by girls who spouted sweet talk and grabbed at our crotches.

"How much would you pay for a woman?" one of them asked me.

"I wouldn't pay anything for a woman," I said laughing. I'd never paid for sex and I certainly wasn't going to start with a trashy hooker at a grimy club in the Zimbabwean jungle.

She pouted and moved on to one of the Germans.

Around 2:00 a.m. we met a drunk cab driver who drove us into a raunchy part of town. We were hungry and he suggested a restaurant that was closed, but would open up just for us. On the way there it was dark, so dark we couldn't see more than ten feet or so in every direction.

After eating a bland dish of chicken, rice, and potatoes in the empty restaurant, we followed the cabbie through a dirty alleyway and around the corner to a shebeen. Music was blasting and there were a lot of people. We were the only white people there and it was now 3:00 a.m. We were a bit of a spectacle, as we were doing shots of whiskey with the cab driver and dancing and talking to everyone.

"How many of these girls are hookers?" I asked the cabbie.

"All of them."

One girl in a skimpy, stained skirt came up to me (after approaching each of the Germans first) and grabbed at my crotch and ass and kissed me on the cheek and neck, standing uncomfortably close. She smelled like dick.

"I like you," she kept saying. "Will you be my friend?"

"Nnnnnno."

On the way home, the cabbie was too drunk to drive, so he let one of the Germans drive his cab. I was taking pictures from the backseat.

"Do not post these photos to the Facebook!" the cabbie said. "My wife will kill me!"

We roared with drunken laughter all the way back to Shoestring.

· · · · · · ·

THE NEXT MORNING, THE Germans were off to a game reserve in the car they rented, so we said our goodbyes.

I ate breakfast and headed for Victoria Falls, just a fifteen-minute walk, but the route took me through town, so again I had to fend off swarms of hucksters trying to sell me bullshit. One guy named Mark, a young, lanky black local from whom I had purchased a couple items from the day before, walked with me the entire way, and I knew he would be waiting for me when I left the falls. He and his fat partner, who called himself King George, were manipulative salesmen, sharp as a whip. They practically guilt tripped me into buying one hundred dollars worth of animal figurines, which probably cost next to nothing to make.

"It costs sixty dollars just to get the material to make these," they had said.

I knew it was bullshit, but I wanted the figurines for my mom, and they wanted to charge me more than I ended up paying.

"Oh, Justin my friend, we are losing hope," King George had said when I almost gave up on the whole transaction.

"So am I."

In the end I got ripped off, but what're ya gonna do? My mother will appreciate the gift.

"You know, we are brothers," King George had said at one point, referring to himself and Mark, who shook his head. Later, Mark told me that that was bullshit, which I had picked up on.

"That guy, always talking business," Mark told me privately.

Like an idiot, I didn't bring a plastic bag or rent a raincoat or umbrella for the falls. Big mistake, considering I had my passport, wallet, cigarettes, and camera in my pockets.

The falls are so massive that, all the way from Shoestring (a couple miles away), you can see a towering cloud rising up. Once inside the park, I walked along a narrow path through a rainforest, essentially. The closer I got to the falls, the harder the river rain poured down on me, a constant shower pushed up from the bottom of the valley high into the air as the hot sun burned bright.

I walked the entire length of the falls and found a vibrantly colorful double rainbow down in the middle of the Zambezi River, which serves as the border between Zimbabwe and Zambia. The rainbow dove down into the water, past the massive Victoria Falls Bridge, which people bungee jump off of. I had heard stories about the ropes breaking and people falling into the harsh rapids below. I'd gone skydiving before, so I passed on that. I'd had my fill of that sort of adrenaline, though apparently not the sort of adrenaline that naturally comes with traveling across a place like Africa by myself. I was soaking wet, but trying desperately to keep my camera and passport dry, to no avail. The camera was done. So stupid. Still, I couldn't help but throw my arms in the air, lift my head to the sky, and laugh hysterically as the river rain relentlessly drenched me in the middle of this Zimbabwean jungle.

Mark was waiting for me as I exited the main gate. I wasn't thrilled that he wouldn't leave me alone, but since the Germans had left, I didn't have anyone to hang out with at that point, so I didn't tell him to get lost. I followed him down a side dirt road and a small path through the bush to a hidden view of the Zambezi River before it hits the drop and becomes several waterfalls. It was so hot and I wanted to go swimming, but the current was way too fast and dangerous. Incredibly, a lion with a GPS tag on it actually crossed that river over to Livingstone, according to the previous day's paper.

I dried out the items from my pockets in the sun, then we walked across the road and into a dense bush. We walked over huge piles of elephant droppings and down some railroad tracks, then back into the bush. We came to a clearing where locals had set up small huts and lined up their stone-carved statues. It was a shame my camera wasn't working, though I suppose it was for the best. Some things are just supposed to exist in the moment and the memory, not to be recorded or shared. I could see several spots where people had recently built cooking fires, and several dirty warthogs walked around us looking for food. Mark told me the villagers eat the warthogs, which made sense.

"Is a good meat," he said decidedly.

Eventually, we came out on the other side of town, closer to Shoestring. We walked to a broken-down mall, half of it under construction. It looked like a bomb had gone off on one side. The open shops displayed decades-old advertising for various excursions around Vic Falls, such as the bridge bungee jumping. We found an electronic repair shop, and I talked to a guy with a big crack running up and down his nose about fixing my camera. He said he could do it for thirty dollars, and to meet him in an hour and a half at the shop. I went back to the hostel and met mine and Norma's new roommate, another gorgeous blonde girl from South Carolina named Melanie. Now, it was just the three of us in that eight-bed dorm. *Score.* Life has little gifts, if you know how to see them.

I went back to the repair shop at the specified time, but Cracked Nose wasn't there and the shop was closed. Did this guy seriously just steal a broken camera? Mark helped me look all over town and after about an hour we found him in a bar. He told me that he had to let a certain type of glue set overnight in order to fix the main gear that was keeping the camera lens from opening. We arranged to meet at the shop the next morning at 10:00 a.m. I was so pissed at myself, not so much because I broke the camera, but because if Cracked Nose couldn't fix it, or if he didn't show up (like earlier that day), documenting the rest of my trip would be very difficult and I would miss a lot of important moments.

Later that night, I met several locals, both white and black Zims, at Shoestring's bar, which was clearly a popular hangout for them. About ten of us, including Norma and Melanie, got drunk and decided to drive to a white Zim woman's new backpackers, a chill but plain lodge with a pool, lounge area, and hammocks. It still needed a bit of work; the owner had told us how hard it was to start a lodge like that in Africa because every day something would break down or go wrong.

We sat around a table and drank Jim Beam Black and smoked bud (including Melanie, which we all laughed about because no one expected her to hit the joint when it was handed to her—she looked too innocent and acted too proper). A thirty-year-old Iranian man (originally he said he was Persian) who was staying at Shoestring also came along. He was the first Iranian I had ever spoken to in any meaningful capacity, and we both seized the opportunity to discuss international affairs. He was not a fan of the Iranian regime, and said the people of Iran did not support the government. We talked about the nuclear weapon situation.

"I don't think the Iranian government has the balls to build the bomb," he said.

"Really? You don't think so?" I asked.

"No way. If they do, they know America, Saudi Arabia, Israel, everyone in the region will up their supply of bombs, and if Iran fired one bomb they know it will be the end of them. The entire country would just be obliterated."

"Yes, but that also gives them negotiating power."

He described the systemic discrimination against him just because he has an Iranian passport. For instance, every single time he goes through airport security he gets called out of line, searched, and questioned extensively. He recalled one story he had heard where an Iranian was brought to a large, padded room tucked away somewhere in the bowels of JFK airport in New York City, where police forced him to strip naked then proceeded to color him with shots from a paintball gun for no reason at all.

Someone brought out a paper-thin lantern cover shaped like a balloon, and we all wrote something on it. I wrote a line from one of my poems: *"i don't want to get where i'm going to, cuz you won't be there to melt into."* We set the lantern on fire and released it into the dark, starry sky.

Marvin, who had big glasses with black plastic frames that ran only across the top of the lenses, was a very cool cat with an ironic sense of humor, and highly political. He explained to us that he was a member of an underground political party called the DPP.

"What's that stand for? The Double Penetration Party?" the Iranian said. Melanie accidentally shot whiskey out of her nose.

"The DZimbabwe People's Party," Marvin replied after everyone stopped laughing. "With a silent 'D' that serves to make the pronunciation of the 'Z' stronger and to pluralize Zimbabwe."

"Oh," said the smirking Iranian. "That makes more sense."

The group decided to drive to another spot that the locals knew about. We got a motorcade going: two cars, a 4x4, a couple motorbikes, and the Iranian's black Mercedes taking up the rear with Marvin and myself in tow. I sat shotgun, Marvin was in back.

"I feel like the *President*, bein' driven around in a Mercedes at the end of this motorcaaade," Marvin slurred.

We drove to a dark, secluded property, and walked into an abandoned, half-built, open-air building made entirely of concrete. We couldn't tell if it was supposed to be a mansion or a hotel, because it was about five stories tall and unfinished. Using lamps and phone lights we made our way through the darkness and up the uneven flights of stairs, which headed upwards in a square pattern, leaving a dangerous, gaping hole in the middle.

We didn't know if anyone was squatting there. Someone could have jumped out at us at any moment. We were also all piss-drunk and stoned, and I had taken one too many Xanax that day. I jumped over part of the bottomless pit in the middle to reach the next set of stairs.

"Whoa!" Marvin exclaimed. "Justin, goddammit. Alright, everyone, let's establish some ground rules here, people. No careless, irresponsible shit here. It's too dark and too dangerous."

"I knew what I was doing," I said.

"Nah, man, you're drunk. Don't jump over big fucking holes in the stairs."

I wasn't just drunk. I was also on Xanax, so I guess he had more of a point than he thought, though I didn't agree with him at the time. If I had fallen through, at best my legs would've been broken, and I highly doubt I would've received the best medical care. Also, everyone's good time would have been ruined. You always think you know what you're doing until you don't.

The top floor had no roof, providing an unbridled view of the sparkling sky overpopulated with empty planets, the moon that supports our marine life, the vast asteroid fields, white dwarfs, black holes, and the suns that are collapsing in on themselves. We could even see the large, Technicolor gas clouds of the Milky Way, our backyard. The walls of the top floor, which had rebar sticking straight up into the air, also had several openings which led to a walkway on the outer rim of the building.

"Everyone be careful up here," Marvin said. "Justin, maybe you should stay away from the edge."

The earth was pitch black until it reached the Zambezi River and Zambia. That area, the city of the famous Livingstone, I presume, was well lit, even urban. To our right, the big mushroom cloud produced by Victoria Falls loomed over Zim and Zam like the beginning carnage of an atom bomb.

· · · · · · · ·

THE NEXT MORNING, I strummed Marvin's acoustic guitar in the red, and yellow, and green garden and ordered breakfast. As I sat there, mentally preparing myself to pack up and move on, I realized I hadn't even thought about heroin in weeks. Highly unusual for me. I began to think that maybe this whole Africa thing was actually working. I tried to think of ways I could extend my trip or find a job. I came to the conclusion that I wanted to be a diplomat. It was like a revelation. I loved traveling and I loved staying in foreign countries for extended periods of time. I loved interacting with people, and I thought I was good at diffusing tense situations. I loved the statesmanlike dignity that is associated with diplomats, and I loved Africa.

I knew I couldn't make a living as a freelance journalist in the States. It's just not possible. I was struggling back home. I was afraid to go back because I knew there was nothing waiting for me there: no job, no job opportunities, no girlfriend, and no prospects for a girlfriend. I had unreliable fair-weather friends and by the time I got home from this trip, I'd have no money. I'd have to start paying back my student loans to the government. I had to live with my grandfather because I couldn't even afford my own place, or my own Internet, or my own cell phone, or even my own food. I still received food stamps. I had been on welfare for four years. I worked so hard every day to find a full-time job, but nothing was taking. I subsisted on reporting stories and writing articles, which did get published, but I got paid a freelancer's rate: fuck all.

Maybe I could eke out a happy existence for myself here in Africa. Get a respectable job, make a difference, have crazy adventures, and write, write, write. I decided to look into what it would take to become a diplomat once I got settled in Uganda.

All I knew was that back home, I was nothing but a junkie.

· · · · · · · ·

SOMETIME DURING THE NIGHT, the entire town had lost electricity. The four German guys came back to Shoestring and told me they didn't have enough money for the national park, and ended up hanging out with three guys carrying AK-47s. They seemed worn out. All the drunk, fun-loving energy they exuded the other night at the shebeen had dissipated.

I went to the shell of a mall in town to meet Cracked Nose about my camera. To my surprise, he was there. Unfortunately, he was unable to fix the camera. Maybe that's why he showed up. I would have to buy a new one in the next town. I was leaning towards Lusaka.

I checked out of Shoestring, said goodbye to Norma and Melanie and the Germans again, always saying goodbye, and headed for the Zam border. It's like you're saying goodbye before you even get to know who a person really is. One has to fill in the blanks themselves. The people one meets while traveling might as well have been figments of our own imaginations.

The electricity was still off when I left, and I didn't know why it went out in the first place. One of those things you just have to accept as an inevitability in Africa.

From here on out, every time I entered a new country, I would have to pay fifty dollars for an entry visa. Ridiculous. At the Zimbabwe/Zambia border, several baboons were walking around as bored police officers sat in the shade and taxi drivers jockeyed for business. A baby baboon was clinging upside down to its mother's stomach. They roamed around like they were people.

I caught a ride to Livingstone, Zambia, to buy a bus ticket to Lusaka, the country's capital. The bus station was a small office in the middle of a dirt lot filled with people, tin and tarp shack markets, small stands with room temperature drinks, and a few buildings alongside the lot.

I had to wait a couple hours for the next bus to leave and had nowhere to go, so I pulled out my playing cards and started setting up Solitaire. Three Zambian guys immediately came over and several others watched as the four of us sat and played an African card game in the dirt.

I won.

MZUNGU

I WAS ON THE BUS to Lusaka, Zambia, but after that I had no idea where I was going. I planned on taking a breather in that city, then to catch the two-day Tazara train to Tanzania, the next country over to the east. But I didn't know where I was going to get off, what my destination would be, or what I would do once I got there. The road from Lusaka to my hazy final destination of Mityana, Uganda, was completely mine to create.

As it happened, however, I more navigated it than created it. Africa had a knack for throwing curveballs at me.

On the bus to Lusaka, a skinny, energetic Zambian man was talking loudly in the local language about his wife and girlfriends, how he couldn't let them know his PIN number or all his money would be gone, how women aren't good at business. The man sitting next to me translated for me. The skinny guy talked about hitting his women, which really got all the women on the bus arguing with him, and everyone else on the bus laughing hysterically, including me and my translator. The debate went on for hours. It was funny but sad, and I thought the guy was pretty ballsy to launch into an argument with a group of female strangers about the inferiority of women. He was just so matter-of-fact about it.

I thought he was a misogynistic anomaly, but the further north and east I traveled into Africa, the more I realized that women in general were treated like second-class citizens, or worse. *What a bummer.*

My translator had a friend picking him up in Lusaka, and he offered me a free ride to Kalulu Backpackers, a small hostel on a bland, rectangular property with an intimidating security gate out front. I ordered a Mosi beer at the backpackers' bar, next to a fat, drunk, white man, whose slurred words were nearly incomprehensible.

"Wwhhyy are yyourrr EYES sso big?" he asked several times.

"You mean my glasses?"

"No no no, yyourrr EYES!"

A black "old queen," as he described himself, bought me a beer. He said something about there being a number of "old queens" around. I figured he meant the fat guy who wouldn't stop staring at my "eyes."

"Oh yeah, who?" I asked innocently, half-committed.

"I can't tell you, that would be rude," he said, a little shocked.

I meant nothing by it. I realized how scary it must be to be homosexual in Africa. I was surprised he had been so open about it with me. It was one of the first things he said to me, though he really didn't have to say anything at all.

I took a much needed shower and hit the sack. Another beautiful, blonde Dutch girl was in my room, as well as a knowledgeable and adventurous Israeli named Shai. *Interesting how I hung out with an Iranian in Zimbabwe and an Israeli in Zambia.* They weren't that different from each other. Africa is often like that, a melting pot.

The next day, Shai and I went walking into the center of Lusaka, a bustling city with half-finished skyscrapers and secondhand markets lining the sidewalks in front of "proper"

A postapartheid South African flag waves over the maximum security prison on Robben Island where Nelson Mandela spent eighteen of his twenty-seven years behind bars.

A dog wanders the streets in front of the Jam Alley Tavern in Khayelitsha, one of the poorest townships in Cape Town, South Africa.

Whites, blacks, and colored play in the water of what used to be a whites-only beach in Fish Hoek on the False Bay side of the Cape Peninsula in Cape Town.

Justin poses with a vendor next to his wares near the Cape of Good Hope.

A troupe of dancers at Lion's Park in Johannesburg, South Africa.

A pride of white lions munch on lunch as people watch from their cars at Lion's Park in Johannesburg, South Africa.

Sunlight spills into the lobby at New Kapiri Mposhi station as passengers await the arrival of the two-day Tazara train.

Locals sell food to passengers through the window of the Tazara at a stop in a Zambian village.

The mighty Tazara train snakes through the jungle in Tanzania.

Children run up to the Tazara train as it speeds by.

A fisherman and his boats on Zanzibar island.

Laundry dries in an alleyway in Stone Town, Zanzibar.

In this photo taken in a Ugandan village, the women had to sit on the ground while the men were allowed to sit in comfortable chairs, despite Justin's protestations.

Ugandan villagers watch as a mechanic attempts to fix Father Odo's car.

A little smart-ass tries on Justin's glasses.

Justin poses with a group of children in a Ugandan village after a game of soccer. Photo by Mary.

stores. We must have walked five or six miles by the end of it. He was looking for a phone and propane for camping (which he kept calling "balloon gas" for some reason). He was eager to go on safari, and wanted me to come along, but I didn't have the budget for that. I bought a better-quality camera than the one I broke in Vic Falls for about 120 dollars. Not a bad deal.

"Are you hearing this?" Shai quietly asked me.

"What?"

"They're calling us *mzungus*."

"Uh, what?"

"It means white person."

After he mentioned it, I did start hearing it everywhere. *How had I missed it? How long had I been missing it?*

At every corner Zambians were calling us *mzungu* ("muh-ZOON-goo"). The word originally meant traveler, then European, and now served as the common word for white person.

Wherever I went with other white people, whether it was a taxi or eating at a restaurant, they tried to charge us more than the standard rates, and we always haggled.

"What is this shit?" we'd say. "Mzungu prices? Come on, man…"

That night, two absolutely gorgeous Dutch girls, Miriam and Emma, arrived at Kalulu. They were in their twenties, brunette and dirty blonde, bright-eyed, smooth-skinned, with wide, white smiles. They were the kind of girls who enter a room and instantly make everyone horny. The kind of girls everyone wants to be around. Shai and I started chatting them up immediately, and I offered to braai them up a dinner. They both had boyfriends back in Holland, so they said, but it's always nice being in the company of lovely ladies that are genuinely interested in talking to you. We ate and drank and smoked and played cards late into the night.

Miriam and Emma were medical students doing an internship at a hospital in a Zambian village. The hospital had fifteen male beds, fifteen female beds, fifteen pediatric beds, an operating room, three doctors, and the two girls. They said they often lost patients, and saved maybe three or four. The other staff would get up early and work until lunch, then take off for the day, leaving the girls to deal with whatever problems came through the door, as well as the problems that already existed. The first weekend they were there, kids broke into their house, but didn't take anything. They were only looking for money. Another night, the girls came home and the word SEX was painted on their room door. In Lusaka, they seemed tired and humbled by the experience, but still wore smiles on their perfect faces.

·······

THE NEXT MORNING I woke up itching all over. I had been getting lazy about using my bug spray, and hadn't used my mosquito net thus far. I had been taking my malaria pills every week on schedule, and was glad that I didn't experience any of the shitty side effects I read about, like skin rashes, psychosis, nightmares, vertigo, nausea, vomiting, toxic encephalopathy, diarrhea, abdominal pain, permanent enamel hypoplasia, dizziness, convulsions, anxiety disorders, hallucinations, esophagitis, uncontrollable itching, confusion, delirium, coma, psoriasis, Bradycardia, sleep disorders, thoughts of suicide, Tinnitus, sinus arrhythmia, and rectal bleeding. It was like when I first arrived in Africa and experienced no opiate withdrawals, even though I should have, scientifically speaking. I could take hardcore drugs and not suffer the consequences.

Maybe I'm indestructible.

Lusaka was the first city where I actually started getting bitten a lot by spiders and mosquitos. I had to start using my mosquito net and bug spray.

It was my last full day in Lusaka. I let the two Dutch girls use my laptop so they could write their case studies and reports, which were due soon. I was surprised that they didn't have laptops themselves, but I didn't ask them why.

Shai and I walked to the Zambian National Museum. In front stood a large statue of a black Zambian breaking the handcuff chains from his wrists. Below that, in big letters, was written FREEDOM. The statue was poorly guarded by a gate that, ironically, wrapped around and enclosed the structure. I suppose the idea was to stop people from tagging the walls of the base, but that gate couldn't keep anyone out.

The museum cost us 20,000 kwacha each, which was about four bucks. For Zambians it was 2,000 kwacha, which we figured was a good thing. It made the museum affordable for locals. The museum had exhibits on witchcraft, the entire history of Zambia, early skulls and bones from before the time of Homo sapiens, villages that you could walk through to see what primitive village life was like, and old newspaper clippings. The museum was still under construction, and between a few cracks I could see some guys working on new exhibits. You could spend hours there reading all the information and looking at the items displayed. I would continue to be surprised by my adventures in Africa. Later on, in Uganda, I was surprised to find that witchcraft was alive and well, scarring many innocent people's lives in ways I didn't expect. I considered it such an outdated, disproved, destructive belief system, though I suppose I felt that way about most belief systems.

After the museum, we walked to the bus station, where we were swarmed by people asking us where we were going, trying to sell us tickets to places we had never heard of. I bought my bus ticket for the next day to Kapiri Mposhi, a small village where I was to catch the Tazara Railway train. The train didn't go all the way to Lusaka, the capital, because the Chinese had only built the train line for access to Zambia's copper. In the other direction the train went all the way through Zambia, crossed the border with Tanzania, and traversed that entire country to Dar es Salaam, the capital of Tanzania, on the east coast of Africa.

When we got back, I realized I had lost the key to my padlock in my room, with several important items locked inside the wooden-doored safe under my bed, including what was left in my Xanax bottle. I searched everywhere for the key with no luck. I thought maybe I dropped it in the backpackers' pool. It was already dark, so I asked Emma to shine a light over the water as I stripped down to my boxers and jumped into the cold, murky pool. I liked getting nearly naked in front of her. I could see her checking me out; I liked being lusted after. Underwater, I felt like a diver looking for sunken treasure. I scanned the entire bottom of that pool, finding leaves, rocks, and nails, but no key.

Emma and I stayed up late, chewing the fat. She was the first person I told about my addictions and why I was really in Africa, because I wanted to lay her, and that was one of my unconscious strategies: to make people feel sorry for me. I was a pathetic, intelligent, handsome, misunderstood, artistic, interesting, miserable, scrappy, young chap, and I was full of love for you if only you would let me love you.

She didn't judge me. I liked that.

"Everyone has their struggles," she shrugged. Her face was angelic and foxy in the glow of the fire. She looked at me and softly smiled.

"How do I stay clean, though, when I'm not even sure life is worth the trouble?" I asked her. I was laying it on thick. I wanted an answer.

"Well, I think you probably need to figure that out for yourself," she said. "Why'd you started using in the first place? What will you gain and lose if you stop? What's missing in your life? What are you trying to fill with drugs? Once you figure that out, then go after the real thing. It's entirely up to you. If you think it's not worth it, then it's not. If you think it is, then it is. Life is truly yours for the taking, so take it."

I kissed her.

She was right, but I had an ulterior motive. Her being a medical student, she knew about the antianxiety drugs I was taking at the time. She knew what Xanax was. Truth be told, I was asking for advice about my afflictions while halfheartedly hoping in the back of my cloudy head that she'd be able to write me a prescription. Plus, I was lonely, and I enjoyed her feminine companionship and attention.

She didn't give me a free pass on the pills, but she did grab my hand and lead me to her room. I'm always surprised when that happens (I'm shocked when my manipulative strategy actually works), but I justified it with a firmly-held belief that I deserved it. She had the room to herself because Miriam was spending the night in someone else's room, so she pulled out a joint. We sat with our legs interlocking.

"Wanna do the honors?" she said.

"Okay." I struck a match and brought the flame to the tip, inhaled deeply, then locked lips with Emma and blew the smoke deep down her throat into her perfect Dutch body. She inhaled as I exhaled, and I was inside her, flanks splayed, lips meshed, loins violently colliding and grinding till all our troubles burst in an explosion of relief.

· · · · · · · ·

IN THE MORNING, I still couldn't find the key to my safe, so I used a butter knife to unscrew the latch (worthless piece of shit) and got my stuff out, then immediately swallowed a couple Xanax. I was running late and didn't want to miss my bus, so I left without saying goodbye to Emma, Miriam, or Shai, and quickly headed to the bus station. I threw my luggage onto my bus, and an employee tried to tell me there was a 10,000 kwacha luggage fee.

"Uh, no," I said. "I'm not a stupid mzungu. I've *never* had to pay to put my bags on a bus."

"Okay, okay, get on bus," he relented.

I stepped outside to have a smoke before the bus left, and a couple Zambians told me I would be fined unless I went outside the grounds of the bus station proper. I stood by the gate and one guy literally pushed me outside.

"Get your fucking hands off me," I told him. "You don't need to push me."

"You must be outside the gate!" he yelled at me.

It doesn't help to get aggressive with guys like this. It only makes them get riled up and respond in kind. Of course the same guy asked me for smokes and money in the next breath.

After the bus ride to Kapiri Mposhi, I took a cab to the New Kapiri Mposhi train station, where the famous Tazara train departs.

The Tazara, built by the Chinese, was a much classier, more comfortable train than the British-built ones in Zimbabwe. It had electricity, showers, toilet paper, and bedsheets, for instance. The basics never felt so luxurious. I had bought a first-class ticket this time, which I had gotten at an office in downtown Lusaka a couple days before.

At the station, kids were riding their bikes outside next to a statue of a whale tail sticking into the air. The lobby was enormous, and filled with people and bags. Sunlight spilled through the large windows. I was a couple hours early, so at first I was the only white person there. Then, I saw a young, white British guy walk in and go to the ticket window. He was about my age, and exuded style and confidence. *Good looking kid.* I watched him as he rummaged through his wallet, then scanned the sea of black faces throughout the station until he spotted me, and made eye contact. He meandered over, like I knew he would, and asked if I was English.

"No, American," I replied.

"Oh, I thought you were British. I only have pounds. I've run out of kwacha and I was hoping to exchange some money with you so I can purchase my train ticket."

"How much do you need?"

"About forty thousand kwacha."

"No problem," I said, handing him a fifty.

"Thanks, mate. I will definitely reimburse you."

He bought his first-class ticket and we talked for a while, waiting for the train. His name was Nick and he was studying architecture and working on building an orphanage from a partially standing structure in a village in Zambia. He showed me blueprints he had designed. He said they put a few kids of different ages together in the orphanages and say, "You're a family now."

"It works quite well," Nick said.

He also told me about a British documentary he saw about the Tazara train. To our right we could see a second floor balcony through the large windows. Nick said that in the documentary there was a shot of the filmmaker walking around that balcony, knocking on the doors and looking for the elusive Chinese engineers that supposedly kept tabs on the train, making sure it ran on time (or at least left on time), watching over their expensive investment. It took the Chinese five years to build the entire track and trains and stations, which is incredible considering the length of the track. It takes more than two days to get from Kapiri Mposhi, Zambia, to Dar es Salaam, Tanzania, more than half of the massive continent.

THE REAL AFRICAN DARJEELING LIMITED

WHEN WE BOARDED THE train, I kept getting switched to different compartments. It was very unorganized, but it worked out perfectly for me because I ended up in a four-bed compartment with just one other guy named Aaron, a sort of Eurasian gypsy with smooth, jet black hair, a nose ring, a mustache, and a Maasai bracelet. He was thirty and clearly storied. I asked him where he was from and he said he didn't know. He was born in Denmark, his mom was Thai, his dad was Swiss, and he had lived in the Netherlands, France, Italy, Switzerland, Boston, Los Angeles, Berkeley, Thailand, and Kenya. He worked as a contractor for local governments around the world. Luckily for me, he was currently stationed in Zanzibar, an exotic island off the east coast of Africa.

"You ever been?" he asked, handing me an unfiltered cigarette and opening the window. We sat on our beds across from each other, a small pullout table in between us, as the train pulled out of the station more or less on time. Nick was in his room, a few doors down the hall.

"No, this is my first time in Africa," I said. "I'd like to go, though. Sounds trippy as fuck."

"So you don't have a plan, or a destination?"

"No."

"Where you from?"

"Southern California."

"What're you doing in Africa?"

"I'm a writer."

He took a drag of his stogie and said, "I'll help you get to where you need to go once we get to Dar es Salaam. Point you in the right direction."

"Thanks, man."

"Yep. There's a lot of cool stuff to do in Zanzibar. You like reggae music?"

"Of course."

"You'll like this one place called the Old Fort. This fuckin' place was built by the Omani Arabs, and now it hosts reggae nights. It's amazing. Real authentic reggae, too. *Tre danceable* stuff, man. Sometimes the DJ'll throw in some jazz, some afro beats, some *taarab*."

"What's taarab?" I asked, enthralled.

"Popular East African music. Very cultural and historical."

I introduced him to Nick and the three of us talked, drank, and smoked all night, and indulged in some Zanzibari hash that Aaron had smuggled aboard by wrapping it in beef in case there were dogs, though at that point I had never seen a drug dog in Africa (and neither had anyone else I talked to).

"I figured I could tell the cops, 'What? Of course the dog wants beef,'" Aaron half-joked, as he took a bite out of the beef. "If I was really in a spot, I could just throw the beef on the ground so the dog would eat it."

"That plod pup would be trippin' balls, mate, eh?" Nick said. Aaron almost choked on his beef laughing.

Before long, Aaron offered for Nick and me to stay with him at his mansion on the beach in Zanzibar. Nick was on his way to Kenya to check out some orphanages for his project, so he politely declined. It was an offer I obviously could not refuse, however. *Zanzibar? Sure, why not? I got nowhere to be...*

The train made lots of random stops along the way. Zambia was relatively uneventful in terms of the view from the train, rather drab and dull. But Tanzania was just gorgeous. It was like night and day, in more ways than one—Zambia is heavily Christian, Tanzania heavily Islamic—and the switch happened immediately after we crossed the border. It took a day to reach the border between the two countries. When we got to the border, several guys jumped on the train to sell phones and SIM cards and to exchange money to Tanzanian shillings. I got a SIM card and changed all my US dollars into shillings, which turned out to be a bit of a mistake. The visa to enter Tanzania was one hundred dollars, but I thought it was fifty dollars, so I had to go around and find an American to help me out with some cash.

I was charging my phone at the bar in the first-class lounge near the back of the train, and unbeknownst to me the Zambian immigration officials were going around stamping people out of the country. They missed me, so my passport never got an exit stamp, which means I can't go back to Zambia, at least not with my current passport. Not that I have plans to go back, but the Zambian government technically still thinks I'm in Zambia somewhere.

"Fuck, dude, are the Tanzanian officials going to let me in?" I asked Aaron.

"I dunno, man. I've never seen this happen before."

The Tanzanian immigration officials collected our passports and congregated in one of the first-class compartments to go through them. It took forever. My stomach hurt from the anxiety and anticipation. I swallowed a couple more Xanax and smoked a cigarette, nervously pacing around my room.

"Just relax, man," Aaron said. "What's the worst that could happen?"

"The worst that could happen? They'll kick me off the train and leave me in fucking Zambia."

Finally the main official knocked on our door. Aaron opened it and the man handed him both of our passports.

"Chapman?"

"Yes?"

"The Zambians didn't stamp you out."

I started to explain but he wasn't interested. He just left.

"Okay then," Aaron said, throwing my passport to me. "Why not? Shit. It's not their problem, after all."

The train moved on.

We passed rolling green hills, people and huts in the middle of nowhere, freight train derailments, kids running alongside the train and waving at us, people selling bananas, and water, and guava, and other food at all the stops, kids sitting on steep cliffsides, slanted stone walls with plants growing out of the cracks, tunnels, bridges, murky rivers, tropical jungles, business-suited men riding bicycles, huge palm fronds, swamps, tall grass fields, small lakes, miles of flat plains, women plowing fields, men swiping machetes in the bush, rivers running alongside the train covered in millions of green lilies with bright blue and yellow and red flowers blooming up out of them, wheat fields, rice fields, maize fields, purple mountains rising up behind the jungle with huts hidden between the thick bushes, tall trees, coconut trees, and palm trees. Nick called it a "green house in Cuba." I spotted one Tanzanian guy climbing vertically up a palm tree, waving to us as the train rolled by.

The train bounced up and down and jolted a lot, so when going to the toilet or taking a shower it was like doing so on a trampoline. I was in the small, dark shower room, ready to clean the grime off me, when the train violently bounced and the soap shot out of my hands onto the dirty floor and I lost my balance. Every time I went to the shitter I had to hold on tight.

It rained periodically, and it was bloody hot all the time. In a Tanzanian town called Mbeya, we were delayed a couple hours so the front car could "get serviced." There was no loudspeaker system, they didn't tell the passengers what was going on; we just had to ask around and even then we'd get as many different answers as the amount of people we'd ask.

Through the dining car window, Aaron asked a Tanzanian kid about ten years old to go fetch us some sporties—cigarettes. The kid ran off and returned five minutes later, completely out of breath, and handed him the smokes.

· · · · · · · ·

NICK AND I ATE lunch in the dining car on the second day and talked about girls. He said he had a girlfriend back home in England, but that he regularly slept around.

"I've never been unfaithful to anyone," I said. "I don't judge, but my philosophy is that I just wouldn't want her to do that to me, so I don't do it to her."

"Yeah, I get it, mate," he said, cracking open a coconut with a large hunting knife. "There's just so many goddamn beautiful girls."

We drank the milk from the coconut and I told him I was having a hard time establishing much of anything with girls. I brought up the notion I discussed with Emma back in Lusaka, though I left out the part about the drugs. I wasn't trying to get anything from him.

"I dunno man, sometimes I wonder if life is even worth it," I told him.

"Yeah, I know," he said. "It's hard. But look at yourself, man. Look where you are. Isn't this worth it?" He pointed out the window. We were passing a tower of giraffes munching on some trees. "There are things worth living for, like this moment here, now, on this train. It's just brilliant. Surreal, really. We're fucking lucky to be here, mate."

He was right. My depression was petty, self-absorbed, and misplaced. I still didn't quite see a way out of it, though. Not yet.

"Well, I guess one thing that makes it particularly hard back home is the pressure in western society to succeed and always be productive," I said.

"That's true," he said. "It's always go, go, go! Even going on holiday is only so we'll be that much more productive when we go back to work."

"It's a never-ending cycle."

"Certainly something we can learn from them," he said, again pointing out the window. "People who live in villages and have next to nothing are happy and enjoy life. In England and America, people bitch and moan about the most trivial crap. We have it so good we make up shit to complain about, like whether or not life is 'worth it.'"

We passed by marijuana fields so big and thick the smell was strong and rich, wafting into the closed windows of the train. We went through Selous National Park and Nick and I were animal spotting for hours. We saw hundreds of zebras, giraffes, buffalo, antelope, warthogs, and flocks of birds, but no elephants or hippos or crocodiles or rhinoceroses yet, the four big ones I had yet to see. *How the fuck could I miss an elephant in Africa?*

It was nearly impossible to take good photos from the train. As soon as I saw something I wanted to take a picture of and got my camera out and turned it on and pointed, a bush would slice its way into the shot, or the thing I wanted would be gone.

We arrived in Dar es Salaam a few hours late. Aaron and I said goodbye to Nick, who I knew I would miss. Had we lived in the same city we'd have been great friends. But his companionship and insights, however brief, were not lost on me.

I went with Aaron (there were actually taxis waiting on the train tracks) to the only place we could find a cheap room in town, the YWCA. *Yes, we slept at the Young Women's Christian Association, what of it?* Quite superb beds with mosquito nets, and a powerful ceiling fan, and a sink in the room, and a free breakfast. I didn't know men could sleep at a YWCA. The female receptionist didn't ask any questions, just rang us right up.

Dar was a bizarre city. Very big, and very hot, and very dirty, and very crowded, and very wet. It had rained earlier, and the city had a horrible drainage system, so there were huge, unavoidable puddles everywhere. The other thing about Africa, and it was quite apparent there, is that the surfaces everywhere were so uneven: potholes here, missing stone steps there, huge holes in the middle of walkways. Dar had impressive skyscrapers, like palm trees reaching for the sky, while people and small shacks and dirty, dank alleyways surround the foundations like the weeds and moss around the base of trees.

We met up with a couple of Aaron's friends and walked to the New Africa Hotel and Casino, a very posh place with neon lights and comfortable chairs and crisp, clean interiors. We went to the ninth floor, which had a swanky bar with a view of the harbor, where we could smoke and have a cocktail. Then we walked through dark alleys to a tavern called Florida Bar. The alleys were empty except for a few guys here and there sleeping amidst the rubble in the street. It reminded me of a Bright Eyes lyric: "No one ever plans to sleep out in the gutter / Sometimes that's just the most comfortable place."

We got rather drunk and played billiards on the second floor of the bar. There were no windows, so it was chokingly smoky in there. Several Tanzanian guys silently watched us shoot pool from the periphery, in the haze.

One of Aaron's friends, a Swiss filmmaker, was leaving the next morning for New York to have one of his documentaries about local African fishermen screened at a film festival.

When we got back to the Y, I asked the filmmaker for his business card. He reached into his wallet to get one and found two tabs of LSD, which seemed to surprise him, not to mention me.

"I forgot all about these," he said. "They must have been in here for two or three weeks. Shit, can I bring these through customs at JFK?"

"I wouldn't risk it," I said, knowing full well airport security would never, ever find two small, square pieces of paper. Much larger, smellier contraband gets through all the time. "I could give them a good home, if you're that worried about it."

I was all for having harmless, fun adventures on drugs that weren't opiates. I kept telling myself that it was the opiates I really had to avoid. Anything else was fine.

He looked at me and then back at the tabs in his hand, then back up at me.

"Okay, I'm not going to risk it," he said. "You can have them, but it's for you *and* Aaron, alright?"

"How much do you want for them?" I asked, closing my hand around the tabs.

"Don't worry about it," he said. "It's a gift for you and Aaron, so just make sure you give one to him."

"No problem. Are they good?"

"They're top notch."

STONED IN STONE TOWN

AARON AND I WOKE up early on the twentieth of April, International Weed Day, during what was supposed to be the rainy season in East Africa, though it never rained once while I was on the island. I had celebrated the holiday for years in various places, like Berkeley and San Francisco, but spending it in Zanzibar had to take the cake.

We ate our free breakfast at the YWCA in Dar (dry eggs, crumbly toast, and stale coffee), and then headed to the port and bought our ferry tickets to get to the island. Aaron's ticket cost considerably less than mine because he had a residency permit. He worked for the Department of Public Health and had a contract with the government to revitalize the dreary, inhumane hospital situation on the island.

We made good time on the ferry, and when we pulled into port the famous centuries-old Stone Town architecture was revealed to us in all its ancient glory. I sported a gnarly sunburn from the ferry ride the rest of my time on the island. We had to get our passports stamped again, and it was the first (and ultimately only) time I was asked to show my International Certificate of Yellow Fever

Vaccination, something I paid 120 dollars for back in the States, which I handed to a woman in a full white burqa. A good majority of the women on the island wore them, only revealing their eyes. In that humid heat, I couldn't understand how they didn't all drop dead from dehydration or heat stroke. Talk about dedication (or repression, depending on how you choose to look at it).

• • • • • • • •

BEFORE I VISITED THE distant island, when I heard the name Zanzibar, I imagined it as similar to Timbuktu or the Bermuda Triangle. For most Americans, Zanzibar (Ungula to the locals) is an exotic place that doesn't really exist in our sphere of influence or effluence. When I came to Africa, I had no plans of visiting the mysterious island in the middle of the Indian Ocean. As happenstance would have it, I came to learn quite a bit about the Zanzibar Archipelago, which contains several islands that used to be their own country. Aaron told me that it was, incredibly, the only (semi) working joint government that existed on the entire continent. The former president of Tanzania offered to make the former president of Zanzibar the official president of both the island archipelago and the enormous country of Tanzania, both predominantly Islamic. The Zanzibari president returned the offer, reasonably explaining that Tanzania is much bigger and therefore should have more control over the country's domestic and foreign affairs. So, and good for them, a compromise was reached. Not all Zanzibaris are happy with this, however. In fact, Zanzibar itself is still a semiautonomous country with its own president and parliament, though it imports all of its electricity, drinking water, and most nontourist financing from Tanzania. The military, the police, and the private security companies are all Tanzanian. Zanzibar has a "revolutionary government," though there are hardly any tangible signs of it, give or take a few actual signs that read "The Revolutionary Government of Zanzibar," as well as worn campaign posters plastered on every public surface that will hold them.

Despite these political, militaristic, cultural, and religious divides, the people of Zanzibar were outstandingly friendly to me. Unlike some places in Africa, I felt completely safe and unthreatened walking around anywhere at night by myself. A sort of mob justice internally governs social and daily life. If someone is caught stealing something—anything—and you scream for help, several strangers will chase the thief and burn him or her to death. This remains true in Dar es Salaam as well. That sort of mentality really makes you think about your priorities from many different perspectives: Is recovering the item the person is stealing really worth ending that person's life by fire? What can you do without?

. . . .

IT WAS ABOUT A fifteen-minute drive from the port to Aaron's place, which was outside of Stone Town proper and reachable only by a discrete dirt road that anyone would miss if they weren't looking for it. Goats were chained to trees along the walls. His place was enormous by African standards, with a metal gate guarded by a local twenty-four hours a day, a garden with white and yellow flowers, a xyst with rocky paths covered by winding roofs of vines and surrounded by palm fronds and yellow bushes, and a hammock tied securely between two palm trees.

One of the paths led to another, smaller, metal-gated door with a locked latch. Beyond that lay the pearls of paradise: a 180-degree view of the beach, stone steps leading down to the sand where local fishermen had their boats tied to trees or out at sea, and carried around spears, bundles of fish, and automatic rifles.

The fishermen taught me the local Swahili greeting. You say "*Mambo*," which means "How are you?" and the recipient answers with either "Fresh" or "*Poa*," which means "Cool."

The fishermen mostly went about their business, depending on whether it was low or high tide. High tide came right up to the stone steps, covering any walkable sand, and low tide sank so far back that you could walk close to a mile in what was otherwise deep, coral-infested ocean. The fishermen chopped wood or worked on their wooden canoes, which had parallel poles stretching out on either side of the boat like bent arms balancing the cargo by grappling with the water.

Walking down the steps, the jungle ended and the long (or short) beach began. During low tide the fishermen slid their boats, anchored to rocks under the surface or trees on the shore, as far out as they could stand. Far down the beach to the left was an almost impenetrable mangrove thicket.

The room I stayed in was huge, with its own bathroom and a king-sized bed draped with a quality mosquito net. I had stumbled upon as close to a utopia as one can find. But I know the thing about utopias: They never last.

Up the dirt road was a small shack market where Aaron and I bought our sporties. From there, we proceeded half a block down the road to a bar and inn he knew of in search of bud to celebrate the holiday. He didn't seem worried about getting arrested, so I wasn't either. There were several cone-shaped straw huts that contained circular tables and benches, each hut about twenty feet away from the next one. On the outside, the stone, circular walls were painted with various themes. One had a marijuana leaf over the word "stoner," and next to that an

African girl smoking a joint next to the word "Rasta." We had come to the right place.

We approached two Rastafarians (there were plenty on the island amidst the Muslims, locals, and Italian tourists) and Aaron asked in broken Swahili if we could buy some *bunge*, the local word for weed. One of the guys immediately hopped on his bike and rode off to fetch it for us. We bought a couple beers while we waited and chatted with the other Rasta, who spoke poor English.

Before we finished our beers, the first Rasta rode up on his bike and revealed a large amount of marijuana packaged in blunt-sized, brown-paper-bag rolls.

We were ready.

· · · · · · ·

IT TURNED 4:20 P.M. as we walked the few rural blocks to a small, cornered center where the *dala dalas* (minibuses, essentially) picked up passengers, so we sparked one up. We weren't yet ready to take the acid. We planned on saving that for the next day. It was silly to make the number 420 so significant. Really, it was just an excuse to get high. I was also able to buy Xanax and Valium without a prescription at a pharmacy in Stone Town. At the time, I wasn't concerned that partaking in so many other drugs might lead to a heroin relapse. I was being careless at a time when my so-called recovery was as fragile as glass.

The dala dalas were the cheapest way to travel, and one brought us right where we wanted to be: to the overflow of humanity and petrol fumes known as the "bus station," a large concrete lot packed with so many minibuses I didn't know how any of them got out onto the road. There was a system, for sure, I just didn't understand it.

We walked across the street (every time, we risked our very lives trying to dodge the cars and dala dalas and Vespas—there's no such thing as pedestrian right-of-way; it's kind of like Texas, actually) to the indoor fruit and fish market, where the locals auctioned off their catches and finds. It smelled horrendous. The fish they serve in Africa comes to you on a plate intact, gooey eyes, cartilage tails, and all, but the setup of the market itself was intricate and beautiful. So was the architecture and centuries-old "urban design" of Stone Town that lay west of the market. Without a guide or someone who knows where they are going (even Aaron got lost a bit) one can easily spend hours wandering the winding, narrow alleys of that laborious labyrinth. Street signs didn't exist, maps were useless, everything looked the same and completely different all the time. Every turn there was something new: dozens of weather-worn mosques, I could hear the loud, torturous call-to-prayer five times a day; small squares where children in Islamic school uniforms bounced around like atoms creating circles around an old, stone-walled cemetery; Vespas, motorbikes, bicycles, and even cars racing around the bends like there's no tomorrow, which there wasn't. Some areas looked like an Islamic French Quarter, with balconies stretching out of the tall structures that surround you everywhere, so you can't get your bearings even if you want to.

I bought a Maasai club called an *o-rinka*, a hard wood cane with a knobbly handle made from the distorted roots of the leleshwa shrub. Apparently, the members of that culture used the clubs to throw at animal's and people's heads, not to beat people to death with (though anyone easily could if they wanted to). I felt even safer walking around with that piece of wood that was bigger and stronger than a policeman's baton—*Don't Fuck With Me, Motherfucker...I am Ahab.*

We walked along the beach, stray cats everywhere, and beside the harbor's stone shoreline on the boardwalk, and ordered a couple Zanzibari pizzas, a bizarre and delicious local street food creation where they take beef, and curry, and onions, and minced red chilies, and shredded cabbage, and garlic, and tomatoes, and cilantro—anything you want, really—throw it all into a large, round piece of dough, and cook it with a runny egg on a small, well-worn stove. As we sat and ate, several stray, feral cats swarmed around us. There must've been thousands of the things teeming around the island. I wondered how they got there. *Who brought them?*

After eating, Aaron and I, along with a sizable crowd, watched a group of about twenty local teenagers run, flip over a stone wall, and dive into shallow water. They had to belly-flop their landings or they'd dive straight to the rocky bottom and break their necks. A few did some rather impressive side- and back-flips, but surely the best of them was one guy who uttered a silly, rapid-fire guttural noise from the depths of his vocal chords as he jumped. His dive was not particularly exceptional, but the noise had the crowd in hysterics, including two baked mzungus.

IN ZANZIBAR RAINBOWS

WE NEARLY DROWNED AT sea the next night when we met up with a group of about twenty of Aaron's friends on the beach. The majority were white something-or-others who had lived on Zanzibar long enough to have connections with the locals. They had arranged for all of us to sail on a *dhow* (think a small pirate ship) to a sandbank that the water only revealed at certain times of the tide. We were all going to get naked and nicely toasted once we reached the disappearing sandbank. On the beach, we had to take off our shoes and wade into the water to climb aboard the wooden boat that was not made to hold twenty people, especially not twenty drunk people scrambling around to find dry seats. It was an attractive group to converse with, though there was a weird vibe. Not everyone knew everyone else. There was an unsteady wooden stepladder that led up to a square seating area, where there was nothing to hold onto.

The first hour or so of sailing in the dead of night was, well, beautiful. We drank very sweet East African semigin that came in pouches. Yes, alcohol in pouches, like small space-bags, that would have tasted much better mixed with soda. The bags hold 500 milliliters, so you can actually take as many as you want on a commercial airplane. We watched millions of undersea fireflies, phosphorescent waves of sparkles produced by the bow of the dhow, as if the sea was literally replicating the dark, starry sky.

After about an hour we realized that the locals, two Rastafarians who were steering the dhow and searching the seas with a weak flashlight, were lost, and could not locate the sandbank where we were to start a fire, get naked, dance, braai, and drink to our hearts' content. At the same time, the waves were getting way too big and rocking the dhow side to side, almost flipping us over. Large waves splashed onto the boat, drenching us all. I still can't believe that the people on top, who had nothing to hold onto, did not fall off into the pitch-black sea. A sense of hopelessness, and the instinct to survive, should the dhow tumble, rumbled through me like a fat line of methamphetamine. I smoked a joint with the two Rasta's to calm my nerves.

Eventually, we gave up and headed back to shore. We had been out to sea about three or four hours, half the time laughing and drinking and the other half scared shitless and drinking. After we landed, we built a big bonfire in the sand on the beach. We continued drinking, though no one got naked, and I got bored, so I decided to jump over the tall flames.

Aaron started to roll a joint, but he got extremely paranoid when it came to his attention that a Tanzanian police corporal was standing against the wall behind him by about twenty or thirty feet, watching our makeshift party. Aaron quickly buried the weed in the sand, but one of the locals gave the cop a bottle of Tequila and he let us smoke.

I don't remember how we made it back to the seaside mansion that night.

· · · · · · ·

THE DAY AFTER 420 was a bizarre, and magical, and nearly tragic day.

I learned in Berkeley, California, that tripping on LSD-25 had a hip euphemism in the fifties and early sixties: To be on it meant you were "in rainbows," (the title of, in my humble opinion, one of the greatest albums ever made, and certainly Radiohead's finest among their many masterpieces).

Aaron and I drove into town to stock up on supplies. It was his first time tripping. In Africa, you have to return the empty bottles so the retailer can redeem the recyclable value before you can buy more beer from them, so we returned a crate of bottles and bought another case, as well as mango juice, chocolate, several liters of water, bags of chips, bread rolls, eggs, packs of sporties, and a couple toffees to mix with and help dissolve the tabs of acid in our mouths. We made a quick retreat back to the mansion, then took a long walk down the beach towards the mangrove thicket as we rolled the chemical toffees around on our tongues. I tried to give him as much information as I could about the acid experience while still letting him figure some things out for himself. I didn't know how strong these tabs were, and beside that, each trip is different, and each person is affected by LSD differently.

We found a very secluded spot under some mangrove trees with our own small, private section of beach. I went for a swim before the acid kicked in, lounging under the Zanzibari sun and paddling my way through a drowning forest of trees: High tide was coming in. I could feel the current lift me up, vertically, and north, directionally. It was amazing enough being sober swimming through the flooded forest, each tree within arm's reach, menacing looking crabs scrambling into the water before I could even grab the dead tree stump they had previously clung to. It was amazing enough to be in the Indian Ocean, not knowing what lurked beneath and around me. It was amazing enough being in Zanzibar, in Africa in general...but once the chemicals took hold, the multiverses revealed themselves to us, and we were both instantly and gradually transported to a realm of infinite consciousness.

The tide came closer and closer, erasing our private beach. To the right, about a hundred feet away, two men answered the public call-to-prayer and sang holy songs by the water, lost in their own, just as meaningless, state of mind. I could see the sand breathing, I could hear the nearby military base's tasteless music, I could feel the water slowly and quickly coming up to swallow us whole. It became next to impossible to walk back to Aaron's mansion, but we had no choice. Our decision-making process had become obsolete. We had to boil it down to a simple yes, no, or maybe.

As we slipped deeper and deeper into the endless positive and negative layers of the mind that LSD shows you (and tripping out as we literally started sinking into quicksand under the mangroves), as we tried to suppress our ceaseless giggles and conversations, as the sand disappeared under the water, we had to make a decision.

Aaron and I gathered our stuff (quite a task) and trekked our way past fishermen, who had absolutely no idea what we were laughing so hard about, through the highest tide back to the mansion. We took quick showers (which was fucking intense, just being indoors changed our outlook completely, what with the sun setting and the light and walls pushing in and out at us at unmanageable depths), grabbed more beers, and walked to the inn down the road to see if we could score some weed. Unfortunately, we walked into the wrong crowd. We quickly exited stage left and walked to the corner where the dala dalas picked people up to take them into town.

"At this point, Aaron, I put my life in your hands," I said, because I did not know the island, the customs, or the language, and he did (at least to some extent).

"Don't say that, man," he replied.

We walked to a shady area under an enormous old tree where several Rastas were sitting around, doing nothing. We tried to maintain our demeanor and asked for *bunge*. They tried to rip us off at first, and even I noticed it, but Aaron talked them into giving us as much as they had for a good price. This method of acquiring marijuana was not typical. Everyone in the small town was watching us, wondering to themselves, *Did those mzungus just walk up to those Rastas and openly buy bunge? Yes, yes they did. Okay.*

Nobody did anything about it, so we hopped on a dala dala and made our way to the stop that led to Aaron's friend's backpackers, down and around several jungle alleyways, each bend revealing something new: a trash fire, a concrete building with wooden poles holding up the roof, children playing in the "backyards" of their homes, women washing clothes in dirty water. Once we arrived we felt safe, momentarily. It was a new property with an empty, hour glass-shaped pool. At this point, only Aaron and I could understand each other. Everyone else looked at us like we were mental, which we were. It had also gotten dark, so I repeatedly warned Aaron not to devolve into negative thoughts for fear he would have a bad trip.

We drank beer and smoked sporties and joints, and Aaron kept saying, "Cool," and, "Wow, nice" in a definitive tone, referring to what he was seeing and feeling. But he could see how it could spiral out of control if you let those demon instincts in. Once they get inside, it's very difficult to get them out. For instance, I had to go for a piss, so I went to the bushes in the corner of the dark yard. My mind started playing tricks on me. I swear I saw four or five small, black leprechauns sitting on the little hill where I was pissing. I could even hear them making noises. Of course they weren't real, and I was glad to hear Aaron's distant voice, speaking to himself in one- or two-word sentences, bringing me back to reality. Still, I backed away from that long piss slowly, tepidly until I could be certain it was safe.

I instead turned my attention to the stars, one of them a projector controlled by unknown forces that was showing my life for the entertainment of unknown audiences in the cosmos. I hoped they were getting their money's worth.

We were waiting for a friend of Aaron's to show up, to rescue us from this complacency we had wedged ourselves into, totally unable to make decisions for ourselves. In the meantime, we drank and smoked, and it was a wonderful sight to see Aaron, who was older than me, explore the intricacies and delicacies of his own mind for the very first time. Our conversations went nowhere, and, at the same time we were connected to each other and totally separated from everyone and everything else. One of us would get two words into a sentence and the other would know exactly what the first one meant, causing us to burst into uncontrollable fits of laughter. The gardener (who was pretending to water the grass, since the sprinklers were on) was obviously listening in on our half-assed but best-attempted conversations and must have thought we were insane.

"There's a theory that proposes that water created life, from single-cell bacteria, to ancient sea monsters, to fish that evolved tiny legs and crawled out of the oceans, to dinosaurs, to mammals, to various types of monkeys, and eventually to human beings, to move itself (water) around the Earth," I told Aaron. "Humans created aqueducts, dams, rivers, lakes, canals..."

He laughed, nodding. "Is there water on the moon or on Mars? No? Then we're gonna fuckin' damn well bring it there!"

"Who are we to say that water is not more intelligent than humans (clearly it is), that it takes eons upon eons to figure out what it wants and where it wants to go (much like humans, but on a *much* longer scale), and that it has a form of consciousness that we can't even *begin* to comprehend? If it doesn't like what we're doing: hurricanes, floods, famine, disease, tornadoes, volcanoes, tsunamis, you name it. Each and every one of us is made up of seventy-five percent water. When the water is done with us, it takes the other twenty-five percent back."

"The water giveth, oh yes, and the water taketh away, yessir," Aaron interjected.

"That is not to say that water is unified in any way, shape, or form. There is a *fierce* battle going on between fresh and salt water. The ice caps are melting. The shores are receding. Venice is sinking. The Netherlands are, well, you get the idea. At one point in time the entire Earth was covered in water; it just chose to reveal bits and pieces to intelligent life forms such as us, perhaps because the surface layer was jealous of the marvels that the depths enjoyed, or perhaps because the depths were disgusted with what they had to deal with all the time and decided to let humans and other life forms channel the surface layers into different areas over trillions and trillions of years."

Gibberish.

· · · · · · ·

FINALLY, AARON'S FRIEND SHOWED up, and we took a taxi to another friend's party. He either lived in, or had rented out, one of the biggest buildings in Stone Town; that is to say, one of the biggest buildings in all of Zanzibar. The party was on the roof, right next door to a cathedral with two massive, spiky pillars penetrating the sky. I recognized a few people from the failed sandbank trip the night before.

That's when it all started to go wrong.

Not five minutes into our arrival, Aaron was in midsentence on a couch on the roof when his consciousness gave out and his head fell to the floor in a face-planting motion. I was the closest to him and knew what was happening, though I'd never seen it happen on acid before, and grabbed his forehead just before it hit the concrete. I pushed him back slightly and his head flipped back. His arms and legs went stiff, his pupils rolled into the back of his head, and he was unresponsive.

Holy fuck. Now what?

Other people started noticing as I grabbed him by the shoulders and shook him around a bit, yelling, "AARON! Aaron, come on, buddy! Snap out of it!" to no avail. Now everyone on the roof, about thirty people (the whole party) took notice. I grabbed him by his head and shook it around. His eyes blinked opened, his limbs slowly loosened, and I grabbed the closest liter of water and put it to his lips.

"Open your mouth, Aaron," I pleaded desperately. "Open your fucking mouth!"

He nodded and opened his lips. I poured water down his gullet and said, "Tell me when."

He nodded again and snapped back to reality, pushing away my hand holding the water bottle and sucking in big gulps of air. I breathed a sigh of relief, but the rest of the crowd was not too happy with the bad element they assumed I had introduced to the party. It was an awkward, awkward scene. A few of the girls who knew me from the night before talked to me, but it was mostly about whether or not Aaron was going to be okay. He had ventured six or seven floors downstairs to a flat for a rest. He said his stomach didn't feel right.

"Maybe it was my ulcer," he said, groaning.

"Well, that probably had something to do with it, yes."

Even from downstairs, though, I could hear people on the roof talking about the situation in a negative way. All I heard was, "acid," "acid," "acid," "acid..." and on and on. As Aaron pointed out, it was a terrible word for it.

Once I made sure Aaron was sorted and had water near him as he lay on a couch, I went back up to the roof and talked to some of the girls. I was still tripping balls. It was a small roof. I could either sit on the couch by myself or try to join circles of people in midconversation. I walked up to a group of girls I knew from the night before. The look on their faces told me I wasn't wanted.

"So...how is he?" one asked.

"He'll be fine," I said. "I don't know what happened. That's really not typical of acid."

They nodded awkwardly. *Yep, yep, yep...*

One of them asked me a question, but I was focused on a melting building behind her head.

"I'm sorry, what did you say?" I asked, snapping out of it.

"I said, *I once thought about doing acid, but there's no way now.*"

"That's really a shame," I said. "What a beautiful experience you'll miss out on. Seriously. Whatever happened to Aaron, I guarantee you it had nothing to do with acid. He has a stomach ulcer, and he didn't drink enough water or eat enough food throughout the day, that's all."

Maybe I was just tripping, but I felt like to the majority of them I was just this California drug pusher who almost killed Aaron, their good friend. I was annoyed by the notion. I didn't force Aaron to take the acid. I didn't even go looking for it or buy it; it literally fell into my hands. I did my best to tell him what to expect, while keeping a safe distance so he could enjoy it without expectations. At the same time, when things did go wrong, I was right there to bring him back.

But they don't know me, I reminded myself. I might've thought the same thing in their shoes.

As the party wound down, one of the girls, who was actually being nice to me, wanted to meet her boyfriend at the Old Fort for Reggae Night. I was most definitely down, but Aaron was not up for it. He took a cab home, and I went with her to the Old Fort, a mammoth, stone fortification that wore its centuries on its sleeves. It was dark inside, and the atmosphere was loungy. Deep bass riffs, skanky guitar rhythms, and tight percussion hits floated through the hallway as we walked into the main area. There was a crowd of locals surrounding a pool table on the right, and another crowd on the dance floor to the left. I watched the regulars play pool. There are very different rules for bar pool in Africa. Certain balls have to be made in certain pockets at certain times and in a certain order. It's much more structured. The balls themselves are smaller. Whenever someone made a good shot, everyone would tap the edge of the pool table twice with their fingers as a way to say, "Nice shot."

I went over to the dance floor and met a Zanzibari named Saul, who, I was told, danced perpetually. I pointed out that the news was playing on a television that had no sound and that no one was watching. He asked, essentially, how I leaned politically.

"Uh...I tend to lean towards...democratic socialism," I replied honestly, though I don't like putting labels on things of such import.

He immediately turned away from me in disgust and started another conversation with someone else. When I explained it to Aaron, who was a communist, the next day, he basically explained that they don't like that particular political genre 'round these parts.

Oh well.

I took a cab back to the mansion and decided to take my mosquito net to the hammock in the garden by the beach. I used the net as a blanket (but still got bit worse than ever) and slept under the palm trees, letting the sound of the tide, low and high, slip me into unconsciousness under the stars.

A HEAVY FALL
OF THE BEAUTIFUL

I LEARNED THE NEXT DAY that Aaron had actually coughed up blood at some point during the night. The next two days inevitably brought the feel-good times to an end, a heavy fall of the beautiful.

He was scheduled to visit three village hospitals that he was helping restore, restaff, and supply water to further inland, and he brought me along since I had nothing to do. We drove deep into the island. It was a Sunday, so the hospitals were closed, but he wanted to take pictures of the situation.

Once we entered the jungle area of the island, where the vast majority of mzungus do not go, livestock was everywhere, and the roads, if you can call them that, were in horrendous condition. If another car was coming at you from the other direction, one of the two would have to pull off into the bush so the other could pass. We stopped at a couple small village clearings that had one-hundred-foot-deep wells with less than a bucket's worth of water at the bottom. A lorry came by every now and then to sell the people clean water. They don't fill the wells because they become too dirty.

The hospitals, themselves, at the least the exteriors, were not in too bad of shape. One was right by the beach. About 200 feet from the gated, new hospital still stood the old, stone hospital, which must have been built a century or two before. It is run down now, no windows or doors, graffiti covering every inch inside and out. One room had two stone steps leading nowhere. There used to be an entire flight of stairs winding up to the second floor, but the rest of the steps must have been removed or weathered away, though there were no signs of any rubble on the ground from what used to be there. We could still see a line where the stairs used to lead. Now there is no way up to the second floor.

As we drove in-between hospitals, we picked up a mzungu hitchhiker. He had come from Vancouver, and had been walking around the island barefoot for four days. He asked if the Department of Public Health was doing a good job when I told him what we were doing out in the middle of the island.

"Oh, good god, no," Aaron said. "If they were, I wouldn't be here. I have a job because they're doing a bad job."

We traveled down a somewhat better road, slightly out of the bush, that was lined on either side by hundreds upon hundreds of trees for a few miles, give or take. Aaron told us a story about the trees.

"The story goes that a princess used to live in this area, and every time she had a lover she would kill the man, bury him, and plant a tree here," he explained. "I mean look at all these trees... can you imagine? She must have been very attractive, or the men must have been very daft."

"I'd say it's probably a good combination of both," joked the hitchhiker.

• • • • • • •

AARON AND I SPENT the rest of that night relaxing and recovering at his mansion. He stopped smoking cigarettes and weed and didn't drink any beer for two or three days.

"I can't remember the last time I didn't do one of those things in a twenty-four hour period," I told him.

"Me neither," he replied. "How fucked up is that?"

"It's not like we *have* to do these things, we just do them impulsively at this point. It's just...sobriety is so..."

"...boring," we said simultaneously, which got us laughing again. I told him at this stage, post-tripping, it's important to keep each other laughing, keep each other up. Otherwise it can get very depressing.

· · · · · · ·

HE HAD TO GO back to work the next day, so I took a dala dala with him into Stone Town, and we went our separate ways for the day. The place is a fucking maze, and I needed to get to three different spots within that maze. I asked a guy for directions, and he basically took me on a guided tour of the area, showing me where the mosques were, telling me when certain buildings were constructed, where children were going to school, where different shops were located, which ethnicity was associated with certain doors and structures, and so on.

Seeing that white people were called mzungus, I bought a shirt that read "MZUNGU–SINA PESA," which roughly translates to *I'm white but I have no money*. The guide and the shop owner shook their heads and laughed.

"You are not poor," the guide said, smiling.

He had a point. I know I didn't feel very wealthy at all at that time. It felt like a struggle. But I wasn't broke, either. I hadn't brought all of the money I had saved up with me, (I had my dad transfer allotments from my savings to my checking account whenever I need them throughout the trip), but the funds weren't endless. I had to be careful about my money; I had to make it last. When—if—I got back home, I'd have to find another job and start from scratch. I was certainly wealthier than most of the people I interacted with in Africa, mainly because I had the option to go back to America.

The shirt didn't lie, though: I didn't have money to spare, *and* I wasn't poor.

The guide took me to a very posh but old hotel. We took the stairs all the way to the rooftop bar and restaurant. He was expecting payment for his tour services (which I hadn't asked for), but I didn't have much cash on me. I ordered us two beers as payment and we enjoyed the 360-degree view of Zanzibar. Close by, I could see the cathedral spires and the white roof where the party incident had occurred just two nights before.

I parted with the Stone Town tour guide and walked along the beach, killing time. I didn't feel well, so I made my way through the maze back to the bus station and negotiated with dala dala drivers to take me back to the bus stop corner near Aaron's place. From there I still had to walk for fifteen minutes, but that's as close as I could get without using an expensive taxi, which I didn't have the money for.

Aaron was still at work, so I took a walk along the beach, swallowed a couple Xanax, drank a few beers, and went for a swim in the ocean as the local fishermen watched me. I love swimming in the sea, and basked in the glory of the moment, the Zanzibari sun shining down on me.

• • • • • • •

I BECAME VERY TIRED after that, and it was oppressively hot in my room, so I lay down on the couch in the main room for a nap.

Aaron came home and continued working on his laptop in the same room.

"Hey Justin," he said, after a while.

"...yeah?" I said groggily, waking up.

"Get yourself together."

I thought I didn't hear him correctly at first, so I asked, "What did you say?"

He mumbled something that I couldn't quite make out. I didn't know what he meant, but his tone was standoffish, like I had been doing something wrong.

"Dude, I was just tired from walking around all day, and it was too hot to sleep in my room," I said. "I've only been sleeping for..." I looked at the clock. "...less than two hours. What's the big deal?"

He didn't answer me, or even look at me. He just kept tapping away at his computer. I immediately went to my room and packed my things.

"Where should I go?" I asked myself, looking at a map. Father Odo, the priest who I was going to stay with in Uganda, wasn't expecting me for about five more days or so. My options were to either stay in Nairobi, Kenya, for a couple days, or just push on through to Uganda. At that point I was kind of tired of the constant stop and go. I wanted a place to settle for a minute, so I decided that I would just bite the bullet, take the thirty-hour bus to Kampala, Uganda, and call Father Odo when I got there, hoping he would be ready to take me in. We had never set an exact date for my arrival, but he knew I was closing in. I went online and booked my bus ticket to Kampala via Nairobi, scheduled to leave at 6:00 a.m. the next morning.

I went back into the living room and told Aaron I would be leaving in the morning. I wasn't sure if he was mad at me or not, if he blamed me for what happened. I was just grateful for the whole experience. It was amazing that he took me in to begin with. I got on the Tazara train not knowing where I'd end up, and somehow everything worked out, thanks to him. All over Africa I'd been meeting such welcoming, friendly strangers, essentially, who wanted to go out of their way to show me around, take me into their homes, and offer me their friendship. I left Zanzibar humbled by people's openness and hospitality.

. . . .

IN THE MORNING, AARON called a cab for me and we said our goodbyes. I thanked him profusely.

I enjoyed the boat ride back to Dar es Salaam, watching the mystical island of Zanzibar fade away, then open ocean in every direction, and then small boats, sandbanks, tankers, and finally the disgustingly hot city of Dar.

A cab took me to a guesthouse hotel around the corner from the bus station where usually only locals go to drink and eat and watch soccer. My room was nice and so was the service.

From my fifth floor window I could see the Dar slums, starting right next door down below, stretching out as far as I could see. I'm sure there hadn't been a mzungu seen in this part of town in ages.

SNOW ON
THE EQUATOR

NOTHER MORNING OF WAKING up way too early, around 4:45 a.m. I took a shower and looked at myself in the mirror. My nose and forehead were badly burned, and I had the worst farmer's tan. I looked ridiculous, and my face hurt to touch. I had only been in the sun for a few minutes in Dar on the way to the hotel. *What gives?*

I headed downstairs to get my other, heavier bag from reception. The lady who ran the place told me the taxi ride would cost 3,000 Tanzanian shillings (about two bucks), which made sense, since the bus station was just around the corner. I would have walked if it wasn't still dark out in the Dar slums, and if I didn't have that heavy fucking lopsided bag full of books with a gaping hole where a wheel used to be, getting bigger and bigger the further I dragged it.

When we got to the station, it was already bustling with people and a hundred buses, engines idling. I asked the taxi driver how much I owed him.

"Ten thousand," he said.

"What? Fuck that, the lady told me three thousand."

"Ten thousand! Let's go!" he yelled at me in a decidedly nonnegotiable tone.

Jesus.

As soon as I got my bags out a guy was right there to put them on a luggage cart. I tried to tell him that I could take my own bags but he ignored me and asked where I was going. I told him Kampala Coaches.

"*Asante* (thank you)," I said to the cabbie begrudgingly, adding under my breath, "you cock-smoking pigfucker."

When we got to the Kampala Coach bus, the cart pusher asked for 20,000 shillings (twelve bucks).

"What? No way!" I exclaimed.

"Okay, eighteen thousand."

"Dude, all you did was push my bags two hundred feet, and I told you I wanted to carry my own bags. I didn't ask for your services."

"But this is government cart," he persisted. "You must pay eighteen thousand!"

I knew it was bullshit, but I was too tired to argue, and this guy was going to start making bad noise if I did, so I very reluctantly paid him. As I was waiting for the bus to leave, I went looking for AA batteries for my camera. I had wanted to take pictures of the Dar slums from my window but the batteries had died. When that happened I couldn't even get the lens to close. I went around to all the open shops looking for batteries, but, of course, none of them had any. I bought some mango juice and bread rolls and went back to the bus. The three or four guys operating the bus saw me approaching and said, "There's the mzungu. Let us go, we are going," in a somewhat frustrated voice.

It wasn't 6:00 a.m. yet, so I knew even when I got back on the bus they would not be leaving right away, which they didn't.

We departed that godforsaken city and I was glad to see it go. I slept for a few hours on the bus.

The rest of Tanzania was just as beautiful as it was from the Tazara train: lush, green farms and forests, with purple mountains spliced into sections by flowing rivers, plumes of smoke billowing up and out. It was overcast and drizzled a little here and there, a nice respite from the oppressive heat of Zanzibar and Dar.

Our bus driver was fucking crazy. I'd be staring out the window and all of a sudden the bus would jolt to the left and a large semitruck would zip past us, literally inches from repeating the incident in Plumtree, Zimbabwe.

At each of the few stops we made along the way, I had about five minutes to do all the tasks I needed to complete: look for batteries, get something to eat, smoke a cigarette, and use the toilet. After a long period of straight driving, the bus finally pulled into a small rest stop. My stomach hurt, and I had to drop a major deuce, but I knew I had to prioritize. First, I bolted out of the bus and quickly scanned all the small shops: no batteries. Then I bought something I could eat on the bus. I quickly sucked down a cigarette, then I ran for the restroom: small holes in the ground with wet shit-stains surrounding the floor-level "seat." And there was no toilet paper. I had to use a small pail to scoop up some water from a dirty bucket to clean my arsehole by running the water down the top of my ass crack. I had to do this at every stop because I could not find toilet paper to purchase anywhere, either. When I eventually gave up on the batteries and toilet paper and headed back to the bus, the operators were pissed.

"Come on, we must go. You are taking too long!"

Fuck you. My asshole is going to have a fucking rash by the end of this bus ride.

. . . .

WHEN WE ARRIVED AT the Kenyan border, we all got off the bus and went through customs and immigration. I got ripped off about six dollars by stupidly exchanging money with guys near the border instead of inside the customs building. Since I was just in transit my visa cost twenty dollars instead of fifty dollars just to continue my ride on the bus into Uganda. The officials took a while to approve my visa, so I was the last person from the bus to exit the building. Outside, two of the bus operators were waiting for me.

"What are you doing? You are taking too long! We must go!" they yelled at me.

"It's not my fault, man," I said. "Immigration officials were taking a long time to clear my visa. It's not my fucking fault."

They just ignored me and rushed me to the bus. No time to look for batteries, which meant I couldn't take pictures of Mount Kilimanjaro when we drove by it. The famous mountain was far away but very visible, and recognizable; snow-capped, misty, surrounded on all sides by plains and desert for hundreds of miles, and right near the geographic line of the equator, which we crossed over. It takes people a week to reach the top of the tallest mountain on the continent. I couldn't take pictures, but at least I had seen snow in Africa.

It became chaotic in the middle of the night as we entered Nairobi, jam-packed with traffic in either direction on the highway into the city center. About ten minutes away from the main Kampala Coach office, our bus ran out of diesel fuel. The operators offered us passengers no explanation, even when asked, and we sat there for more than an hour, rain pouring outside. I went up to the front and asked if I could walk across the street to take a piss.

"No," the driver said without looking at me, staring straight ahead into the rain.

"What the fuck? It's raining outside and I need to piss. What's the problem here? How long is this going to take?"

He rudely waved me off without saying a word. I went back to my seat and spoke to the guy next to me, a Ugandan wearing a suit and tie on his way home from a job in Dar, about how unprofessional the bus company and its operators were.

"We are sitting here in the rain in the middle of this busy highway and it is very dangerous," the man said. "They tell us nothing. Like they don't care that they have paying passengers back here."

Indeed it was very dangerous. Cars, and tankers, and semitrucks, and buses were whizzing by us. We could have been hit at any moment. To make matters worse, the other side of the highway, which was separated from us by a grass median, was so backed up that vehicle after vehicle decided to drive over the grass and onto the wrong side of the highway, our side, to go around the traffic. It was a recipe for disaster. We were scared and livid.

"Why don't they just call the main office and send a bus to come pick us up?" the man next to me said. "At the main office, just ten minutes away, they have three or four empty buses just sitting there. You'll see. They are losing customers because they behave this way."

The driver went to fetch diesel fuel, but even after they put the fuel in, the bus still didn't start. Again no information was given to us.

I'm not sure how they finally got the bus to start, because they simply didn't tell us, but when we reached the main office, low and behold, there were three or four empty buses sitting there doing nothing. They told us we had just ten minutes in Nairobi until the bus was going to leave again for the Ugandan border. God-awful jackasses.

I went searching in the wet, rainy Nairobi night for batteries, passing nightclubs, and bars, and restaurants, and shops, and neon lights, and tall buildings, and large puddles, and dark alleys where hookers with umbrellas lingered and loitered, then finally found Eveready batteries. I went to get something to eat and used the Kampala Coach office's toilet, which was located through a narrow, dirty alley that led to a courtyard with metal steps that led up to the toilet. It was also shit-stained filthy and had no toilet paper. I wanted to cry.

In the alley, partially protected from the rain, one of the nicer bus operators asked me for a cigarette. I expressed my grievances to him. He was sympathetic, but said that the office was also not giving them any information.

"Well, you guys knew you ran out of fuel, and you could have told us that," I said. "You could have given us some idea of how long it was going to take. You could have let me off the bus for two minutes so I could have a piss."

I also told him I didn't appreciate being rushed at every stop. I mentioned something about the lack of toilet paper.

"Yeah, well, this is Africa," was his response.

"No, this is Kenya," I shot back. "Everywhere else I've been, there has been toilet paper, even in public toilets, and even the places I've been staying, which are not expensive hotels. They've been the cheapest places to sleep that I could find. So don't give me that 'This is Africa' crap. This is laziness and disorganization and unprofessionalism, that's what this is."

The man just shrugged.

"I just don't understand," I continued. "Is everyone just walking around with poop constantly caked in their butts? Seriously? Does it not give you rashes?"

He laughed and shook his head and walked away.

It was becoming clear to me that I was entering a part of the world where basic necessities were downright luxuries. I wasn't in South Africa anymore; I was in the *Heart of Darkness*, a place where I needed to learn to thoroughly prepare beforehand, and expect to fend for myself. Utilize opportunities, however minor, to solve obstacles when they arise, not when the situation becomes critical and you have no negotiating power.

I got back on the bus and put the batteries into my camera. They were just powerful enough to close the lens, and after that they stopped working. I felt like beating someone to death with the Maasai club in my bag. The Xanax was warping and magnifying my emotions.

• • • • • • •

WHEN I WOKE UP in the morning, our bus was stopped again. I looked out the window to see our bus driver running away from a Kenyan police officer with a large, protruding belly.

Our driver had broken some unknown rule and decided to run, leaving us passengers stranded about ten minutes from the Ugandan border. We just sat there, dumbfounded, watching this fat cop chase this fat driver around. The cop's hat fell off, he ran back to grab it, and then continued chasing the driver. They ran around a square building four or five times, because the cop was too out of shape to catch the driver. It was like a cartoon. Meanwhile, a female police officer stood at the front of the bus, and a couple of the passengers argued with her.

"Why are you doing this?" one man screamed at her in English, ostensibly for my benefit, or perhaps to let her know that there was a white person on the bus. "We are tired. We have been on the bus for a whole day. The children are hungry and tired. At least think of them, and let us go on our way. We paid for our tickets. We do not deserve this."

Another driver, escorted by Kenyan police, brought us to the Busia District police station, where we all got off and wondered how long this totally unnecessary stop would last. The police station's toilets were just as gross, and dirty, and smelly, and paperless as the rest of Kenya. Finally, a police truck rolled into the station with the driver who had run away. One of the passengers told me they were going to torture him inside the building. They brought him inside, and ten minutes later he emerged with a black eye or two; it was hard to tell. He had definitely been roughed up. He probably paid them to stop beating him up. I never found out what he did wrong, only that he "didn't follow the rules."

We all got back on the bus, and that same driver took us to the Ugandan border where I had to pay fifty dollars for my visa, which allowed me to stay in the country for sixty days. It was more than enough unless I decided to apply for a work permit, start writing for a newspaper, and stay there longer. I didn't have a plan, per se. I had been in Africa for a month and a half, and I was just a few days away from being halfway through my entire semiplanned trip.

Thinking back on the past five weeks, I was elated and gushing with pride. I had made it through seven and a half countries—South Africa, Botswana, Zimbabwe, Zambia, Tanzania, Zanzibar, Kenya, and Uganda—by bus, car, boat, and train, *by myself*, carrying way too much luggage, without being robbed and without my life being threatened by another human being (though it was threatened several times by other factors—I didn't count Edgar chasing me in Guguletu; he was really after Roslyn). Oh right, did I mention I did all this while kicking opiates?

How many people can say they accomplished what I just had, at my age?

And I was just getting started.

THE UGANDAN BREAST-PINCHING BRIGADE

UGANDA STRUCK ME AS a much cleaner country than most of the places I'd visited in Africa. Shockingly so. There was hardly any trash on the ground, and the environment had been preserved. Even the dirt looked clean. It was blood red, mixed with greenery so bright that it made me think of Christmas.

I was still pissed that the batteries I bought didn't work, for there were plenty of things along the way that I wanted to photograph, like Mount Kilimanjaro, the Tanzanian scenery, Kenya's nightlife, the Busia District police station, and the Source of the Nile River in Jinja, Uganda. But these breathtaking, multilayered landscapes—farmers plowing, animals grazing, all shades of green trees and yellow plants shining in the Ugandan sun—let the troubles from that shit-show of a bus ride pass from my mind.

But I also knew that those landscapes were fertilized by the victims of the horrific regimes of Idi Amin, Milton Obote, and many vicious rebel groups, such as the Lord's Resistance Army, led by the infamous Joseph Kony. The country had suffered decades of mass murder and misery. Sure, it had smoothed out and calmed down by the time I arrived, but it was still there, under the surface.

A couple days before my arrival, a friend of mine who I had met during a layover at the airport in Johannesburg on my way to Cape Town, had visited Gulu in northern Uganda—the site of much of the kidnapping of children by the LRA. He had reported via Facebook that, "Kony has not been here for six years. It is one-hundred-percent safe. Are you listening, Invisible Children?"

Invisible Children is, of course, the organization that's seeking an end to the LRA conflict and to raise awareness about its activities in Uganda, the Central African Republic, and South Sudan. A documentary by the organization of the same name depicts the abduction of children who were then used as child soldiers by Kony and the LRA. There has been a lot of criticism of the organization, though it seems they have good intentions. Whether or not they're a few years late bringing these atrocities to the world's attention, they want to see Kony and his cronies brought to justice. So do I.

The villages and towns that we passed on the bus were beautiful. Jungles gave way to square, dense forests where hundreds of thin trees gave way to vast expanses of plains and farms. Small towns gave way to tit-shaped hills, each with single trees at the top serving as its nipple, which were surrounded by green fields, banana trees, wheat fields, coffee plantations, and sugar cane stalk. I could smell the life in the air, hard won by a proud, yet still wary, people.

Before we reached Kampala, right as we came into view of the majestic Lake Victoria in the town of Jinja, our bus was stopped by the Ugandan police, next to aluminum factories and old graveyards.

They made everyone get off the bus and I saw several blue-and-white-camouflage uniformed police officers with assault rifles and a drug-sniffing dog. My heart dropped as I remembered

I had several joints wrapped in a sock in one of my bags in the luggage compartment under the bus. Once we were all off the bus, the cops let the dog jump on board to sniff around.

Holy fuck. This is it. I'm done for.

I thought the borders would be the problem, but no, it's the random police checks. Aaron had a good idea wrapping his bud in beef.

I imagined the dog smelling my bag and the cops finding the bud, then arresting me in front of everyone and bringing me to a shitty little police station like the one in Busia District. I'd seen enough episodes of *Locked Up Abroad* to know what would happen next: beatings, forced confessions, more beatings, getting locked away in a cold, small cell with two other maniacs or a hot, large room with fifty people itching to stomp my ass in the shower, stabbings, failed escape attempts, more beatings, humanity lost, dignity never to return again, endless years of lockdown before I even go to trial, only to be given a twenty-five-year sentence with no representation. All for a couple joints. Good times.

Finally the dog came out and I asked a fellow passenger standing next to me what was going on.

"The dog is finished," he whispered back. "He found nothing."

"Okay, good, because I have—"

"Relax," he interrupted me, knowing what I was about to say and cutting me off before the cops overheard and I fucked it all up. "It is over. We go now. Calm down."

My heartbeat slowed a bit and we got back on the bus. Looking back, I never should have been so careless. I was aware of the consequences, but I didn't think they applied to me. That was some stupid shit to pull in a foreign land, where my precious American, civil, and human rights did not apply.

We continued over the river that is the source of the Nile and eventually entered Kampala. It was the craziest city center to drive or walk around, packed with endless people and vehicles. It was first come, first served on the streets as tens of thousands of *boda-bodas* (motorcycle dala dalas), bicycles, trucks, lorries, minibuses, and cars vied for spaces to wedge themselves into, to slowly squeeze through the traffic.

My bus *finally* arrived at the Kampala Coach office at about 1:00 p.m. (mind you, we had left Dar es Salaam at 6:00 a.m. the previous day), and I hired a taxi driver to take me on a few errands.

After withdrawing money from an ATM, the driver and I went searching for Duracell batteries. We must have visited ten stores in that bustling city.

"Do you have AA batteries?"

I had to show them what batteries looked like every time I asked.

"No."

"Of course not," I would say. "Why would you? Fuck's sake."

"Yes, I have," one said, and pulled out a packet of EverReady batteries, the kind I already had which didn't work.

"Goddammit, no."

We eventually found a store that had Duracell, and I was finally able to close the lens of my camera and get it working properly. Then we went in search of a Ugandan SIM card so I could call Father Odo, the Catholic priest who was going to host my stay in the Pearl of Africa.

"Father Odo, this is Justin! *Oli otya*," I said, which means "How are you" in Luganda, the major language of Uganda.

He laughed on the other line and said, "Hello, Justin! I am good. Where are you?"

"I'm in Kampala. I'm a few days early."

"Yes, I thought you were coming this weekend. But that's okay. This works out better because I am in Kampala, too."

He was at the Pope Paul VI Memorial Hotel for a three-day regional conference of about fifty priests from all around Uganda.

"Why don't you call a taxi and meet me here?"

"Okay, I'm with a driver now. I'll give him the phone and you can tell him where to take me."

I made one last stop at a pharmacy to buy some over-the-counter Valium.

· · · · · · ·

I WAS DIRTY, HUNGRY, underdressed, and tired from my bus ride when Father Odo and I finally met for the first time in person in the lobby of the Pope Hotel. He was a young priest, maybe thirty-eight years old. He carried himself with confidence and ease, and something about his demeanor made me feel safe. He was an endearing, gentle giant: a bulky, broad chested, handsome Ugandan with a square jaw, a deep voice, and a small gap between his two front teeth.

I knew him through my mom, who knew him because he visited her church in California, the church I was raised in. He and I had talked on the phone a couple times when I was planning my trip, but we had never met. It was a joyous occasion. He suggested that I spend a night at the hotel since the conference was still going on until early afternoon the next day. That way he could drive me to his church and home in Mityana, about two hours west of Kampala.

I checked in and went to my room. It was an impressive, quality hotel, with excellent service. The lap of luxury, sure. I was overjoyed at the sight of toilet paper and a clean shower in my bathroom. I even had a balcony, though it only overlooked a courtyard with concrete pillars sticking out of the ground, rebar still poking up out of the top. They were being used as clotheslines to dry laundry. Beyond that, I had a view of Kampala, for the hotel was built on one of the higher hills near the outskirts of the city.

I took a glorious shower, and had a glorious shave, and ate a glorious meal, and drank several glorious local beers called Nile Special after that bus ride from hell. Refreshed, I did some writing and got some much-needed sleep. I woke up late and went out behind the building, where only employees were supposed to be, and saw a shockingly large Marabou stork. It was so beautiful, I had to get as close to it as I could. I regretted leaving my camera in my room. I came within ten feet of it, enough for me to see its intricate, colorful details, before it lifted up its enormous wings and fully flapped them a couple times to launch itself into the air. Its wings made loud whooping noises with each flap as the bird soared over the city.

When Father Odo returned around 2:30 p.m., he drove me and three other priests into the city center so I could pick up my order from the pharmacy. The traffic was a nightmare, even worse than Los Angeles because of its concentrated size. After I picked up my prescription (if you can call it that), one of the priests and I began making our way back to where Father Odo had parked. We passed a police checkpoint and one of the cops said, "Hey you, mzungu, come here."

We walked over to him.

"*Oli otya, ssebo* (Hello, how are you, sir)?" I said to him.

"What are you doing here?" he asked coldly, ignoring my attempt to practice what little Luganda I knew.

"Uh, I'm visiting friends," I said.

"Where are you going?"

"Mityana, to visit a priest who is a friend of mine."

"Where do you come from?"

How to answer the question without being here all day?

"I just came from Kenya, but I'm from California," I said. "America."

"Do you have your passport?"

"Yes, sir," I said and pulled it out of my pocket, handing it to him. He handed it right back to me.

"You open it up and then you give it to me."

I opened it to the page where my Uganda stamp was, which could have been easily flipped to because it also contained my folded visa receipt.

"Here's the stamp, here's my visa receipt," I said, pointing and subtly challenging him to find something wrong with my papers. The reason he stopped me was because I'm white, and he wanted to find something that he could say I needed to pay a fine for. *Fucking crooked cops, the world over.*

He looked at my passport and visa receipt, and I looked at the rifle around his shoulders.

"How long do you have?" he asked, referring to my visa.

"They gave me sixty days, and I've only arrived yesterday, so... if everything is in order..."

"Okay, go away," he finally relented.

The entire time the priest who accompanied me never said a word, just stared at the officer, who never asked for the priest's passport.

We made it back to Father Odo's car and I told him what happened. He shook his head in disgust.

"The police here are crooks," he said, as we passed hundreds of uniformed officers getting ready to go to their posts in various parts of the city and country. "Two groups of Muslims are fighting right now," he continued, "so the police fear there will be violence. Thank God they do not have their guns today. Or at least not yet. Today it is peaceful, but if you are in the city when the police decide to harass and beat and shoot people, you want to leave Uganda the next day. It is like being at the gates of death."

· · · · · · · ·

WE DROVE THE TWO hours to Mityana, a midsized town with several confusing market streets off the main highway, which was recently repaved because elections were supposed to happen soon and the government was trying to put on a show that they were restoring Uganda. Father Odo told me the road was terrible before that, just a dirt path with deep potholes and sharp rocks sticking out, turning the hour and a half journey into a three- or four-hour drive.

We went to a market so I could get a few things, then headed down a steep hill off an easy-to-miss dirt road that led into the lush, green property that was Baanabakintu Cathedral, where Father Odo lived and performed mass along with five or six other priests. There were grass fields surrounding the enormous brick veneer church, with hundreds of palm trees and other plants providing plenty of shade, a well-maintained graveyard where the previous priests were buried, and several supporting brick buildings with beautifully colored flower gardens.

It was built by German missionaries in the sixties, and had three half-cone-shaped spires sticking out of the roof which represented the huts that the locals were living in when the missionaries arrived. In front stood a statue of a priest with three sharp spears attached to his back who lived in the area. In 1886, soldiers raided the village and asked for the "believer" to come forth. The man stepped forward and said, "Here I am," so they speared him three times and tied him to one of the trees that still stands in front of the church today. It took him two days to die.

Father Odo introduced me to several of the other priests who lived there, as well as three girls who lived on the property and did all the cooking, cleaning, and what have you. I was instantly attracted to one of the girls, name of Mary. She dressed smartly and professionally, and carried herself with an air of confidence. Unfortunately, she was a devout Catholic, like everyone else there. *What a bummer. No fun at all.*

The girls prepared my room, which shared a courtyard with the rooms of all the other priests. I sat down with those priests and the girls for dinner in the rectory, a cozy, dark brown, rectangular room with posters and crosses and other religious propaganda littering the walls, as well as a few comfortable chairs and the main television, where every night we watched the local nightly news and soccer matches. Most meals consisted of rice, beans, cooked bananas, either chicken or beef, plantains, avocado, bread, juice, and cantaloupe. The girls prepared the meals in a separate, small, red concrete house with aluminum roof panels that sat behind the rectory. A mud path led to the structure, next to a pile of large logs. Large plumes of smoke constantly puffed out through the windows from its stone oven. Everything was delicious.

"I will sit next to the mzungu," said Mary.

No complaints from my side on that.

"So maybe I can become a mzungu," she continued, only half joking.

"What, through osmosis?" laughed Father Odo.

"Why do you want to be a mzungu?" I asked her.

"So I can be like you."

It reminded me of something a Mexican girl, with whom I had had a brief fling in Monterrey, said to me: "I want your life. I want to be free like you."

"You don't want to be like me," I said to Mary. "Do you not like being Ugandan?"

"I want to go to California. How can I do that?"

"Well, that's pretty difficult," I admitted. "You could marry a mzungu. It would be a fake marriage, but it would work."

"Yes, but in the eyes of God…" she trailed off, shaking her head.

"Mary is a very prayerful girl," said Father Odo.

What a shame. What a waste of beauty. She was holding herself back from such wonderful experiences as making love, all for some misguided notion of a nonexistent eternal afterlife. Meanwhile, reality, right there in front of her, was quickly passing her by. I considered it a tragedy.

• • • • • • •

As we ate, we watched the news, which became a nightly habit. A couple days before I arrived in Uganda, the police stopped a woman who was just driving through the city but happened to be in opposition to the government of President Yoweri Museveni. The president had eliminated presidential term limits (which he himself implemented when first elected in 1986) when his two five-year terms were nearing an end. Everyone was debating this when I was there. Even members of the ruling party were speaking out and calling for the restoration of the term limits, which Museveni bullied parliament into eliminating in 2005. Although he had done much to turn Uganda around from the decades of unimaginable violence brought by Amin, Obote, and the rebel groups, many Ugandans believed it was time for Museveni to step aside. Some also feared that a future president would have a lifelong appointment. And if that future person is anything like Idi Amin and the like, it would be more than disastrous for Uganda. I heard many Ugandans comparing Museveni to Amin.

So the police had pulled the woman over and opened her door. The entire incident was caught on tape, which was repeatedly shown on the news show we watched. The priests and I sat transfixed, shaking our heads at the outrageous behavior of the police. The officers were grabbing at her, trying to pull her out of the car. They reached between her legs and one cop kept groping her breast over and over again.

"Leave my breast alone!" she yelled. "Why do you want to pinch my breast?!"

"Are you serious?" I said out loud. "What the fuck?"

Father Odo nodded. "I know. That is how it is."

The next day, hundreds of women walked around the city wearing only revealing bras (with pants or dresses) and confronted the police. Several of them had no bras at all, and carried signs in front of their chests that read "RESPECT OUR BREASTS!" One woman interviewed on the news called the police the "Ugandan Breast-Pinching Brigade," which had the priests and I cracking up. The girls, including Mary, had long since gone into the kitchen to clean the dishes. I realized that the status of women in Uganda, indeed in all of East Africa, was deeply unequal and rather disturbing. It reached far beyond the vile grip of the Ugandan Breast Pinching Brigade: the dynamic played out right there in the church rectory. The message was clear: women are second-class citizens.

BANANA
FIBER FUTBOL

OVER BREAKFAST, FATHER ODO asked me to explain to the other priests why I was agnostic and not Catholic anymore.

I gave them the same reasons I gave Thelma back in Fish Hoek: "I know that I don't know for sure if there's a God or not, and I know that no one else knows for sure," I said.

This evolved into a very long discussion with the priests, whose ages ranged from midthirties to high seventies. Most of them were fairly large men with protruding bellies and hearty laughs, and all of them were very wise. They had all seen some shit in their day.

They asked for my opinion, so I gave it to them. I told them it was possible Jesus was a real person who preached about and did some good things, such as taking care of the poor and promoting peace, but that I don't believe he is the Son of God because I don't see God in a human form. I recognize an energy or mass consciousness that, for lack of a better word, governs the universe, but I think it's a force that human brains cannot even begin to comprehend or understand. If anything, I refer to this force as nature. I think the Bible has some good stories, but that's all they are. The thing was written by humans influenced entirely by the politics of their day, so it is not the word of God. Over the last 2,000 years, religious authorities have changed so many things and produced so many different versions. They left out what they felt was wrong according to the politics and customs of their time, thereby making the Bible an incomplete, inaccurate book of scattered fairytales and political texts. I completely disagree with the *Book of Genesis* and its explanation for the origins of man; I believe in evolution and multiverses and things we don't yet or can't yet know about, things more interesting than Christianity's, or for that matter any other religion's, simplistic, nonsensical, and unsatisfactory explanation for existence, morality, and humanity.

The priests shook their heads and chuckled. I wondered if they ever had to really defend what they believed before. Their reaction was essentially, *Oh, young boy, you have so much to learn,* but at least they weren't too condescending about it, which I liked. They just asked me questions to clarify my position and engaged me in a respectful discussion about a serious topic.

I decided to keep it light and comical, so I threw a biblical conundrum at them: "There is a very critical line missing from the Bible. After Cain killed Abel, there is a sentence that reads something like, 'And then Cain had children with his wife.' Where did his wife come from? At that point, there was only Adam, Eve, and Cain, so did Cain sleep with Eve, his mother? So it was incest?"

They laughed heartily at this.

"That is a very good question," one of the priests admitted. "Very good. I think there are a few lines missing from the Bible as well. Perhaps at that time incest was not taboo, and became taboo later on."

"But even if that's true," I said, glossing over the fact that he had essentially just admitted there were critical lines missing from the book that he believed to be the word of God, "then we are all related and we are all incestuous."

Tears were running down our faces from laughing so hard.

"Justin, we will have to set up a meeting with the headmaster at St. Noa High School soon so you can start teaching there," Father Odo said.

"Okay, yeah, that sounds great," I said.

"But don't tell the students that we are all products of incest," he said, smiling.

A man who ran the parish's Communications Office, Father Pantius, walked through the room. Father Odo asked the correct pronunciation of his name.

"PAN-shus," he pronounced.

"So, not Pontius, huh?" I joked, as in Pontius Pilate, the Roman judge who ordered Jesus Christ to be crucified.

"No, no, no," he said. "Do you want to get me stoned?"

"Well, sure. But not in the way you think."

As I expected, the reference went over his head.

· · · · · · ·

FATHER ODO HAD TWO functions to attend that day: a village mass and a graduation party. I decided to go with him. Mary came along as well, wearing a sharp business suit that made her look like a young professional. We drove in Father Odo's four wheel drive vehicle about forty minutes west of Mityana. We stopped at the graduation party first, which was just getting set up. I approached a few guys in shabby clothes sitting under a square canopy tent, and they handed me a cup without saying anything. From a gas canister they poured a brown liquid with tiny chunks floating around in it into the cup.

"This is the locally-brewed beer," Mary explained. "The men sit under this tent and spend all their money and get drunk all day."

The guy with the canister poured more into my cup after I had tasted it. The chunks turned out to be pieces of sugar cane, and the beer itself wasn't bad. I only had a couple sips when a really drunk dude (it was only 10:00 a.m.) with missing teeth and a ripped-up shirt came up to me and spoke only in Luganda. I thought he was asking for a sip of my local homebrew, so I handed it to him and he drank the whole thing in one gulp.

You fucker. I wanted to try more of that.

Then he asked me for money to buy more of the sugar beer, with Mary translating. She told him to get lost, and we all got back in the car and drove down the highway again for the village mass, with the intention of coming back later. The turnoff to the village wasn't visible from the highway, and I was surprised when Father Odo suddenly drove off the road, basically into the bush. A very narrow and bumpy dirt path appeared, hardly drivable. It was practically impassable. An American driver would see this and think it was a small hiking trail, where cars were not allowed.

We drove deep into the bush, surrounded by jungle, until we came to a grassy clearing. We parked the car and walked up to a midsized house made of mud and wooden sticks. Rows of wooden benches were covered by a yellow tarp that was held up by wooden poles, and about 200 villagers were waiting for mass to begin.

As Father Odo prepared himself, Mary and I walked around to the outdoor cooking area on the other side of the yellow tarp tent. Several old pots covered with banana leaves, and other pots made of wood and bark, wrapped tightly with string, sat over hot coals, cooking the edible interiors.

A small boy led Father Odo and me on a five-minute trek into the dense bush, where one of the many cows in the area was grazing. The cow had been given to Father Odo as a gift about a year before, and he wanted to see how it had grown. Although very wary of me at first, it eventually calmed down enough for me to gently stroke its side.

Back at the makeshift church, the "pews" were filling up with people. All the children, about thirty of them, sat in the front on a straw mat on the ground, leaving their sandals and shoes in the dirt. Everyone was staring at me the entire time, especially the children. They were fascinated because they had never seen a mzungu, especially not one attending a mass in their village.

Mary and I sat in the front row and watched Father Odo, who was now in full priest garb, performing quiet confessions for a few individuals who wished to repent.

I couldn't remember the last time I attended mass, but this was a pretty special occasion, so I didn't mind. I went through the motions, standing when everyone else stood, clapping when the choir sang and the drummers drummed, kneeling when the others knelt, and so forth. I hadn't done the sign of the cross in about fifteen years or so, and caught myself when I moved my hand up, down, right, and left, instead of the correct up, down, left, and right. I tried to suppress my chuckle.

The entire mass was conducted in Lugandan, so, although I remembered most of how Catholic masses go (they're all basically the same), I did not understand what was being said, except when the other local priest introduced me to the villagers.

"Justin, you are most welcome," he said.

He told them I was a journalist, and that I had traveled from South Africa to Uganda by road. He also addressed me in English after his homily, explaining that the special occasion for this particular mass was that a husband and wife wanted to show the community what they had accomplished since beginning their family some years ago.

After an hour and a half, I was quite bored and very relieved when it was over. I had put on my best shirt, pants, and shoes for the occasion. Mary, Father Odo, and I said goodbye to the villagers and got into his car to travel back to the graduation party. About twenty feet after the clearing and back on the shitty, impassible "road," his car broke down. We were stuck. A few of the men from the village came over to inspect the engine, and the theory was that the fuel pump needed to be replaced. We were so far away from anything resembling civilization, that we knew this would take some time.

"So is this where God wants us to be right now? Why doesn't he fix the car for us?" I said to Mary, instantly realizing how mockingly mean-spirited the comment was. She looked away and didn't reply, and I regretted saying it.

I lit a cigarette, but Mary told me to put it out. People may have been chain smokers in southern Africa, but hardly anyone smoked in eastern Africa, especially Uganda.

Father Odo called a mechanic, and as we waited for him the village priest invited us to eat lunch. We walked back to the yellow tarp tent and up two or three dried out, uneven mud steps into a small, battered mudroom that had one small window letting in very little light, though the sun was shining bright that day. The mud walls were plastered with a few small, worn religious posters.

Father Odo, the village priest, and I were allowed to sit in chairs at the table in the middle of the room. Mary and another girl from the village had to sit on a mat on the ground on the other side of the table. They had to remove their shoes and we, the men, did not. Mary and the village girl brought in our lunch and washed our hands for us.

"Why can't the girls sit down in these two chairs like us?" I asked the two male priests.

"Look at them, they are fine," said Father Odo.

"Here, Mary, take my chair and you take this other empty chair," I insisted.

They shook their heads no, embarrassed at the offer.

"We are used to it," the village girl said under her breath.

"It is culture," Father Odo said over her words, but I'm glad I was still able to hear them, for they were very telling words.

"Yes, I know, it is your culture...but I disagree," I said. "I think we are equal."

"We are equal, but..." the village priest trailed off.

But what? I wondered to myself. I should have said it out loud.

"That's not right," I concluded, which was the last word on the subject.

The women were also required to clean up afterwards as us three men sat with full bellies, discussing some matter of import or other. It felt like we were in a special dining area where the secret male elite met to decide regional policy. I felt blessed and ashamed to have been a part of it.

· · · · · · ·

OUTSIDE, I JOINED A couple villagers playing the village bongos. I was banging on the drums when the mechanic finally arrived, and I helped a couple guys push the car back into the clearing so that other vehicles could pass by. Many of the children sat and stood around watching the few men try to fix the car, which was looking less and less likely.

I decided to try to introduce some fun into the hopeless situation. I asked Mary to be a translator as I tried to get a kid, any kid, to grab onto my arm tightly so I could lift them into the air.

"Here, let me grab your hands and I'll swing you around," I said to one small boy, demonstrating what I meant. He quickly backed away, fear in his eyes. He didn't even want to touch me. "Grab my arm, and I'll lift you up!"

Mary put the boy's hands on my arm, which freaked him out to no end. He started to cry and ran away, mortified at the notion of grabbing the arm of a mzungu. Still, the kids stood around me, staring at me, curious, confused, shy, frightened, and obsessed.

Then I remembered a dream I had a week before I arrived in Africa. I had dreamt that I would be in a village, deep in the bush, playing soccer with a group of kids using a ball made of something natural and rubberless. I walked back to the yellow tent and asked a Ugandan in his late twenties if there was anything we could make a soccer ball out of. He had to leave soon, but he grabbed his machete and led me on a hike through the bush towards Father Odo's cow where there were plenty of banana trees. He began hacking off dried, dead banana leaves and showed me how to make the core of the ball. Mary tagged along and made one herself. The man then had me chop off several long banana leaves, which he ripped into thick shredded pieces of fiber and wrapped them around the core until we had two makeshift soccer balls. They were far from FIFA World Cup regulation balls, but they would do the trick. He had to leave, so Mary and I walked with him back to the clearing where the children were milling about, bored to death. I figured this would get them going.

I started to take off my nice shoes but Mary told me it wasn't a good idea. As soon as I started kicking the two balls into the crowd of children, they instantly got the idea and I was filled with emotion as their faces lit up with excitement. I had gained their trust, finally. We played for two hours as the men worked on the car, just me (essentially playing goalkeeper the entire time) against thirty children. A few of them, especially one young girl about ten years old, were very good. They scored a few goals on me, but even with two balls and thirty kids I managed to hold my own.

Whenever I would take a break, to go to the car and drink some mango juice, or sit down because I was so goddamn out of shape, the kids would gather around me, staring at me and waiting for me to continue playing. They wanted it to go on forever. My shirt was drenched with sweat, my chest hurt, and I was getting blisters on my feet inside my nice shoes that were not made for playing soccer in an African village with thirty kids. But I kept on going. I had to, really. What other choice did I have? The dream I had before I came to Africa was now realized, exactly how I had envisioned it in the depths of slumber where I usually only experienced nightmares.

The mean-spirited comment I made to Mary earlier about God wanting us to be there and not fixing the car returned to my mind, and I realized that yes, maybe there was a reason.

"You are making the children very happy," Mary told me. "They will all be talking about you, the mzungu who they played soccer with, to all their friends and family, for a long, long time."

· · · · · · · ·

WHEN THE CAR WAS fixed, Father Odo gathered the children around and had them repeat after him in English, "Thank you very much, Justin." He told them where I was from, how I had traveled across Africa to Uganda, my profession as a journalist, and so on. Then he had them sing two songs for me, essentially meaning "Thank you very much."

The four of us got into the car, I waved goodbye to the children, and, as we sped off back toward the smooth(er) road, all thirty of the kids ran after the car yelling and cheering, "Mzungu! Bye, mzungu!" I stuck my head out the window and watched them disappear in the dust we left behind.

"AFRICANS ARE NOT PEOPLE"

ONE DAY AFTER MASS at Father Odo's Baanabakintu Cathedral, a couple state soldiers enrolled dozens of kids in a "disciplinary" program, and proceeded to train them in the fields outside the church by having them march around, repeat slogans, and what have you. "Soldiers of Christ," one of the soldiers called them. An oxymoron, if you ask me. It reminded me of Kony's methods, brainwashing young children who didn't know any better.

I played soccer with the kids, and at night they created a large bonfire and the children danced around it, singing. Out of nowhere, it began pouring rain, so I retreated to the nearby community room and sat outside in a chair under a tin awning, the liquid prison bars restricting me from going anywhere. One of the soldiers, Charlie, a tall, ripped Ugandan with a scraggly beard, sat next to me as the kids went inside for more lessons and supper. It was midnight. He smoked with me as the fire continued to burn. The rain could not put it out because of the condensed way they had constructed the wood, he told me. Charlie offered to escort me to Rwanda, the Democratic Republic of the Congo (DRC), and Semuliki National Park, where he said there was a pygmy village. I wanted to go, but money was an issue, as I would have had to pay for myself and for him. Also, he sketched me out a little bit. Something was a little off about him. Later on, I ended up doing that exact trip, only with a local journalist instead of this army soldier. A slightly better travel companion, in my humble opinion.

I asked Charlie about the controversial government plan to destroy 4,000 homes and compensate the homeowners so the government could build a brand-new highway from Kampala, the capital, to Entebbe, where the airport is.

"It is still in the planning stages," he said.

"I know, but what do you think about it? Do you think it's a good idea or a bad idea?"

"Uh, I work for the army, for the state, so I cannot give you my opinion," he replied.

Therein lay his answer.

· · · · · · ·

THERE WAS A MENTALLY ill man in ragged clothes who wandered the parish property, yelling and muttering gibberish or idioglossia, a mixture of Luganda and who knows what else. He used to be a policeman. Now he's batshit insane, but completely harmless. He was more scared of others than anyone was of him. He mostly stayed near the church's cemetery, where the priests were buried. Still, whenever I walked by he yelled nonsense at me, and it was unnerving.

Father Odo and I drove around town. There was a big soccer match planned for that Saturday between Mityana's team and the neighboring county's team. The locals were constructing a tall, brick wall around a large grass field called Ssaza Playground because the kabaka (king) of central Uganda (called Buganda) would be attending. This was a very big deal. He rarely left his palace in Entebbe, and only visited Mityana once a year. The people there absolutely adored him, so all week they were building the bleachers in the playground where the kabaka and his VIP entourage would watch the game, and the large, square archways made out of bamboo and wood called *kiyitirirwas* that were placed every half-mile or so along the route the kabaka would travel to the game, and making other preparations. The town had also been partying nonstop since I arrived, and every night I could hear the drumming and singing from my room, which was next to the cathedral and a bit remote from town.

I bought a USB modem from a company called Orange so I could have access to the Internet from my room or anywhere I wanted instead of going to a café all the time. The service was inconsistent. Sometimes it worked great and other times it was terrible. The Internet in Africa, in general, was just dogshit.

I also rented a bike and rode around town. At the top of a hill overlooking the town, I met a man named Ben. He said he worked at the subcounty office that we were standing next to. We talked for a while about why I was in Mityana, and then he said something that shocked me.

"Would you like to take my daughter?" he asked.

"What do you mean 'take' her?"

"You know, to marry her," he said. "She is very loyal."

My body tensed up. I couldn't believe what I was hearing, though it wasn't the last time I was offered someone's daughter or sister. They wanted their female relatives to marry a mzungu so that they may have a better life. They didn't understand that it's just not possible nor desirable on my part, unless I actually loved the girl and she actually loved me. She'd also have to be somewhat close to my age.

Charlie the soldier also had me meet his sister, who was in the sixth grade. I knew it made sense to them, but it made absolutely no sense to me. I groaned internally as she offered me a gift of candy, lemons, tomatoes, and avocados. I took the gift and thanked them, but told them that I wasn't interested. I gave the food to the girls at the rectory who prepared our meals. They cooked the items and served them, along with the rest of dinner, to the priests and myself.

There was a tiny kitten that lived in the residency house, smaller than my hand, and after dinner I brought him to my room and he slept in my bed with me. Mary kept calling him pussy, not knowing the alternate meaning of that word.

"Here, pretty pussy," she'd say when she was looking for it. "Bad pussy!" she'd yell when it scratched her. "Oh, what a dirty pussy," when she found it rolling in dirt outside.

"Does she know what that word means?" I asked Father Odo.

"What does it mean?" he said.

"It's a dirty word for vagina."

"Oh, well don't tell her," he said. "She'd be so embarrassed."

· · · · · · ·

THE NEXT DAY, I met Noah, a very well-connected and knowledgeable journalist who wrote for New Vision (a government owned media company based in Kampala) and filmed short news segments for Bukedde TV (a local broadcast station based in Mityana) in front of the cathedral. He was short, about my height, and always wore argyle sweaters and khakis; a handsome Ugandan with a self-satisfied glint in his eyes. His energy was laid back and confident, and I instantly picked up that he was really intelligent. He took a liking to me right away, and we bonded on an intellectual level. We discussed what I wanted to write about in Uganda, and other details of my stay there, and made a plan to carry the ideas out. He took me under his wing and showed me the ropes of how journalism worked in Uganda, which had similarities and differences to how it worked in America.

The day I met Noah was Uganda's Labor Day, so a large mass was held, followed by a conference. He was going to interview a beautiful female member of Parliament who was in attendance. *How did she become a member of Parliament in a country where women are servants?* I should have asked her.

Noah and I set up a time for us to meet and discuss the details of my reporting the next day. I went to sit and watch the conference and listen to the Parliament member speak to the sizable crowd in Luganda. Afterward, several members of the crowd came up to offer the priests gifts, mostly reams of paper and office supplies.

The next day, I met Noah in town and we took a dala dala to Kampala. We went to a posh hotel, where we caught the end of a press conference held by the board of the Human Rights Network for Journalists, Uganda, of which Noah was a member. They unveiled a new report entitled "Media Liberalisation in Uganda: Threatening Journalists' Rights and Freedoms." Some of the injustices they focused on included the fact that Ugandan journalists didn't have health insurance or other benefits, and that they received lower pay than journalists in other countries. They also spoke about police harassing and beating journalists as they covered protests and fracases.

After that, we walked to the New Vision Group headquarters, a large, government-owned media house that produced several newspapers, and TV, and radio broadcasts. The security guards had to write down the serial numbers of my camera and laptop before we walked through a metal detector and into the building. We went upstairs to the newsroom, and I was very impressed. It reminded me of the newsroom in *All the President's Men.* There was a long, rectangular room with at least a hundred different half-sized cubicle walls, so everyone could see everyone else. Each section (Features, Editors, Subeditors, Opinion, Sports, etc.) was labeled and there were people working at almost every desk. Every piece of equipment needed to run such a large media house was present. The computers were brand new. Reporters and editors were hard at work: writing stories, reading stories, cropping photos, listening to audio reports on headphones, chatting on Facebook, playing solitaire on their computers...

Noah introduced me to several reporters as well as to the Features editor, Chloë. She and I talked about a couple story ideas I had for New Vision, and we agreed to start with a feature story about my experience traveling alone from South Africa to Uganda with my American perspective. After that was published, we would discuss more opportunities for me, such as opinion pieces and hard news stories. I hoped it would come to fruition; to be published in a Ugandan newspaper would be a significant personal victory. I would become an internationally-published journalist.

When we entered the newsroom, I saw on a television that US Special Forces had joined the Ugandan army (UPDF) in the Central African Republic, a sort of state within a state (the Democratic Republic of the Congo, or DRC), where Kony was thought to be hiding. The regime in Khartoum, Sudan, was supplying him with food and ammunition. Since many of the Lord's Resistance Army's (LRA) commanders had died, defected, or fled, it was believed that there were only 250 rebel fighters left in the bush. It felt as though US and Ugandan army officials were on the cusp of capturing or killing Kony. Tales of the Special Forces' exploits and other Kony-related news dominated the headlines every day.

I got ahold of the number for the Communications Officer at the US Consulate in Kampala and called him to see if I could be embedded with the US Special Forces as they hunted for Kony. He gave me the email for the Major who was heading the team. I emailed the Major, detailing my request, and he replied, "Justin, thanks for the note. Unfortunately we are not accommodating journalists right now. Last week was a preplanned escort trip. If you're truly interested in embedding, I would suggest contacting UPDF." I looked up the spokesperson for the UPDF and sent him an email with the same request. I never received a response. Perhaps it was for the best.

. . . .

BACK IN MITYANA, I was just about to go to sleep in my room in the rectory courtyard when I heard loud singing and drumming coming from up the long path to the main road. It was about midnight, but I decided to walk up there to see the excitement, which was generated by the upcoming kabaka's arrival (the people loved their king and hated their president). A large, drunk crowd had gathered around a circle of drummers, dancing the night away next to one of the *kiyitirirwas*, which were still under construction. A few men from the village stood there, arms crossed, making sure nothing happened to the archways. I joined in on the drumming and the dancing, and the crowd went wild with excitement.

"Mzungu! Mzungu!" they chanted.

"Mugandans!" I said, which is the term for individual Ugandans.

Everyone wanted to talk to me and pull me in this and that direction. They also wanted me to drum and dance in the Ugandan style, a bouncy, energetic movement, but I wasn't very good at it and just wanted to do my own thing, follow my own rhythm. They thought my style was hilarious.

One tall, skinny Ugandan with dark skin and a gnarly scar over his left eye, who was about my age, approached me.

"What is your name?" he asked.

"Justin."

He busted out laughing. "Oh my, that is funny!"

In Uganda, Justin is a girl's name. Every time someone asked my name, they'd laugh. I had to explain every time that in America, Justin is a boy's name and the female version is Justine. Ugandans spell it with an "e" at the end but don't pronounce it.

His name was Adam, and he offered to buy me a beer. He led me down a dark, dirty alley to a shebeen where he bought me two beers and fetched two cigarettes for me, because I was in my sandals and pajamas and hadn't brought any money with me. We talked and drank for a couple hours, mostly about how he loved mzungus and was helping me because he knew that at some point in his life a mzungu would help him out in return. We had an instant connection. It was like we were old friends.

He left for about ten minutes at one point, and when he came back he was distraught and full of despair. I asked him what happened as we walked back to the drum circle.

"I just went to my wife's house, just now, and I caught her sleeping with another man! Oh my god! Oh my god!" He paced around the shebeen. "I am so confused! How could she do this to me? I worked so hard for her. I gave her everything. I bought her a motorcycle. And she does this to me? She is not serious. Oh my god..." He sat down and put his head in his hands.

I felt really bad for him and tried to calm him down. We sat down in another shebeen across the alley and I distracted him from his troubles by talking about other things. Back at the drum circle, people were pulling my arm to drag me somewhere else to show me something, or grabbing the beer out of my hand, when one of the sober *kiyitirirwa* builders pulled me aside.

"Justin," he said. He knew my name but I didn't recognize him. It startled me. "This guy, that guy, that guy, and that guy, do not trust them. They are bad people. You should be very careful. Finish your beer and go to sleep."

It was sound advice, sure. I wasn't sure if Adam was one of the guys he pointed out. Then he muttered something I couldn't believe.

"Africans are not people."

I immediately headed into the darkness back to the path that led me to the cathedral. As I was walking away, the drum circle was just beginning to disperse, and I could hear someone (I think Adam, but I wasn't sure because it sounded like a woman) yelling, "Justin! Justin! Where are you? Chapman! Justin!"

I walked faster and didn't look back.

WITCH DOCTORS
AND CON ARTISTS

THE SUN BEAT DOWN on the small, African town in the middle of the supposed rainy season as I traveled around Mityana with Noah on a *boda-boda* (a motorcycle taxi). It was the cheapest and most convenient way to get around town, but also the most dangerous. The roads were shit, mostly dirt with divots and potholes and sharp drops where the concrete streets met the dirt paths. There were so many of the boda-bodas along with all the lorries and cars, and everyone was driving like there was no tomorrow. The drivers took so many risks.

We went to the various posts where people were still building the *kiyitirirwa* archways that the kabaka's convoy would be passing through the next day. We stopped at each one, where people were drumming and singing and dancing nonstop and cleaning the bamboo poles that were to be added to the *kiyitirirwas*, and Noah was filming them doing their thing, and interviewing a few people in Luganda for a Bukedde TV segment.

We went to the Ssaza Playground, where the big game was to be played. The brick wall, interior fence, and bleachers were still under construction. I played soccer with a few guys on the field as Noah interviewed important people from the town, such as chiefs, and heads of counties, and a very rich businessman who owned two hotels in Kampala and was the head of the Mityana Trader's Association. Every shop, no matter how small, had to register with his association.

We were trying to get Noah's video clips to Kampala, but he couldn't find any transport, and his deadline was looming. The head of the Trader's Association drove us from the playground to the house where the kabaka would be sleeping the next night, after his arrival, passing a nearby field where about twenty prisoners in bright yellow uniforms were hacking away at the tall grass with machetes, watched by one rifle-wielding guard.

In the middle of a small roundabout that sat in the middle of the main intersection of the town there was a small, straw hut. We stopped there to film a pretend healer (a guy with straw and leaves around his head who invited us into his hut). We removed our shoes and went inside. It was about five feet tall and shaped like a triangle, around five feet from wall to wall. There wasn't much inside. The man did a little dance, sang a little ditty, and shook his shakers to entertain us. Afterward, I put 1,000 shillings (about forty cents) into his wooden cup. I guess Noah had left the hut before me and filmed me pushing aside the cloth door as I left, because that shot of me exiting the hut was included in his TV news segment about the preparations of the playground and the *kiyitirirwas*.

After Noah had given his tapes to a dala dala driver to deliver to the New Vision and Bukedde TV headquarters to be edited, we rode on a boda-boda about halfway to Kampala (an hour's ride) for a witchcraft ceremony, which Noah was scheduled to cover. He had begun taking me on all his story assignments in an effort to show me the ropes. I'm very grateful to him. Without his guidance, I wouldn't have had much journalistic experience in Africa at all. I probably would have wandered around aimlessly, perpetually fucked up.

The driver turned off the highway onto a walking path that led us deep into the bush, to the village where a man named Donald had been accused of practicing witchcraft, or, at the very least, hiring witch doctors to curse a nearby family. A man in the family had died, the husband was supposedly acting crazy, like he was possessed, and the wife was ill.

Several villagers had attacked Donald's house the week before, and he had fled the village, landing hundreds of miles away. Riot police had to come and shoot tear gas into the crowd so they'd disperse. The villagers called a traditional healer to come and use his powers to confirm or deny whether Donald had, in fact, been practicing witchcraft.

The Ugandan constitution allows all kinds of worship, but it includes a (very weak and stupid) provision from 1957 called the Witchcraft Act that sets forth punishments for those who practice it. However, a court later voided the sections about witchcraft for having vague definitions. You are not allowed to threaten someone with witchcraft, but proving that someone has practiced it, let alone succeeded in utilizing evil spirits, is impossible at best. The whole thing was open to interpretation and manipulation.

Noah told me that the villagers were wary of modern hospitals and doctors, and that once they were convinced that witchcraft was being practiced, the sick wouldn't visit a hospital because they thought the doctors wouldn't be able to find, let alone cure, the problem.

"That's tragic," I said. "What if someone has malaria?"

"If they believe witchcraft is the source, they will not go to the hospital, and they'll just die."

When Noah and I arrived, there were about 300 people from the surrounding small villages there to witness the ceremony. I was the only mzungu there, obviously, and I was wearing my "MZUNGU–SINA PESA" shirt. Of course, everyone was staring at me, like, "Is this guy serious?," but they knew I was with Noah and that we were filming the ceremony for Bukedde TV. This gave us access that the crowd didn't have.

Under the Ugandan constitution, large gatherings of people are not allowed without permission from the police and without police presence. Indeed, there were several uniformed officers, who stood in front of the crowd (which was compacted together on a hill twenty feet from Donald's small, battered house, with people watching among the trees, cows, pigs, and chickens in the bush) while riot police, automatic rifles at the ready, stood at various points in a circle about forty feet from, and circled around, the crowd.

The traditional healer, a well-dressed bald man in his late fifties wearing a pink button-down shirt, an expensive watch, and a disinterested, arrogant expression on his face, had to get clearance from the local police as well as the chiefs of the village before he arrived.

The healer took his time, walking around the square house and tapping at various things with his black walking stick, which curved near the top like a handle, then continued up another foot (supposedly the source of his powers), before entering the house to look around. He didn't bring a bag, but two men came with him and one of them wore a thick, black rain jacket with many pockets. The healer exited the house and the three of them took canisters filled with local brew and walked around the perimeter of the house, splashing the alcohol against the outside walls of the house. They did the same thing with canisters of milk, then one of the guys tossed small stones up to hit the tin awning that stretched out beyond the roof. The crowd watched their every move, completely silent.

The healer then placed a bag of flour and a wooden bowl filled with an unknown substance at the foot of the door. He lit his pipe, smoked slowly, answered his smart phone and talked for a minute or so, then looked around at the crowd like they were figments of his imagination, and used his stick to mix the substance in the bowl. After smoking for a few minutes, he went back into the house with his associate. Noah and I followed. I saw the man with the black raincoat pull a cone-shaped item out of his pocket and put it in a bag on the floor in one of the bedrooms. We went outside. The healer emerged with that bag and another one, which he said he suspected contained the witchcraft items. After another few minutes, he opened one of the bags (a soft, weathered briefcase) and pulled out the curved, cone-shaped wooden handle with herbs sticking out of the top. He held it up to show the crowd, which went wild with excitement, for this was supposed to be the witchcraft item used by Donald to bewitch the family. I already knew the whole thing was bullshit, but when I saw what he did, I realized the scam. The man who was wearing the black raincoat had put the cone-shaped handle, which he had hidden in his jacket pocket the entire time, in the bag. It wasn't in the house originally, so Donald didn't use it to utilize evil spirits. I wasn't sure why, but the healer never looked at me or even acknowledged me the entire time. It was odd, because everyone else was staring at me.

Now all riled up, people from the crowd began throwing large pieces of wood into a pile in front of the house to make a fire. They brought two chickens over and removed the feathers from their necks, then sliced the heads off right in front of me and threw them into the pile. A guy doused the wood with kerosene and lit a fire. The healer threw the bags in, as well as the witchcraft item, which supposedly contained all the evil spirits. People grabbed whatever they could and threw the stuff into the fire. More gas was splashed on, and it became the tallest, hottest bonfire I'd ever seen. Everyone had to back away about twenty feet because it was so hot.

Then the already-elated crowd marched behind the healer down a path to the victim's home, about one hundred yards down the hill. Noah and I ran in front to get pictures and film the single-file hikers. When we got there, the healer approached the sick woman and rubbed the curve of his stick around her head, muttering a few words, and gently lifted his hands to the air, as if to say, *Evil spirits be gone.*

I followed the healer into the victim family's home, which he inspected thoroughly but with complete disinterest. I saw the room where the family members slept, on thin mats on a hard floor.

The crowd was angry. They wanted vengeance. Everyone marched back to Donald's house with the intention of destroying it. The police were there to stop them, and Noah told me, "If there is violence, stand behind the police, because they will shoot in front of them into the crowd, not behind." So we stayed behind the police, who stood between the crowd and the house. I was surprised to learn that Donald's father, a very old, frail man on crutches, was there. He claimed that his son was innocent. The police told the crowd to disperse. The crowd slowly backed off, though they didn't leave, and they would surely be back later to demolish the house.

The police told Noah and me that they were leaving and that we should leave as well, because if something happened they would not be able to protect us. I wanted to see some action, but it's probably better that we got back on the boda-boda and booked it out of there, following the healer who also rode on a boda-boda.

"We're not really in danger, are we, Noah?" I asked.

"Well, the villagers know they can be identified on television, and so, when the police leave, they could potentially attack us. It is better that we leave."

"What's going to happen?"

"The villagers will go looking for Donald, and if they find him, or if he ever returns to the village, he will be killed," Noah said. "Many people die this way. People practice witchcraft in Africa for various reasons: They are jealous of someone for having more money or beautiful children, they are mad at their spouse for having an affair, anything. And people are killed and their homes are destroyed because of it."

Meanwhile, the traditional healer was paid between 500,000 and 1,000,000 shillings (200 to 400 dollars) for his "services," which was a fuckload of money for villagers to cough up. He was ripping them off, and he also added to the confusion by spreading rumors about certain people practicing witchcraft. It was a business, and business was booming.

Noah and I went back to Mityana for beers and grub. He took me to his favorite bar, an unnamed tavern across the street from a petrol station called Gaz. We started calling the tavern Gaz Bar for identification purposes, as we ended up meeting there nearly every night for the rest of my trip to lick our wounds, bask in small victories, watch the news, discuss the day's events, and plan for the next day. Noah ordered us a couple Nile Specials and veggie samosas.

"According to the Ugandan constitution, in order for the police or a traditional healer or anyone to search your home, they must have a search warrant," Noah said.

"Same in America," I added.

"At this ceremony, they had no search warrant, and yet the healer and others were allowed to enter Donald's home, search it, seize items from it, burn them, probably destroy the house, and later most likely murder him."

Noah said that if Donald knew the law—which he doesn't because he's ignorant of it plain and simple—he could sue the police, the healer, and others. He could say his name and image were tarnished and be compensated 2,000,000 shillings for that, as well as for the destruction of his home and property, such as the bags and the chickens. The chances that he would win the case were extremely high, because how can anyone prove in court that evil spirits were the cause of the victim family's illnesses and death?

"Wow," I said. "I want to help Donald. Can we give him the pictures and footage we took of the ceremony so he can use them in court to prove he was not served with a search warrant?"

"Donald can only use our footage and pictures if we what? Broadcast them on television or publish them in the newspaper," Noah said. "If we supply him with the raw clips and photos, the villagers will think we were what? Spies trying to help him the whole time, instead of attending the ceremony to write and shoot a legitimate news story."

His use of the word "what" was a common Ugandan idiom. It came from the way they were taught English in school. A teacher would say, for example, "In order to pass my class you must what?" Pause. "Study hard and pay attention."

If we gave Donald the evidence he needed to prove his innocence, we would be outcasts in the community, and since Noah lived there and people knew who he was, he couldn't do that for Donald. It was all so frustrating. If these people really wanted to hold onto this outdated belief system, fine. But why not try a healer *and* a real doctor in a real hospital? What have they got to lose? They just think it's a waste of time, because the real reason for unexplainable things is invisible spirits and powers that can't be proved. The priests back at the cathedral made fun of the villagers who believed in witchcraft, but the basic concept wasn't that far from what they believed themselves.

How interesting. How bizarre.

Of course, there is no such thing as absolute truth, is there? At the end of the day, my worldview was no more valid than the priests', the villagers', or even the traditional healer's. I thought they were all living a lie, and they almost definitely thought I was doing the same by indulging in drugs and espousing of a lifestyle dangerously close to nihilism. I say they're wrong, they say I'm wrong, add up the score and everybody's wrong. For what it's worth, I was glad to be able to witness an entirely different world from my own, even if, and especially because, I didn't agree with it.

· · · · · · ·

NOAH AND I STOPPED by his home and I met his young son and his wife, who was too shy to greet me because she grew up in a village where the custom taught to her mandated that, because I was a man and she was a woman, she could not approach me or greet me without putting a mat on the ground and kneeling in front of me. She was searching everywhere for a mat, and I wanted to greet her, but I could sense her hesitation. I looked at Noah, who didn't seem to notice the awkward situation. It was rather ridiculous: A woman couldn't talk to me because she didn't have a mat to bow on, while the next day I was going to see the king.

WITH GREAT BEAUTY COMES GREAT PAIN

IT WAS FRIDAY, THE day of the kabaka's arrival. The people adored their king. I mean they fucking loved him. People wore shirts with his image (a bald man blankly staring up and out, completely expressionless). They waved banners and flags, played drums in the streets, gathered along the roadside by the thousands. The town's weeklong excitement, which had been building up and bubbling under the surface since I arrived in Mityana, finally exploded in a festive, frenetic citywide party.

I met up with Noah with the idea that we would travel to Kampala to film and photograph the kabaka's convoy arriving from Entebbe, where his palace was, then leaving Kampala for Mityana, but we couldn't find transport to the capital. Noah became more and more despondent as time went on, and we learned that the kabaka had left Entebbe and, about an hour later, Kampala.

While we were waiting, someone called Noah and told him that a nearby village was going to slaughter a cow in honor of the kabaka. I said I wanted to go witness the offering, so I got on a boda-boda while Noah stayed behind at Kolping, a bar in the center of Mityana. When I got to the site of the sacrifice,

I instantly recognized the place: It was where I met the man named Ben, who had offered me his sister, when I first rented my bike and went for a ride around town. Ben was there, along with fifteen other people, and told me that the cow slaughtering had already taken place down the road and the villagers had already cooked and eaten the cow. However, they were preparing to slaughter a goat right then and there. *Lucky me.*

As several guys played drums, others placed a makeshift mat of straw on the ground and brought the goat over. They allowed me to take pictures as one of the guys took a small machete and slit the goat's throat open. The creature at the gates of death made no noise, but a look of instant shock washed over its face. It was hard for me to watch, being a vegetarian and all, but also hard to look away. Blood spilled out of its throat and its body writhed around pathetically. Everyone stood around watching it.

"It's still alive," I said. "Why don't they kill it?"

"It will take a couple minutes," was the unsatisfactory reply.

I knelt down close to the goat's face, its sad eyes looking into my equally sad eyes, and breathed a deep sigh as it experienced its final death throes. Then the men grabbed the goat by the legs like it was, well, a piece of meat, and tied its hind legs to the top of a straw hut so it hung upside down, blood dripping everywhere. One guy used his machete to make a straight cut down the middle of the body, from the testicles to the neck, then carefully cut the skin apart from the interior, like opening the pages of a book. When he was finished with that, he sliced open the belly and used his bare hands to remove all the internal organs, causing a thick, chunky, green liquid to spill out of the open wound in the goat's throat, its body swinging slightly, helpless, lifeless.

Finally, they chopped the head off entirely, and one guy held it up to me, put his hand up its neck, and used his fingers to open the eyelids and to move the lips from inside its head as he pretended the goat was talking. Something like, "Hello, mzungu, how are you? I am dead." And so forth.

"What are you going to do with the head?" I asked.

"We're going to cook it and eat it."

They were dead serious. Nothing like a bloody caprine sacrifice to whet one's appetite.

I played the bongos with a few of the guys, and although they thanked me for playing and therefore contributing to the kabaka, they didn't like my style of drumming. They wanted me to hit the bongos with Ugandan rhythm, a manic, bouncy beat with specifically choreographed movements that I just couldn't seem to master.

· · · · · · · ·

NOAH HAD FOUND A man with a car who said he would drive us until we found the convoy on the main highway, but he was taking his sweet fucking time. He knew Noah was on deadline and had to get the clips of the kabaka to the New Vision office in Kampala, but as we waited in Kolping for the driver to be ready, he started several conversations with people in the bar. Noah sat there glaring at the man.

Then the driver said he was ready, but ordered a beer first. Time was of the essence, and the town was abuzz with activity and anxious anticipation. The kabaka's convoy was going to be there any minute, one of the biggest stories of the year in Mityana, and Noah was practically missing it. Finally, the driver was ready. A woman rode shotgun and I rode bitch in the back seat of the car, with Noah to my left and a young Ugandan man to my right. We drove for thirty or forty minutes, passing everyone who lived in town and near the highway lining the streets, waiting for the kabaka, until we finally saw the convoy coming. We pulled over and Noah and I jumped out to take pictures and footage. The SUV carrying the kabaka, as well as the rest of the entourage surrounding his car (which consisted of several police and army vehicles and three or four other SUVs), zoomed by at breakneck speed. The thick crowds lining the sides of the road cheered wildly as he drove by. People cheered from on top of rooftops and hilltops and treetops.

Right behind them, thousands of boda-bodas, dala dalas, cars, trucks, and other vehicles followed, all Ugandans following their king across the country, packed tightly together in a dangerous race to keep up with the kabaka's convoy. The noise was almost unbearably loud. People were screaming and hooting and blowing horns and honking. The vehicles were all decorated with branches and leaves and signs. Some cars had no doors; one guy sat on the top of a dala dala. Even the boda-bodas had crammed as many people as they could fit onto the motorcycle seats. People ran along the sides of the road, jumping for joy.

After filming the kabaka's vehicle drive by, Noah said he was going to head to Kampala to deliver the video clips. He had to beat his competitors. It is the curse of the press: Delivery of content outweighs all other considerations. He told me to ride with the same driver back to Mityana with the convoy.

I got back in the car and we joined the convoy. There were still vehicles coming from down the highway, as far as the eye could see.

I rolled down my window and sat outside of the car with my hands on the roof and my feet inside. The young guy sitting next to me followed suit on the other side. It was a dangerous thing to do, because there were so many vehicles weaving in and out and fighting for space to get ahead. A truck could have tried to squeeze by us and hit me, and I would have been done for. Besides that, the road was terrible, littered with shitty little speed bumps and potholes. Everyone was waving at me and cheering, "Mzungu! Mzungu!" I couldn't help but smile and laugh the whole ride back. We were so close to other vehicles that random guys would put out their hands to fist bump mine as we sped along. I gave a thumbs up to some people cheering at me and they shook their heads. I found out later that a thumbs up signals support for the hated president. *Shit!*

At one point, about five minutes before we reached Mityana proper, we slowed down a little bit for fifteen or so people, who were standing in the middle of the road and waving aside the vehicles around them. As we slowly passed by, I saw they were surrounding a man who was lying dead in the middle of the street, a pool of blood circling his head. I wanted to get out of the car and find out what happened, because I didn't have enough time to snap a picture for Noah's story from the moving car, but the driver said it was too dangerous for me to get out and walk around there, and he was probably right.

There must have been tens of thousands of people participating in the convoy, which entered Mityana and turned off the main road down one of the dirt paths towards Ssaza Playground where the official soccer match would be held the next day, and then on to the guest house where the kabaka was to sleep that night.

I was supposed to meet up with a photographer named Moksa. He worked with Noah and was told to get pictures of the convoy's arrival and the after-party while Noah was still in Kampala. While the car I was in slowly navigated through the crowds of people on the street, Moksa ran up to me as I was still hanging out the window. I had never met him before, and was a little surprised he knew who I was. But I suppose I stood out like a sore thumb. He ran alongside the car and we had about ten seconds to tell each other where we were going to meet up (Kolping Bar, in the center of town) before the car moved faster than he could run.

After reaching the kabaka's temporary Mityana house, the convoy turned around and headed back into town, where people were partying the night away. It was a huge celebration. It felt like the night Barack Obama was elected president, a feeling of overwhelming joy. I remember being in Berkeley, Obama Country, that historic night in the fall of 2008, throngs of jubilant people flooding Telegraph Avenue, everyone wearing a smile.

I got dropped off at Kolping and ordered a beer as I waited for Moksa to arrive. It was served warm, a common occurrence because refrigeration costs money. Many East Africans actually preferred warm beer, they were so used to it.

When Moksa showed up, I asked him to take a boda-boda to the spot where the guy had died in the middle of the convoy to find out what had happened. A few minutes later he came back with photos of the circular blood stain in the road. I asked him where they took the guy's body, because Moksa did not get any information about what happened. He said Kampala was too far, so they probably took him to the main hospital in Mityana.

"Okay," I said. "Let's go."

. . . .

WE TOOK A BODA-BODA to the hospital. It was about 9:00 p.m. I put the press pass Noah had given me around my neck, and followed Moksa through the gate onto the hospital grounds. He explained to the three or four guys there that we were journalists and we wanted to take pictures of the guy who had died in the convoy for the newspaper and find out what happened. The man in charge wanted 5,000 shillings (just two dollars) to let us take pictures. In journalism school, they teach you that it's unethical to pay for any kind of access for a story, but I didn't want to be denied entry to the mortuary. I could have argued, but I didn't. I paid the money, but instantly regretted it, not because I broke the rules of journalism, but because I should have argued with the guy that it was my right to go in that room of death for free.

Three guys escorted us through the hospital grounds to the mortuary, a small, one-room square, stone structure, about ten feet by ten feet, with one door. They unlocked it and we all went inside. What I saw there will haunt me forever.

The deceased, who was only twenty-five years old, was lying on the cold, concrete ground. Against the back wall was a sort of operating table, and I don't know why his body was not resting on that. The stretcher they used to transport him to the mortuary was leaning against the table, and it was drenched in dried blood, as was his shirt. His eyes were open but lifeless. He looked like he was in shock. A large pool of blood had leaked out of the back of his head, and pieces of his brain sat in the middle of the pool. I'll never forget that revolting smell.

Moksa and I took pictures, and had the worst, most disgusting feeling doing so. I kept shaking my head in disbelief, grieving for this twenty-five-year-old. Someone or something had finally stolen his carbon, his sensory departed. I walked around his body to the other side to get a couple feet of distance from him. As I backed up, one of the hospital employees suddenly jumped at me and pushed me forward.

"Watch out!" he said.

I turned around to find another dead body, completely wrapped up and lying next to the side wall. I hadn't noticed it before, and I had almost just stepped on it.

What. The. Fuck.

I asked the man who spoke the best English what the twenty-five-year-old man's name was and what had happened. I didn't know this until later, but the guy I was speaking to was a reporter working for another station. He told me they only knew his last name, Nsenji, and that they were waiting for his relatives to arrive that night. Nsenji had hired a boda-boda from someone to drive in the convoy that day. He had no passengers. In his excitement, he let go of the handlebars to pump his fists in the air and cheer for the kabaka (apparently every time the kabaka visits, people die; the previous year, five people lost their lives in the convoy). He lost control and fell off the motorcycle, hitting his head on the ground. A large truck coming from behind had no time to stop and slammed into him, cracking the back of his head open.

A few days later, on Bukedde TV, they showed a segment of how the people and police handled moving his body to the mortuary. They were all screaming at each other. A boda-boda can fit three people, uncomfortably. To transport Nsenji's body, one guy drove the boda-boda and another guy sat in the back, holding Nsenji's lifeless body in the middle, his head flapping from one side to the other as they sped along. I wasn't so much distraught about seeing death firsthand as I was disturbed at how casually, and at times carelessly, death was handled in Uganda.

We spent about twenty minutes inside that mortuary, that dirty, disgusting temple of death. As we left and they locked up the building, I almost cried walking back to the boda-boda. Those images of the goat and of Nsenji are burned into my brain forever.

May you rest in peace, I thought, reminded of an old Irish blessing, *and may you be in heaven at least half an hour before the devil knows you're dead.*

GAME DAY

STILL TRYING TO RECOVER from the horrific, mad scene I had witnessed and participated in that night in the dank, blood-soaked mortuary, I returned to Baanabakintu for some respite and rest. I told the priests all about it, and while they were sympathetic and saddened, they had no words of solace for me, nothing in their infinite religious wisdom to calm the storms rumbling in my head.

I wasn't surprised, but I was still disappointed.

Father Odo, however, did offer something else: the chance to go to a live concert at the playground that night. I had to think about it for a minute, but realized that music and dancing would be the perfect distraction, and the perfect end, to my living nightmare.

Mary came along as well, and the three of us drove to the playground. It cost 5,000 shillings to get in, the same amount the mortuary gatekeepers wanted. Everything was so unofficial there. We had to buy our tickets from a woman sitting in the dark in a car parked next to the playground wall. The exchange took place through the half-opened window of her car.

We went inside and joined about 300-or-so people, most of whom were sitting in white plastic chairs that had been set up on the grass in front of the stage. The same musicians played most of the night (except for the one break they took, when a Ugandan rapper played music he had composed through the speakers and sang live), and they were all very good: the drummer, the bassist, the guitarist, the keyboardist. The genre was a mixture of Ugandan country and reggae, sometimes slow and pretty, sometimes fast and rockin'.

But after three or four songs, a new singer would come on stage and replace the previous one. After one song, the crowd would start yelling for them to leave the stage. They didn't seem to be enjoying themselves.

Out of the hundreds of people there, I was among only a handful (including Father Odo) who actually danced. Mary tried to get me to dance Ugandan style, which involves vigorous gyrating of the waist and hips and a lot of jumping and flailing of the arms. I attempted the dance, causing her to burst out laughing. Of course everyone around was watching me, but I was there to have a good time, *to hell with them*. One man kept yelling at a female singer, even attacking her dress (which I thought was a beautiful, sparkling, shimmering gold, but was supposed to be worn only for special occasions such as weddings and what have you), telling her in Luganda to get off the stage so the mzungu could dance, because he saw that I had stopped while she was performing. I was just taking a break. But even though his comments were rude, they were pretty funny, and everyone laughed and looked at me.

I often felt like an animal in a zoo, held in self-imposed captivity to be gawked at by the locals. But I didn't fear dancing at all, anymore. I was always the first on the floor.

I was waiting for Noah to come back from Kampala and meet me at the playground. Toward the end of the show, I saw someone taking photos of the crowd, and noticed that the person was wearing an argyle sweater. I walked quickly around the crowd to the front of the stage, and sure enough, it was Noah. He took me backstage and said it would be alright if I went on stage and took photos of the musicians up close. I was hesitant, but he said it was fine. I walked up the crooked wooden steps to the stage and kneeled in front of every musician as they played, taking photos. They each nodded their heads to me, and I returned the favor. I could hear the crowd yelling something about the mzungu.

By now, everyone in town recognized me.

* * * * * * *

SATURDAY WAS GAME DAY. Noah, Moksa, and I went to the playground around 2:00 p.m. There was too much confusion at the front gate, and we were late getting our press passes, so we walked around to the back gate, which was the VIP entrance. The UPDF and police officers searched my backpack and used a metal scanner, asking me what was in my pockets, then let us inside.

The playground held a total of about 20,000 people, the vast majority of them were standing behind the interior wire fence that blocked them from walking onto the field, and packed them together like sardines. They stood there for hours. Some of them were sitting on top of the wall or had climbed a couple nearby trees for a better view. I was allowed on the field because Noah managed to get me an official press badge. He introduced me to all the journalists there. We mostly hung out with them in the press section, which moved to various places as two young teams played an intro game and the dignitaries began to arrive: bishops, chiefs of villages, heads of counties, representatives from five East African Community countries, the kabaka's security force, UPDF and Ugandan police officials, community leaders and businessmen, people from all over Uganda, and so on. The dignitaries had special bleachers and seats to sit in, covered from the sun by canopies.

Before the kabaka arrived at the playground, members of Parliament played a short soccer match against a group of referees. Noah and I and the other journalists were allowed to go on the field to take pictures, and I met several members of Parliament.

Out of nowhere, the sun disappeared behind a dark cloud and it began pouring rain. Everyone ran for cover. All the reporters slipped their cameras under their shirts and rushed to a corner of the field and packed together under a plastic banner that was being used as an advertisement on the fence, but which we all held up above our heads with our hands. Water flowed off the edge like a waterfall. The rain lasted about twenty minutes, and then stopped as suddenly as it had begun, just as the kabaka arrived with his security in tow. The crowd went wild with excitement, blowing horns and cheering. Noah and I and about twenty other journalists rushed to the field to film and take photos of the kabaka greeting the members of Parliament, other dignitaries, the referees, and the players of the two teams of the official match: Ssingo (the local Mityana favorite wearing white uniforms) and Buweekula (from the neighboring county wearing red uniforms). As the kabaka slowly moved along the line of people he was greeting, his security and the UPDF kept pushing us back forcefully.

"Take one photo and go!" one of them said.

I ignored him and kept jockeying for a better position. I was no more than five feet away from the kabaka. Another official came up to me with mean intentions in his eyes and grabbed me by the shoulder.

"Let go of me!" I yelled at him.

He grabbed the press badge that I was wearing around my neck and saw that I had official credentials, so he apologetically, and silently, fucked off.

Sometimes it's good to be the press.

As far as I could tell, I was the only mzungu there, out of thousands of people, and I was on the field, just feet from the kabaka, who Bagandans, or citizens of the central region of Uganda, would have given their lives for (and many do, every time he visits...).

At one point, the army, police, and security officials began arguing and screaming at Noah's colleague, who was once an army soldier and was there to help Noah get footage of the game and of the kabaka. The colleague told the official that he was going to "box him," and it almost came to that, because the king's security kept trying to push us away from different areas. They would tell us to go stay in one section, then the security guys there would tell us to go back. Eventually, Noah and I joined a couple other journalists on one end of the field, sitting just a foot away from the out-of-bounds line between the right goal post and the corner kick. We watched the game from there.

The kabaka, finished with his greetings, waved to the crowd and walked over to his special seating area, which had a roof that blocked him from any rain or sun, a fan to keep him cool, and a fancy throne, which he sat in the entire time he was there. Even when he was walking, two or three of his personnel held a large umbrella over him to block the sun. I found out later that Ronald Muwenda Muteba II, the kabaka's real name, had supported himself as a freelance journalist when he was in exile in London with his father during the second Obote regime. His family members were the largest private landowners in East Africa, and landownership rights for Bagandans remained one of the biggest areas of contention between the king and the federal government. He was named heir apparent by his father in 1966, when he was just eleven years old.

Everyone stood for the national anthem, and the kabaka and I, who were facing each other directly about twenty feet apart, were probably the only ones not singing the words. He looked me in the eye and nodded.

Noah leaned over to me and whispered, "Remove your hat."

I took off my hat and looked back at the kabaka. We smiled at each other. For me, it was a look of recognition and respect. He didn't know me, but he acknowledged me. I like to imagine he was admiring me, thinking it was no small feat that this small, young white boy was standing on that field in front of him, smack in the middle of the Dark Continent. Or maybe it was just the generic, meaningless smile of a politician.

After the anthem, the kabaka walked to midfield along with his security, and all of us journalists followed to film him "officially" kick off the ball. He went back to his throne and the game was ready to begin.

Noah and I went back to our spot between the goal and the corner, where we watched the entire match. My feet were literally touching the out-of-bounds line, just unreal access compared to where most of the town's residents watched the game from, and at one point the game ball came hurtling towards me, right into my hands. I threw it to the Ssingo player, who set it up for a corner kick.

· · · · · · · ·

THE GAME, WHICH WAS jam-packed with fouls and yellow cards, was a big disappointment, especially for the majority of the crowd, who were locals. Ssingo just didn't play as well as Buweekula. The local team (in white) seemed tired, unprepared, unfocused, and disorganized. Except for a couple nice headers and bicycle kicks, each pass from a Ssingo player went directly to a Buweekula player. The visiting team in red was much more organized; their passes were precise, their speed instantaneous, their offensive attacks strategized, their energy relentless, their defense impenetrable, their months upon months of practice and preparation obvious. Most of the action took place on Ssingo's defensive end of the field.

Buweekula scored two goals in the first half; the second goal, however, was a bullshit call. The field referee had blown the whistle to figure out some kind of foul or other. Both teams' players slowed down, thinking the game had come to a brief halt. As a lark, one of the Buweekula players playfully tapped the soccer ball into Ssingo's goal. The line referee called it a fair goal, even though the field ref had stopped the game. There was a lot of commotion and arguing and yelling, and even though the field ref knew it was a terrible call, he did not exercise his authority to overrule the line ref.

In the last fifteen minutes of the game, Ssingo finally scored a goal, making it 2-1, though it should have been 1-1. The crowd became excited and Ssingo actually started playing a proper game of soccer. I suppose the crowd's energy pushed them to try harder to tie up the game before the ninety minutes were up, but it was not to be. Mityana residents (the majority of the peanut gallery) and other local citizens booed and hissed, and an unsettling, dejected energy settled over the town.

The kabaka left immediately, back to his warm, safe, secluded cocoon of a palace in Entebbe. The visiting fans and dignitaries rushed onto the field when the final whistle was blown, elated at their jaundiced, lopsided victory. Final score: Buweekula 2, Ssingo 1.

The citizens of Mityana sulked back to their homes, an entire town butthurt. If they had won, there would have been a citywide party until well after the sun came up. It made me wonder, as Noah and I met a couple colleagues of his at a virtually empty bar, which was more important: the kabaka being there, or winning the game? It seemed the latter. Perhaps they were ashamed of losing in front of the kabaka.

. . . .

NOAH SUGGESTED WE GO to a *boîte* or discothèque, the equivalent of a nightclub. I was up for dancing, but Noah said I couldn't just show up and dance with any girl. I had to arrive with someone. So

I asked him to call a cute Ugandan girl with super-short buzzed hair who we had met earlier. Her name was Charlotte. She was nineteen years old and getting ready to finish her secondary school exams to enter university. She also had a tight little bod and beautiful eyes, so, sure, I was down to buy her a couple sodas so she'd dance with me. Nothing more. Yet.

Before leaving, I left my flask full of Ugandan Bond 7 whiskey at Gaz. The *nyabo* (woman) who ran Gaz asked Noah what was in the metal container, referring to my flask, which we were asking her to watch.

"Poison," he replied, sipping his beer. And he was right.

Charlotte showed up an hour late (probably on purpose), so we missed the concert and headed straight for the discothèque, a multilayered, multi-neon colored interior with an underground main dance floor. Charlotte was nervous at first; she didn't know what I wanted from her. I just wanted to dance, which we did, and when I grabbed her waist to pull her closer to me, she said, "Ooh, that's what I was afraid of..." She didn't want to take the initiative of the already awkward situation. But once we got going, we connected. Dance is a representation of many things. A couple Ugandans tried to grab her hand and pull her away from me to dance with them, but she refused and stayed with me.

"Why does every Ugandan want me to dance their way?" I asked. "Why can't I just do my own thing?"

"They were just teasing and challenging you," she replied. "But you challenged them, and you won."

We met up with Noah and went back up the neon-lit stairs to the street to get some grub. A man with a broken foot was beating a guy on the ground with one of his crutches. A couple people tried to break it up, and another couple tried to attack the crippled man, who attempted to hobble away, then turned around and smacked one of the guys in the face with his right crutch. The man fell to the ground. I tried to get closer to see what was going on, but Noah and Charlotte dragged me away. Probably for the best.

Charlotte and I had a long discussion about what we wanted from each other, and once she was convinced that I didn't just want her as a sex object, or to pay her for sex, she wanted to find a room and just sleep in the same bed, which was fine with me. I was dead tired, and pretty drunk.

Noah helped us look for a cheap room somewhere in town, but had no luck. I was more concerned with the super-full moon in the clear sky, a large, spherical, bright ring that circled it, a hundred times the size of the moon. The lunar eclipse was beautiful, and although it was past two in the morning and we needed to find a place to sleep, I was still more interested in the wonderful loveliness of the super-full moon's lunar eclipse.

"Why don't I just bring her to my room at Baanabakintu Cathedral?" I asked.

"Because," Noah started, "it would be..."

"Disrespectful?"

"Yes."

But everywhere we went the rooms were all full on account of the kabaka's arrival. Eventually, Noah gave up and went home and I took Charlotte to the rectory. I knew the priests were sleeping, and luckily the front door was open, because I didn't want to let the priests know that I had a girl sleep in my bed without their permission. I knew it was wrong; I did it anyway.

Charlotte and I kissed and slept in my bed in just our underwear. We were trying to take it slow. We were building mutual trust, and since I didn't insist on having sex or anything else besides kissing, she became immediately attached.

Oh boy, I thought, wrapping my arm around her body from behind, lying on our sides. *Where is this going to go?*

AIDS! THE SAD REALITY

GRAVELY AFFECTING CHILDRE

PRODUCED BY UGANDA COMMUNITY BASED ASSOCIATION FOR CHILD WELFARE(UCOBAC) WITH FINANCIAL ASSISTANCE FR

THE MZUNGU
OF MITYANA

AWOKE IN THE SHITTIEST mood. I felt horrible. Maybe it was the "poison" in the flask, maybe it was the dancing around, maybe it was going to sleep too late and waking up too early. For whatever reason, I was short with Charlotte and tried to get her out of there as soon as possible. All the priests were at Sunday mass, so I snuck her out the back trying not to be noticed, but the cleaning girls saw us.

I had long since run out of Xanax, and the pharmacy in Mityana only carried Valium, which isn't as strong. So I started taking more Valium to compensate for the decrease in potency. As soon as Charlotte was gone, I took too many Valium and passed out until 2:00 p.m. I still felt awful when I got up, and the cleaning girls, who got to sleep and eat at the cathedral residence for free, were letting my dirty clothes pile up. They did everyone else's laundry, but not mine. I wondered if it was out of spite. Mary had left to attend school, so I no longer had an ally among them.

A couple hours later I felt slightly better, and one of the younger priests invited me to play a game of soccer up the road with some other guys. I was hesitant at first because of my hangover, but I always tried to remember, *Fuck it, I'm in Africa.*

Just do it. So I borrowed shin guards from him and we went to the shabby, slanted soccer field on the cathedral property. I was too out of shape and smoked too much to be as good a player as I once was.

There was only one goal, without a net, and no goalkeeper, so the idea was that if a member of the other team touched the ball, your team had to pass it all the way back midfield to a dirty line in the grass in order to proceed towards the goal. We had a referee and everything. At one point, the ball flew in the air towards my general direction and I jumped up and back to try to head it, knocking over a player behind me from the other team. The ref saw the foul and I technically received a yellow card, though the ref didn't have any actual cards, but since I was a mzungu and it was unintentional, the ref blew his whistle and let our team continue the game with possession of the ball.

By the end, I was drenched in sweat, my lungs hurt, I was filthy and sunburnt, and it was hard to breathe. Apparently, these guys played every day, starting when the sun was at a certain point in the sky. When I got back to the residence, the girls hadn't even started washing my clothes, so I used a couple sweatshirts as towels after showering. I ended up washing my own clothes in a bucket after that.

A truck drove by announcing through a loudspeaker that there would be a meeting of Ssingo fans and leaders at the back of the Kolping Bar in a town hall conference room to discuss changes that needed to be made to the team's organization. I decided to go, and, unsurprisingly, ran into Noah there.

About one hundred people showed up. The leaders of the team ran away, because there was talk of mutiny. There was a lot of commotion. Eventually, a few guys convinced them to return, and the meeting began. Noah quietly translated for me. In the end, the crowd decided to vote out the old cabinet and elect new leadership.

Noah told me, after the meeting, that our segment about the witchcraft ceremony still had not played on Bukedde TV like the editor said it would, which was bad news. The people in the village gathered around a shop that had a projector every evening and waited two nights in a row to see themselves on television, but it wasn't to be. They kept calling Noah asking why it didn't play, but it wasn't up to Noah; it was up to the editors and subeditors back in Kampala at the New Vision office.

. . . .

EVERY SINGLE DAY, THE hydroelectricity went off, shutting down all the power in the whole town. This made it very difficult to write. The blackouts lasted about thirty minutes, as did the periodic pouring rain that appeared out of nowhere, the sun shining bright one minute and the sky overcast the next. It provided for a constant feeling of uncertainty.

Charlotte kept calling me, but I was either asleep or in the freezing cold shower. She sent me text messages saying she respected that I didn't force her to have sex the first night, that she was ready for "anything" now, and that she loved me.

Goddamn, nineteen-year-old girls are so emotionally immature.

I couldn't blame her, though; both her parents had died of AIDS, which is why we thought it best to have her go to the main hospital to get tested. She called me and said the results were negative, but that her doctor requested that I attend with her at some point so we could both get tested together and I could see her official results.

"Be careful," Noah told me over beers at Gaz when I told him about the situation. "There is a pill that someone who is HIV positive can take that will make any test show up negative. Tell her one day that you want to hang out, not mentioning the hospital beforehand, and then spring it on her when she arrives so she can't trick you."

. . . .

THE NEXT DAY I met up with Noah and we took a boda-boda to the main police station, a rotting series of buildings with several interview rooms, shogun-toting officers, and gigantic turkeys walking around rusted semitrucks. We went to the station's "health barracks," dirty stone structures, where a nurse explained to me the different drugs she was preparing. Next to her sat a woman in her late twenties, holding her baby, who had just been born the night before.

Apparently, she had thrown her baby into one of the disgusting latrine holes in a nearby village. A neighbor noticed that she did not exit the restroom with the baby and called the police, who arrested the mother for attempted murder. Her arrest was the only thing that saved her from being lynched by a village mob. The baby was cleaned and given antibiotics. At the health barracks the mother sat there with dried tears on her cheeks, cradling the baby she had tried to murder the night before. She had told the police that she thought she had to use the toilet and the baby popped out, but they knew she was bullshitting them.

Noah interviewed her, and she opened the kanga cloth to show me the baby's face. I didn't think she was fit to raise a kid, but the problem was that if the police charged her with attempted murder, it would be like arresting the baby as well, because there were no nearby childcare centers that took newborns, and a jail cell is no place for a newborn baby. It was becoming clear to me that daily life for many in Uganda was an unflinching barrage of raw human tribulations. It was certainly nothing like my life back in California, nor anywhere else I'd traveled around the world. My problems were quite petty and conquerable by comparison.

In the police station interview rooms, a few suspects were being questioned. One had stolen a chicken. Noah knew all the high-level police investigators and introduced me to them.

"Noah, can I ask you a stupid question?"

"Of course."

"Do you think one of the cops would sell me their hat?"

He laughed. "What do you think?"

"No."

"That's right."

We were able to walk around the grounds, no questions asked. They didn't even have a portable metal detector to check my bag or my person. You can get away with so much more in Uganda than, say, America.

• • • • • • • •

NOAH AND I HAD discussed many options since meeting a couple of weeks before: he had a meeting scheduled with an investor who had the money to contribute towards creating a new radio station that would be managed by Noah's limited media company, which he had yet to register officially, and I needed to fill out my application and take a written test in Kampala the next month to try to get a job as a diplomat at the US Embassy. We had talked about me coming back to Uganda later that year and applying for a Special Pass so I could live in Uganda for up to two years, then apply for a Work Permit, which would require a letter from Noah's company saying they would hire me if the Ugandan Immigration Department approved my permit, and we needed to forward the request letter to the kabaka's press secretary to ask that I be granted an interview with the king (if that happened, I would be on the front page of the biggest newspaper in Uganda).

But the most pressing piece of business was our impending three or four day journey to Rwanda, Semuliki National Park in western Uganda, and a pygmy village. Noah and I were leaving that night for Kampala to catch a bus to Kigali, the capital of Rwanda. There were many preparations to be made, and time was running out.

As we discussed these plans at Kolping, I finally saw two fat, female mzungus, either Dutch or German, passing by, the first white people I'd seen in Uganda. I felt violated.

I am the Mzungu of Mityana. How dare they?

• • • • • • • •

I CALLED CHARLOTTE TO "hang out," not letting her know that I was going to bring her to the hospital so she wouldn't have a chance to take the pill that makes an HIV test null and void. I wasn't so sure such a pill existed, as there was quite a bit of misinformation regarding HIV throughout Africa, but I wasn't taking any chances. When she showed up, we took a boda-boda to the main hospital. Apparently, she had an American family sponsoring her and providing her with money, some of which went to her personal doctor, so we were able to walk by the forty or so people waiting around the dirty outdoor sitting area and go right into the doctor's office. He took samples of blood from both of us and said it would take about thirty minutes to get the results.

In the meantime, Charlotte and I walked to her place, a dark, dank building constructed of old concrete with no electricity and about a dozen rooms. Hers was modest but comfy. We lay on her bed, a small cot, and talked. It was muggy, and we were both sweating. When we were ready, we headed back to the hospital. The doctor told us to wait outside for a few minutes. I had to buy a small notebook for him to write the results in. He brought us into a private room and sat us down. I did not have a good feeling about the look on his face. It was the look of a human being tasked with telling another human being that they had an incurable, fatal disease.

The doctor was holding the notebook with the results in his hand, but he took his sweet fucking time getting to it. He asked us many questions and spoke very slowly. After asking me all of these questions, he asked the same ones to Charlotte, just as slowly.

"Okay, Justin," he said. "I have administered an HIV test for you and for Charlotte, yes?"

"Uh, yes."

"There are three kinds of results: one, completely negative; two, completely positive; and three, negative and positive, which means we would have to do further tests."

"Okay."

"Why did you want to get an HIV test?"

I looked at Charlotte.

"I've been traveling throughout Africa and it has a high HIV rate, so I wanted to make sure I'm okay."

"And you, Charlotte?"

"I just wanted to make sure my life is okay."

"What will you do if you are HIV negative?" the doctor asked me.

What the hell kind of question is that?

"Umm...go on living my life?" I said.

"And what if you are HIV positive?"

"I don't know...I don't know...that would be very difficult."

"What will you do if you are HIV positive and Charlotte is HIV negative, or if you are HIV negative and she is HIV positive?"

When he asked that, my heart stopped beating. The tone of his voice, the look in his eyes, the question itself...I could sense that a bad news bomb was about to be dropped on us.

"Then there will be no sexual contact between us," I replied.

"Okay, now," the doctor said. "If you are HIV positive, you will have to get treatment and talk to a guidance counselor."

Yes, yes, I know all this. Get to the fucking results already!

"Now I will show you Charlotte's results, and then I will show Charlotte your results."

I know he was required to say all that first, but, *Come on man, our lives are hanging in the balance, here.*

He opened the notebook and showed me Charlotte's page. He pointed out where he had written her name, age, marital status, etc., like I cared about that, and asked me if it was accurate. I didn't answer him and scanned the chicken scratch writing looking for the words "negative" or "positive."

I saw "negative" before he said, "And here are her results. It says 'negative.' That means she is HIV what?" *Pause.* "Negative. Now I show her your results."

I already knew my results; I'd been tested many times. Though I *had* used needles again since being tested. I suppose you never know. Again he pointed out my name and other information before saying to her, "And here are Justin's results. It says 'negative.' That means he is HIV what?" *Pause.* "Negative."

As we walked down the road, Charlotte said quietly, "Thank you, Justin, for bringing me there to make sure I am okay. I have never been sure if I was negative because of my parents. No one has ever cared about me like you have cared about me."

I'm not sure if that meant she was lying earlier about her first test, or if she was just speaking generally.

I would have brought her back to her place and banged her right then and there just to relieve the stress if I wasn't late to meet Noah.

· · · · · · ·

I RAN BACK TO the cathedral and packed my things and took a shower, then ran to Gaz with my travel bag to meet Noah. We took a minibus to Kampala, where I bought us each bus tickets to Kigali, Rwanda. It was leaving at 1:00 a.m., so we had a couple hours to kill. We knocked back a few beers at the nearest tavern. I played a couple games of pool with some Ugandans, but the pool cues in Uganda were so crappy and worn down, it was nearly impossible to make a shot. Either way, both games came down to just the eight ball, and these guys were really good, so I thought I did okay. Noah teased me and said he would have bought me a beer if I had won, but too bad.

"Why don't *you* go try playing against those guys and see if you come anywhere *near* as close to winning as I did," I playfully challenged him.

As we got back to the bus station, the bus was already pulling out, and as it was moving the driver opened the door so Noah and I could jump on. Made it just in the nick of time. We had the entire back row to ourselves. I tried to get some sleep because it was a long way to Kigali, but the roads were so bumpy and shitty, it was not a peaceful rest.

DIRTY POOL, RWANDA, DIRTY POOL

WANDA. THE VERY NAME conjures horrific, unbelievable images of people being hacked to death by machetes, and for what? Because the Belgians, when they had control of the country way back when, decided to split the people into two groups, the Hutus and the Tutsis? The only difference between them being the size of their noses. For one hundred days in 1994, the world watched and did nothing as 1,000,000 people, just one seventh of the population, were brutally murdered at a faster rate per capita than the Jews under Nazi Germany. It gave me chills just seeing a Rwandan with a machete, hacking at some weeds or tall grass.

When I was in East Africa, everyone talked about how Rwanda had completely turned around. They said the country was now clean and safe, the people were friendly, business was picking up, there was so much to see.

Bullshit. It was all propaganda.

True, when I woke up on the bus it was early morning and we were passing through Rwanda's famous Land of a Thousand Hills, mist shifting between the lush, green, cultivated, and layered jagged mountains, and it was breathtakingly beautiful. There were farms on hillsides, very well organized and maintained. Rivers flowed throughout the valleys as we drove along a road carved out of a mountain, past animals drinking and bathing in the dewy early morning hours.

But that beautiful countryside was fertilized with the victims of the genocide. And all that talk about Rwanda having turned itself around, well, Noah and I were about to find out that it wasn't true. There's no turning something like that around.

· · · · · · · ·

I GOT SICK AT a police checkpoint once we had entered Rwanda (I think from Noah's pure coffee beans that I had chewed on). The police came on the bus and I tried to hold it in, but couldn't do it. I rushed to the side window, threw it open, and hurled my guts out onto the highway. The police saw but didn't say or do anything.

The capital itself, Kigali (pronounced chee-GAWL-lee), was rather small, and definitely not clean or well-organized like Uganda. It was underdeveloped and there was a mean energy permeating the air. As we got off the bus at the station, I looked around and thought to myself that everyone at least twenty years or older had either participated in murdering people or watched their friends and families being murdered right in front of them. They all wore mean expressions, and their demeanor was very aggressive. Noah and I did not feel safe there. The last time I hadn't felt safe in Africa was all the way back in Johannesburg. I had an uneasy feeling in the pit of my stomach the entire time we were there. I swallowed a few Valium.

All over the hilly city, I noticed several people that had to drag themselves along with their arms because their legs were crippled. I saw people hobbling along on crutches, who were missing a leg or an arm.

"You think those injuries are from the genocide?" I asked Noah.

"I'm pretty sure if you were attacked, you were either killed or you escaped," he said. "There were no injuries, you know what I mean?"

A fair point, but there were more people with unnatural injuries than usual, for sure.

We worked our way through the crowded, bustling bus station to find some breakfast. Walking down one alleyway I saw a row of women tapping away at old typewriters. I didn't know what they were typing, but I wanted to take a picture of them. I asked if it was okay. Most Rwandans don't speak English, they speak French. So it was difficult to understand their response. Eventually they had to write it down: 5,000 Rwandan francs, something like ten dollars or more, just for a photo or two.

"No way," I told them, and walked off. They just laughed, unconcerned about missing out on a better deal. That's one thing I learned very early on in Rwanda: there was no negotiating with people. Riding boda-bodas, for example, required a fixed price. Noah tried to haggle for a very long time whenever we had to ride one in an effort to get a cheaper price, but it never happened.

There was really not much to see in Rwanda. Our first stop was the Hotel Des Mille Collines, the actual building that the movie *Hotel Rwanda* was based on. It had undergone substantial renovations since those days, but I could still recognize the exterior of the building. An employee said we were free to walk around downstairs and outside to take pictures, but that we weren't allowed to go upstairs to the hallways where the rooms were.

Downstairs, as we walked around a large, clean pool, as well as a fully-stocked straw hut bar and hammocks along the grass overlooking the city, another employee, who looked more official than the first guy (more security than concierge) came up to us and asked us what we were doing and why we were there. We explained and he said it was okay to take pictures, but not of the hotel itself. He and several other employees watched us as we walked around, but we took pictures of the hotel structure anyway. We had traveled a long way for this.

I asked someone at the front desk if there were any pictures or a tribute or a mention at all of Paul Rusesabagina, the hotel manager who saved almost 200 people from being slaughtered in 1994, and they said, "No." Not one word or picture of gratitude for the man and what he did. They even seemed standoffish at the question, like, *How did he have the gall to even ask that?*

"Something doesn't seem right, Noah," I said. He nodded.

Our next stop was the Genocide Memorial Center, where 259,000 people were buried in mass graves. A very old United Nations truck was parked outside. We went in, and although the entry was free, it cost twenty dollars to take pictures inside the museum. Ironically, we were allowed to take pictures for free outside, where the large, stretching, rectangular concrete graves were located, bundles of flowers placed on top. They even had open graves, where piles of wrapped up bodies lay there for anyone to see. Although it was tastefully set up, Noah and I felt nauseous. The result of the senseless, brutal mass killings were on display right there in front of us, and we didn't know what to say to each other. I don't think we even looked at each other while we were there, though we were on the same page.

The site itself was beautiful, at least, with pathways leading to various sites, vines providing a sort of roof as it began to drizzle. There were also very pretty reflecting gardens with fountains, and statues of animals, and circular rows of flowers. One fountain spewed out water from two sides with fire burning in a bowl held up by a pole in the middle.

Inside the museum they had thousands of pictures of the deceased (when they were alive), as well as testimonials from those who survived. A ten-year-old wrote about running away from the carnage behind, passing a man who had been struck in the head by a machete but was still lying there breathing, his life very slowly and very painfully slipping away. There was a room with dozens upon dozens of actual skulls. We could see the cracks from the machete blows, lots of teeth missing, and some skulls that were split wide open. There were also piles and piles of human bones.

"This is too much," Noah said, heading for the door. "I'm out."

I watched him go, then turned back to the skulls and bones. I understood how he felt, but I was mesmerized. I stared at the skulls in awe, trying to imagine each one's traumatic story, and popped a couple more Valium.

. . . .

AT 1:30 P.M., JUST a few hours after we had arrived, we were done with Rwanda, so we went back to the bus station and bought a ticket for 3:00 p.m. As we were waiting, we saw the police arrest eight or nine young people, one of them a minor, just for idling and walking around town. They did absolutely nothing. One guy was handcuffed to a pole in the back of the open-air, caged police truck. He kept screaming in the local language, "Why the fuck am I being arrested for doing nothing?"

Everyone in the bus station just watched. Noah told me not to take pictures of them being arrested, for I would have been arrested as well. I was depressing that Rwanda was still struggling nearly two decades later. The place wasn't a genocidal hellhole anymore, but there was still something evil and choleric lingering under the surface. My Valium intake was rapidly increasing.

Noah wanted to interview a few Ugandans who were living and working in Kigali. They were just a five minute walk away. We could have easily gone over there and interviewed them with Noah's video camera, but Noah wanted to take the official route and go to the same police post where the men had just been arrested to ask for permission. The officer, fresh from arresting a group of young people for no good reason, was very suspicious. He kept asking why Noah wanted to interview Ugandans in Rwanda, and asked to see his press credentials. After looking at Noah's journalist ID card thoroughly, he said he had to call his police commander to come and question Noah first.

"Noah, why didn't we just go interview the Ugandans without asking?" I said. "If the cops came, we could've just said it's our first time in Rwanda and we didn't know the protocol."

Not everything has to be done officially, especially with journalism. If you ask for permission, of course they're going to say no. You don't ask, you just do.

Noah didn't answer, but it occurred to me that he was employed by a state-run media outlet. He had to play by different rules. His livelihood depended on it.

Noah called a friend who lived in Kigali. The friend told him not to bother with the police commander.

"They'll just question me, look at all my photos and footage, and go through your stuff," Noah relayed to me. "They can keep us here for two days and then still say no."

"Let's get out of here. You hungry?"

All the restaurants, it seemed, were run by Muslims, so they didn't serve beer. We had to walk across a busy street and up a couple flights of stairs to find a couple of cold beers. We were disappointed and disgusted with this city, and we wanted out. Three o'clock couldn't come fast enough.

As we talked, we saw a shirtless Rwandan who had painted his entire face and body blue and white in support of a local soccer team. The next thing we knew, he was up on the same level as us and sitting at the table next to us. I asked to take a picture with him, and he joined our table. He was enthusiastic about life but obviously crazy. Noah tried to converse with him, but the guy spoke about four different languages, mixing them together in the same sentence. We asked if he was Hutu or Tutsi, which he didn't want to answer (meaning he was Hutu), and whether Hutus and Tutsis got along now, if they could be friends, if they've moved on. He was hesitant to answer the question, and did so in a roundabout way. He said the only way to tell the two apart were their noses, and finally admitted that no, the two groups still didn't get along and couldn't be friends.

That was the clincher, for me. The point when I realized the country hadn't come that far after all. They weren't killing each other anymore, that's true, but they still hated each other. I lost a little hope for humanity's capacity to love that day.

Noah and I were all too happy to board our bus and head for the Ugandan border. I had to pay another fifty dollars for a single entry visa, even though I had only left Uganda for a few hours. The immigration officer gave me the visa sticker for my passport, but he didn't give me a receipt. Noah told me that meant the officer pocketed my money.

It's a scam, it's a scam, it's a scam.

A RIPTIDE RELAPSE
IN A PYGMY OPIUM DEN

PARTS OF THE MAIN "highway" (a bumpy dirt road) to Semuliki National Park in western Uganda were even worse than the roads in Kigali, which is saying quite a lot. It was the second leg of Noah's and my trip. We had to take several long, tiring buses and minibuses to different small towns, past the Bwindi Impenetrable Forest, and along the Rwenzori Mountain border between Uganda and the Democratic Republic of the Congo to get there, but we were glad to be out of Rwanda. At one point a bus driver forgot to drop us off in the town we needed to be in to catch our next bus, and we ended up at the Democratic Republic of the Congo border at 4:30 a.m.

This was easily one of the most dangerous places in the world to be. There was no one in sight.

We were running on empty: just a couple hours sleep and very little food after a two-day journey, and it was starting to wear on us. Our trip was only half over.

Another bus finally showed up and we made it to Fort Portal, a small town that served as a regional transportation hub and the last main stop before our final destination. We grubbed down and caught a minibus towards Sempaya Gate, the entrance to Semuliki National Park. We still had a bit of a drive to reach the town where the Batwa pygmies lived. I remembered reading about pygmies in a cultural anthropology class in college; when I had an opportunity to meet them I jumped at the chance. All I knew about them was that they were hunters and gatherers, they lived in the forest, and they were very short people.

The view on the way was beautiful: huge, rolling, green hills split down the middle by a deep gorge and sprawling valley. But the road was terrible: winding, bumps every twenty feet, some parts partially paved, and we had to make several stops for Chinese and African workers using dump trucks and Caterpillars to try to repair the shitty road.

It felt like the end of the Earth.

From the gate, we had to take a boda-boda to the nearby town of Ntandi, surrounded on all sides by hills, and jungle, and the bush. The main town looked like an African version of the American Old West: one long, wide road with one-story buildings on either side that looked like saloons and sheriff outposts. This place had a bad vibe to it; we did not feel safe.

We were led out of town by a local, down dirt paths and small huts, to the Batwa pygmy village, a small place with small people. We were greeted warmly; they lived off visitors like us, and they only received about ten visitors a month at the most. We met the *mbewo*, or king, the smallest of them all, who was forty years old. Everyone was smoking cigarettes and pipes, indoors and out. There were about thirty pygmies there, mothers holding babies, naked kids playing in the dirt next to empty gas and alcohol canisters, black and white goats meandering about, and shirtless, hairy-chested men building fires. Their village was a clearing carved out of the jungle, their houses were mud huts and straw tents. They didn't seem surprised to see a mzungu, which surprised me.

They were short, for sure, but there were also nonpygmies present. The actual pygmies were about half my size. I'm 5'6", not tall by any stretch of the imagination, and I towered over them. They looked like they should have been kids, but their faces were old and compressed. They looked like black Benjamin Buttons.

The pygmy king's name was Nzito Jofuley, and he was wearing a tattered red shirt that read, "Every One, Every Day, Every Way." His crown was a small yarmulke-like hat with dozens of long, colorful feathers shooting up every which way into the sky. He had one wife, who was taller than me and definitely not a pygmy, and four children (three sons and one daughter). The king and several pygmies and children led us into the king's home, a mud house that the European Union gave them money to build, in order for us to explain the intention of our visit. It was hot and we were all sweating. We sat down on the dirt floor in a small, empty room. Old, cracked paint was peeling off the walls. They were all carrying small, wooden stringed instruments, like mini harps, and colorful pipes that, presumably, they wanted us to buy. They also had a fee for anyone visiting their village, so we negotiated a price. Their local language was Lukswa (though they knew some other languages spoken in the Congo), so the Speaker, a twenty-five-year-old pygmy named Julius Balyebulye (who had two wives and four sons), had to translate for us because he was the only one who also spoke Luganda and English.

The original pygmies, he told us, were half the size of the ones we saw. The reason for their growth in size was because they had begun intermarrying with regular-sized Africans after many women died in the forest. They originally lived in a forest called Mawoyo in the Congo, where they were hunters and gatherers. Once the animals they hunted were gone, they resettled in Semuliki in 2007 and became Ugandan citizens. They began hunting animals in the park until the Game Rangers and the Ugandan government stopped them, allowing them to only fish and hunt monkeys. This forced them to begin cultivating the land, but they said they didn't have enough land to sustain themselves. They arrived here with a population of about 200, which was reduced to eighty six, and had since gone back up to 116, though Julius said their numbers were dwindling and we only saw about forty people in the pygmy camp at any given time. He told us the rest were in the forest hunting and would be back the next morning. They had relatives in the Congo, and once a year they crossed Lake Semuliki by boat. When a married couple has a daughter, they all travel to the Congo to exchange the baby girl with a Congolese relative's daughter. If one or the other does not have a girl to exchange, they get seven dogs instead, which help them to hunt for food.

Noah asked them if they ever felt discriminated against. Julius said that sometimes they did, but never for their size, only their supposed laziness. At school their children were called smelly, because they used to live in the forest and didn't bathe, though they said they did now.

They needed more help from the government. They had written to government officials many times but received no response. They needed more land to cultivate, they needed more money to build better homes, and they needed better health care. The hospitals were too far away. They either needed a hospital nearby or they needed funds for transportation. They used to take herbs from the national park, but the Game Rangers said they were destroying the nature and told them to use the hospitals, which they couldn't get to.

Besides smoking tobacco, they also smoked marijuana (to "give them courage to go hunting") and, unfortunately for me, opium, both of which they grew in a secret location in the bush. As soon as he said opium, I knew I wanted to try it.

"Will you take me to the marijuana and opium fields?" I asked Julius. I wanted to see how big they were and if pygmies were working the fields.

"Okay," Julius said.

"Justin, if you go there you will be attacked and killed," Noah warned me. "They're not just going to let some stranger see their drug fields and get away."

Noah didn't approve of the use of drugs, but he knew he couldn't stop me from making my own decisions.

I decided to follow his advice and not pursue visiting the actual fields. Julius did show me a few marijuana plants he was growing behind his house, though. Instead, I just smoked weed with Julius and the king in a small room in Julius' house. Noah watched, but didn't partake and didn't say anything. Once the small, dank room started filling up with smoke, he went outside to take photos of the village and the people.

The king then brought out his long, wooden, hand-painted pipe and offered me opium. I was in some alternate universe: I had traveled halfway around the world to escape my heroin addiction, and yet here was a three-foot, forty-year-old, bald, fucking pygmy king with a feather crown handing me a handmade pipe packed with opium in the middle of the jungle.

At the time, I didn't consider it a relapse, because I didn't consider opium to be as hard or as serious as heroin, even though heroin is refined from raw opium. I figured, *I'm not sticking a needle in my arm and injecting the poppy resin straight into my bloodstream, so what's the big deal?* The truth is, I just didn't think about it that much; I just did it.

Julius loaded the pipe with the substance, then put hot coals on top instead of using a lighter or matches. As I sucked the opiate smoke deep into my lungs, I reflected on the strange, enchanting fact that I had stumbled upon a pygmy opium den. The high was crap; I barely felt anything. I expected opium grown in the jungle like this to be particularly potent, but I just felt really stoned. It left me wanting something more.

I inquired about law enforcement.

"The police tried to destroy our opium fields but they let us grow marijuana," Julius told me. "But the police do not enter our camp, so do not worry."

"What if someone within the camp were to steal or hurt someone else?" I asked, taking another hit, holding this one in longer.

"They would be punished by the king."

"What would be their punishment?"

"Death."

So there was a sort of internal law enforcement in place there.

"But usually there are no incidents," he added. "We are a peaceful people."

Outside, the pygmies danced and sang for us, but it was quite pathetic and disappointing—they just kind of halfheartedly moved around in a circle and made random noises. The whole affair cost us 100,000 Ugandan shillings (actually it cost *me* that much; Noah did not pay for one single thing the entire four-day trip). I bought the pipe from the king, as well as one of the small instruments, a sort of pygmy harp.

If there are marijuana and opium fields here, that means there's heroin here, which is not good.

I was clearly still lying to myself and hadn't admitted that I had just violated my recovery by smoking opium. I suppose I thought about it for a moment, but then I thought, *Well, the opium I smoked wasn't that good, so it's not really relapsing. I mean, I didn't get that high from it.*

Of course, the truth was that it only made me want the real thing.

If there was heroin nearby, that also meant the main town, which was populated with nonpygmies, was filled with junkies, making it a dangerous place to be. It also meant the town was a drug trading post, a smuggling stop along the way from the Congo to Uganda and other East African countries. I had to get out of there.

In town, Noah and I discussed our options over dinner, which was bland, local food. All the restaurants were run by Muslims, and the walls were plastered with posters praising Moammar Gaddafi, Saddam Hussein, and Osama bin Laden, next to a Coca-Cola advertisement with two smiling Africans that read "Loaded with Happiness!"

We were nervous about sleeping in town. After all, we were surrounded by bush in a dangerous drug town, far away from any official help. If we were attacked we'd be fucked. It was a long way out of there. After weighing our options we decided to stay the night in a shabby back alley "motel," and to keep our wits about us. We were very tired, so after a couple beers we hit the sack in our separate rooms. I kept my Maasai club next to my mattress.

• • • • • • •

IN THE MORNING, JULIUS came to fetch us. He had promised the rest of the pygmies would be back from their hunting trip at the camp, but when we arrived, there were even fewer people than the day before.

"Let's go, Justin," Noah said. "These people played us."

We took a boda-boda up the road to Sempaya Gate and went to the main office to pay our entrance fees to see the park's hot springs. Noah had to negotiate for ten minutes with the receptionist in the main office to reduce the price for me. Finally she relented. The office offered eggs for sale, which we could cook in the hot springs. We bought a few eggs and a tour guide led us into the dense, wet rainforest on a twenty-minute hike. We could see and hear monkeys scrambling around from tree to tree, howling at each other or at us. We eventually reached a clearing and came to the "female" hot springs, a wide expanse of mud, hardened lava rock, a hot lake, and two geysers spewing out white hot magma water, surrounded by rainforest and plants, animals shrieking in the distance.

There was also a "male" hot springs, but it was an hour's hike away, and we were too tired. We spent a good amount of time at the female hot springs, where local women believed their ancestors reside. If they want to become pregnant, they go there to ask for fertility; if they're already pregnant, they go to ask for a safe delivery.

Our guide said the water itself was 103 degrees Celsius, which seemed technically and scientifically impossible, but it was *damn* hot. Huge plumes of steam rose up from the geysers and the lake. We walked as close as we could to the nearest geyser. There was about ten feet of water separating us from hardened rock where we would be able to see the geyser from just a couple feet away. The guide helped Noah, who was wearing sandals, across to the hardened rock. I started to take my shoes off and as I bent over to do so, my camera, the one I bought in Lusaka, slipped out of my shirt pocket and fell straight into the steaming hot water.

"God-fucking-dammit!" I yelled.

I pulled it out as quickly as I could and removed the SD card and batteries. I dried them off, pissed as all hell.

I took my shoes and socks off and the guide grabbed my hand as I stepped on a few rocks and logs that poked out of the water on my way to the hardened rock, which had all kinds of divots, and holes, and lines that had formed from the hot water over years and years.

A witchcraft healer and a large crowd of villagers watch a witch doctor's evil spirits burn up.

Mityana residents pound some bongos as one man slices open a goat, both an offering to the kabaka, or king, of Buganda (the central region of Uganda).

Tens of thousands of people line the streets to witness the kabaka arrive in their small town of Mityana, Uganda.

Justin relaxes with the local reporters in the "press box" at Ssaza Playground before the big soccer match will commence in the kabaka's presence. Photo by Noah.

A UPDF soldier shades the kabaka from harmful rays.

ustin watches the soccer game behind him. Photo by Noah.

Justin poses with a blue and white Hutu soccer fan in Kigali, Rwanda. Photo by Noah.

The pygmy king smokes his opium pipe.

Justin (who is 5'6") with a group of Batwa pygmies. Photo by Noah.

The pygmies perform their ritual dance.

A Coca-Cola advertisement in a restaurant near the pygmy village next to a poster apparently mourning the deaths of Moammar Gaddafi, Osama bin Laden, and Saddam Hussein.

A Ugandan journalist kneels next to the "female" hot springs in Semuliki National Park.

Funeral for the thirty-eight-year-old Ugandan priest who died in a car crash.

Ugandan children study on desks donated by Justin's grade school.

Schoolchildren dressed in pink perform a dance to welcome the Americans.

A giraffe in Murchison Falls National Park, near the River Nile.

Being so close to the geyser actually hurt, it was so hot. There was so much steam it was hard to breathe.

We made our way back and I let the camera dry in the sun, hoping it would work later. Luckily, it was fine just a few hours later, like nothing had happened; I didn't have to spend another 200 dollars on another stupid camera. We brought our eggs to a small hot water puddle and put them in. It took about five minutes to boil the eggs. The guide used a stick to roll them out of the puddle, and we brought them to a circular hut to eat our hot-spring-cooked brunch.

We hiked through the jungle, and when we got back to the main gate, we walked down the road and sat on a pile of rocks in the middle of nowhere. We could see the workers doing construction on the road down a ways. We sat there for two hours waiting for a minibus to pass by and take us out of that place.

"Noah, build us a time portal," I said, becoming a little delirious. "Come on, man, you have everything you need right here in the bush to make one. Transport us to Fort Portal, or better yet, Mityana."

He smiled uneasily at my silliness.

Eventually, we were able to flag down a minibus and took the same winding, bumpy road back to Fort Portal, where we ate lunch and had to catch another minibus all the way to Mityana because there were no bigger, more comfortable buses coming. Every bus and minibus we rode took between four and twelve hours each. We slept the entire way back, exhausted and frustrated with the journey, though neither of us regretted it.

When I got back to Baanabakintu Cathedral in Mityana, it was about 11:00 p.m. I took a shower and immediately rode my rental bike to Charlotte's place.

I needed to get laid.

SEARCHING FOR STAMINA AND PATIENCE

THOSE HAZY DAYS, THEY began to blend together, a smoothie of highs and lows, noise and silence, movement and sleep. A flurry of activity, no rest for the wicked in this pocket of the world. I hoped my body and mind could handle this level of sustained, consistent intensity. Stamina, where art thou?

I submitted an application to the US State Department to become a diplomat and work at a foreign embassy (hopefully the US Consulate in Kampala). Actually, the title was Foreign Service Officer. It took me two hours to fill out the application online. And just when I was about to submit it, the Internet went out across town—like it did at least every other day for about half an hour, totally at random—and I had to redo the whole thing.

I was scheduled to take my written test in a couple weeks. They only had a one-week window for test opportunities per year. They had testing centers at embassies for Americans overseas. My test was scheduled from 1:00 to 4:00 p.m. on a Saturday at the US Consulate in Kampala. If I passed the written test, I would then undergo an oral interview in Washington, DC. I imagined that would probably be the hardest part.

Of course, I'd have to be clean if I was going to get serious about this career. I was at a fork in the road, and there were two different Justins duking it out.

· · · · · · ·

FATHER ODO INFORMED ME that a group of ten female American students from a Catholic university in California were coming to visit. They were arriving at Entebbe International Airport with a nun named Sister Paula. Father Odo, who had invited them to Uganda when he visited their school in California, went to pick them up at the airport, and they were asking him all kinds of questions about me and my journey through Africa on their way back to Mityana. I was excited, hoping there'd be a couple hotties in the group.

I rode my bike in the rain a few minutes up the road to Enro Hotel, a pretty standard place of lodging but nonetheless the fanciest place in town, where they were staying for two weeks. They were still recovering from jetlag when I went to meet them. I sat in the bar and talked to Sister Paula and Father Odo, and two by two the girls began to trickle into the bar from their rooms. I learned that they were between the ages of nineteen and twenty-one.

We sat and talked, and they asked me questions about my Africa adventure. They were going to sleep early, so they gave me a list of their parents' email addresses, and I sent them an email saying that their girls had arrived safely and that they were in good hands.

· · · · · · ·

THE NEXT MORNING, FATHER Odo had business to attend to, so I showed the girls around Mityana. I was their tour guide. I showed them Kolping, Gaz Bar, Stanbic Bank, the Indian supermarkets, Internet cafés, the bike shop, the taxi rank, Ssaza Playground, the discothèques, the fruit and vegetable and fish and meat market, and a few other key places. They got freaked out while we were at the open-air market because a shady looking creeper kept following a couple of the girls and speaking to them in Luganda. I didn't see it happen, and they didn't tell me about it until afterwards. He was probably just trying to get them to buy stuff. We ate at a restaurant where they tried the local food. I taught them several Luganda words and phrases to help them get started on the language.

When Father Odo was ready, we all boarded a school bus (basically the same as a minibus) and headed out of Mityana to Father Odo's farm. He had a team of workers who lived there and tended to the various animals and plants and trees that inhabited the spacious land. Then we visited his mother's home, where he was raised. I saw the room where he grew up and chatted with his mother. The home was on the property of a school and parish, which Father Odo had contributed a lot of time and effort and money to help grow.

A group of about fifty kids gathered around us as we introduced ourselves. I noticed that several of the wooden benches they sat on outside said "DONATED BY ST. ELIZABETH CHURCH, ALTADENIA [sic], CALIFORNIA." I was astonished. I went to St. Elizabeth School for nine years and grew up in Altadena. I knew Father Odo visited that church once a year, but actually seeing the name of my school and the town where I grew up moved me. There I was, deep in the bush in a poor village, and yet I was right at home, still in Altadena.

The girls had come to Uganda to visit various churches and schools and provide water purification systems, seedlings, money, and other supplies, and to explain how to use the water purification systems, start or grow a small business, learn about nutrition and hygiene, and a few other projects. Their intentions were noble, but ultimately their contribution was minimal. Their efforts helped a small amount of people for a few days, though I suppose that's better than nothing at all.

We met with the local women's group, and they explained to us how their husbands spend all their money on drinking alcohol all day, leaving them to take care of their children and earn money. So they made baskets and mats and such. Every single time there was an opportunity to buy stuff, the American girls swarmed around the goods like vultures to a fresh kill. *An opportunity to go shopping?! Holy fucking shit!* The problem was, although the thought of helping these women by giving them business did enter their minds (sort of), they were really just being typical American consumerists. They reminded me of how inane and superficial Americans can be. They reminded me of myself.

As the girls went shopping for mats and baskets, I went to play soccer with the young students. Every opportunity I got to play with a group of people, I took. Of course, I always got sunburnt, and sweaty, and tired, because I was out of shape and it was bloody fuckin' hot. One of the girls joined our game, and she was pretty good. I was impressed. She managed to juke one of the best players quite a few times, causing all his friends to laugh at him because the female mzungu was better than him.

As we drove off in the minibus the children ran alongside the vehicle and yelled, "Mzungus!"

"Aww, they're sooo cute," whined one of the girls.

"Yes, right," I muttered under my breath. "'Look how cute and hungry and sick these children are.'"

I realized that I should have held my tongue, and even though the girls made selfish, rude comments to me on a fairly regular basis, I decided to keep my opinions of them to myself from then on. Easier said than done.

• • • • • • • •

FOR THE FIRST FEW evenings after they arrived, I went back to Enro with Father Odo and the American girls for dinner, but later in the week I decided to get dropped off before they reached the hotel in order to hang out with other friends.

Charlotte kept calling me. She was jealous that I was spending so much time with the American girls, even though I told her I was writing an article about their trip. She wouldn't let it go. All we did was bicker. It was her way of getting attention from me. I decided I needed to break up with her. She had become way too attached way too quickly. I understood why she behaved and thought the way she did, and why she tried so desperately to fill that emotional hole, but she was just as young and immature as the American girls and I just couldn't be that person for her. She thought we'd still be together when I got back to America. That pretty much exemplified her level of awareness right there. I figured she was going to think I used her for sex, which was not true. Or she'd think I was now in a relationship with one of the American girls, which was also not true. They didn't seem interested in me romantically at all, or in any other way, for that matter.

I didn't handle the situation with Charlotte very well. I didn't handle it at all, in fact. I just stopped picking up her phone calls. I knew it was mean, but she was just smothering me, and I couldn't deal with it. She wasn't fun to talk to or be around. She was just mad at me all the time.

• • • • • • •

EVEN THOUGH I DIDN'T particularly enjoy their company, I continued to travel around with the American girls as a way to see more of Uganda with Father Odo. Our excursions to villages near and far were also a way to avoid Charlotte in Mityana, an excuse to not deal with that situation.

One day we drove around hundreds of kilometers of an Indian tea plantation called Kakonde, which was established in the nineteen-tens. The foremen there beat the workers with sticks if they got tired. When we got out of the minibus to take pictures, a guard in uniform began walking towards us. Our driver told us to get in the minibus immediately because we were not allowed to take pictures. The girls freaked out and jumped back into the bus. Sister Paula later said the guard was running at us, but I saw him the whole time.

"The guy was just walking over to tell us to stop taking pictures and to leave," I said. "He wasn't chasing us."

"Well, I'm going to say he was running after us," said Sister Paula. "It's a better story."

But it's not the truth.

•••••••

THE BIGGEST EVENT THE girls hosted, a day-long health and education fair, was held very far from Mityana, about 160 kilometers away, at a place called Our Lady Source of Joy Kasambya Catholic Parish. There was a big sign that welcomed the American group, and when we walked up a path to enter the grounds, dozens of students from the school and parish sang and danced and drummed to welcome us. They led us into the huge cathedral, but as soon as I realized they were going to conduct an entire mass, I grabbed my bag and left.

Noah had come with us to cover the story with me, and he had left the mass as well, so I joined him in the lounge room, where we ate, and drank tea, and watched television on comfortable couches.

"The girls are very pretty," he said. "We should take them to the discothèques in Mityana and have fun with them."

"I've told the girls many times about those nightclubs, but they seem nervous," I said. "I think it'd be a good experience for them, but they're worried that a bunch of black guys will surround them and force them to dance and not let them leave."

"What? It's not like that."

"I know," I said. "Their chaperone asked me, 'What if they want to leave the club?'"

"Just walk out," Noah said.

"I told them there are tons of boda-bodas outside and they just have to say, 'Take me to Enro,' and pay them 1,000 shillings. Maybe if you suggest it to them, because they don't seem to like me."

After mass, Noah broached the subject with a few of the girls. He explained that Saturday and Sunday nights were free for ladies, but they still seemed hesitant. They glanced at me as if they knew I had put him up to asking them, which I guess I had. They never went.

The girls paired up and set up six stations around the large parish property where they taught about one hundred local youth various skills: starting a business, growing food, raising chickens and pigs, nutrition, hand washing and teeth brushing, and purifying water. Each pair of girls had a Ugandan translator, which Noah also helped out with, and the youth could visit three of the six stations for half an hour each, after which they would switch to another station of their choice. It was a fun and successful event, and for the first time I thought the girls' presence in Uganda had some value.

I walked around and took pictures for the article I planned to write about what the girls were doing in Uganda (this event being their main reason), and helped them with whatever they needed (moving chairs, delivering raffle tickets, etc.). It was not the best situation for me to use my digital recorder to capture what they were saying; instead, I made a list of questions about their experiences and expectations and results to interview the girls at a later time.

The local member of Parliament, Patrick Mulindwa of Kasambya County, attended the event with his armed guard, and I was granted an interview. He had been in Parliament for one year and was celebrating his first anniversary later that month. He talked about the poor education system in Uganda, how the youth needed to be taught practical skills like growing a business, that there were so many more job seekers than job creators, and how impressed he was with the American girls' presentations. His presence at the event was significant because it showed the people that this was important and also that he genuinely cared about the youth of his county gaining useful knowledge.

"It is very important that people like these girls come to places like this to share their knowledge," he told me. "But having said that, out of the people here, only thirty percent will understand what the girls were talking about, twenty percent might understand it over a period of time, and the other fifty percent will not understand at all."

After the presentations were over, I helped put the chairs and other items away, and then we ate a delicious lunch in the shade on the grass outside. One of the girls sat with me for a short time, but when she realized the rest of the girls were sitting in chairs in a circle a few yards away, she got up and joined them. They did not invite me over and they did not come over to sit with me. The latter was a common occurrence. If we entered a room where there were couches and chairs while we waited for the day's events to begin, and I sat down somewhere, the first girls to sit down would find a spot as far away from me as possible. The last one to sit did so next to me, but only because there was no other space for her.

What is this, junior high? They just didn't seem to want to get to know me, let alone like me. Who knows what they said about me when I wasn't around? I told myself at the time that I didn't care what they thought, but clearly I did.

I gotta hand it to Sister Paula, though, as every village we visited I witnessed her handing over crisp new hundred-dollar bills to women and priests and schoolmasters who were operating in extreme poverty. Everyone we visited was so happy to see us because they knew the American group had lots of money.

• • • • • • •

BACK IN MITYANA, I went to Kolping by myself and ordered a Nile Special. I watched a group of guys playing pool in the corner and recognized one of them as Adam, the guy I met at the drum circle in the middle of the night when he found out his wife had cheated on him, before the kabaka's arrival.

"Chapman!" he said, walking over and joining me at the table.

We stayed out late and talked. I told him about the adventures I'd had since I met him, as well as the adventures I'd had before I arrived in Uganda. I told him about my acid trip, and he mentioned that he could get marijuana for me, if I was interested. I said I'd keep that in mind. Just when we were about to start heading home, a huge fight broke out. We were in a dark alleyway that was lined on either side with small bars and shops, next to the main road, when all of a sudden a man was kicked to the floor. Two or three guys started kicking him as he tried to protect himself. Dozens joined in the fight. A few people helped the guy up, and it seemed like the fight was evenly split: about seven or eight guys against another seven or eight guys. Some were trying to break the fight up. Everyone was extremely drunk.

The owner of one of the small bars helped push a boda-boda into the bar, then they closed and locked the metal doors. The boda-boda belonged to the guy who caused the fracas in the first place, and he came running over just as the doors were locked and began pounding on the metal, kicking the doors with his feet and screaming at the top of his lungs. The fight continued down the alleyway, then back up, and finally onto the main road. Adam and I just watched the whole thing from about twenty feet away, utterly amused.

"You see, Chapman?" Adam said. "Africans are MAD! Ah! So drunk, and fighting for what? Because it is time to go home? Ah! I wish I was born your color, Chapman. Africans are so mad. And they are so dormant. They are horrible at business. Ah! I cannot believe this. These stupid motherfuckers. Ah! Africans are so mad!"

BLOOD
AND GLORY

THE AMERICAN GIRLS HAD a three-day trip planned to visit Murchison Falls National Park, which features all kinds of wild animals along the Nile River. They were leaving the next day. I emailed the Ugandan woman, Elizabeth, who had organized the trip for the group to see if there was room for me. She said there was, but the price was more than double what I originally thought: 520 dollars instead of 250.

I was limited to the bank notes I could take out of an ATM in one day, about one hundred dollars. I would have to take a small amount out each day. I told her that after the trip, when we made our way back to Kampala en route to Mityana, I could take the money out and pay her the full fee for the trip. I even tried for a week beforehand to visit the only ATM in Mityana where my card worked to get the money out each day, but the ATM was either out of cash or the power was off.

But I had to go; how could I leave Africa without seeing an elephant or a hippo?

The day before we left for Murchison Falls, we were scheduled to visit a parish and primary and secondary school in Kigandi, where Sister Paula had lived and taught a few years prior. We stopped into the Indian markets in Mityana so the girls could get supplies.

I sat in the bus and waited. I thought about the pygmies, which reminded me about the opium, which reminded me that ever since then I had had an unsettling urge to do heroin again. It was subtle but unavoidable, like an inner-ear itch. Something from within, bubbling, and growing, and clamoring for attention. I had managed to suppress it so far by reasoning that I would never be able to find heroin in Mityana, Uganda, that small village town in the middle of Africa. Then, I remembered Adam saying he could get marijuana. Maybe, just maybe, he knew somebody who knew somebody who could get skag as well.

I don't want to wait two months or however long I have left here in Uganda to get high. Besides, who's going to hold me accountable out here? Maybe I'll just ask Adam and see what he says. If he says no, he says no. And if he says yes, well, then I'll be feeling pretty fuckin' good pretty soon.

As soon as I had made up my mind, there was no turning back. I called Adam and told him to meet me outside the Indian market as soon as possible. I told him there was something very important I wanted to ask him. Luckily, he was nearby.

He took forever, though, and arrived just as the girls got back to the minibus and were ready to leave. I had been calling him incessantly. When he showed up, I ran to the middle of the road to talk to him in private on the center divider. I could feel everyone in the minibus staring at us.

I quietly and subtly asked him if he knew where to get it, making a motion as if a needle was going into my arm, and he said he might but it would take awhile. Without questioning it, he was willing to help me, and I realized he would do anything for me. He said he would try while I was gone that day. The heavy wheels of opiate addiction were not-so-slowly starting to swing back into action. I could feel the weight of it already. The possibility was terrifying and exciting.

"Let's go!" one of the girls yelled from the car, oblivious to my internal struggle.

After a long drive we finally reached the parish in Kigandi. We walked up the main road to the primary school, where 800 children dressed in pink greeted us with loud singing and drumming and dancing. It was very overwhelming. We walked through the crowd and sat in the middle of them. The Americans offered various gifts to the headmistress, a nun.

The children danced and sang for us, and performed a theatre production about hunting in the village, with one student on all fours wearing a lion-skin costume as several others captured it with a net.

Outside the classroom buildings there were several slogans painted on the walls: "Say no to gifts for sex," "Stay a virgin," and "Choose life." The irony of me seeing the latter slogan at that particular point in time was not lost on me, but I swiftly chose to ignore it. There were also murals of flowers, insects, animals, and human organs, all with lines identifying different parts.

While most of the Americans went to the secondary school, one of the girls and I went to the nearby private Catholic health center. Although smaller than the main hospital in Mityana, its facilities were much better and cleaner. Perhaps that is because they charged for services (with the exception of things like HIV testing). A lab technician showed us around: there was a woman sick with malaria, a rather small birthing room that still had fresh blood and vaginal juices on the bed and floor, a ward with two young boys who had horrible burn marks all over their bodies from a boiling water accident at home, and an incinerator out back where they burned all the waste produced by human life and death.

When we were finished, we walked by a soccer field to the secondary school where the other mzungus were. We walked inside to find them and ourselves surrounded by at least 1,000 high school kids in one large room, some even poking their heads through metal-barred windows to see us. They cheered when we entered. A DJ played some traditional music, and one boy lip-synched and danced to entertain us. I walked up and gave him some coins as he danced. Then another group of girls danced for us, each of them pulling some of the American girls onto the dance floor against their will.

When that was over, everyone walked back to the soccer field, where a big match between boys and girls was about to begin. One of the American girls and I decided to play. About 1,000 people surrounded the unclear boundaries of the field as we put on our uniform shirts. Since it was boys versus girls, all the boys, including me, had to have our hands tied together to level the playing field. I felt like a prisoner. The field itself was not level; it was so uneven and bumpy, and it was very difficult to run and keep my balance with my hands tied together. I fell a couple times, much to the amusement of the spectators, who cheered and yelled loudly from the sidelines throughout the game. The American girl and I played opposite positions, so we often went head to head, no holds barred, when one of us had the ball. She gave me a serious run for my money.

Near the end of the game, the boys had possession of the ball and were running towards the goal. One of them kicked me a perfect pass, and without even stopping the ball I kicked it straight into the goal with my left foot at an odd angle, ending the game 4-0. Everyone cheered, but I could hear the American girls booing from the opposite side of the field as I raised my tied hands into the air in triumph. *Fuck them; that goal made my day.*

Later, I asked a couple of them if they saw the goal I made.

"We weren't really...rooting for *you*."

"I don't see why you would, it was boys against girls," I replied. "Doesn't mean you have to be a cunt about it."

They pretended they didn't hear me and walked away.

. . . .

LYING IN BED AT the cathedral the night before we departed for Murchison Falls, I decided that I didn't want heroin after all. *You can do without it,* I told myself. *Just enjoy your time in Africa. That's why you came here in the first place, isn't it? So, then, it's settled, you won't buy any.*

Then Adam called me and said he would have some dope for me by the time I got back from Murchison Falls, a few days later, and I fell right back into that bottomless pit again. The longer I went without it after having decided to get it and use again, the more I wanted it.

We woke up at an ungodly hour the next morning and caught a bus to Murchison Falls, a twelve-hour drive on bumpy roads, much like the trips Noah and I took when we went to Rwanda and Semuliki. Each one of the girls had two seats to themselves and took up the whole bus, so Father Odo and I had to sit on very uncomfortable fold-out chairs in the middle aisle. Somewhere along the line these girls had missed a lesson or two in sharing and generosity. Their Catholic university had apparently not taught them how to be decent human beings.

We stopped in a town called Masindi for lunch. Ernest Hemingway had stayed at the very lodge we ate at, so they named the bar after him. I made sure to have a drink there. After that, our next stop was the top of Murchison Falls, which was similar to Victoria Falls. Very powerful, rushing rivers splitting into the Albert Nile and falling down into the Victoria Nile. If anyone fell in, their body would never be recovered. Two beautiful, symmetrical rainbows formed over the raging river. This was a special place.

Back on the bus I wrote a poem:

WHAT TO DO TO DIE TODAY

last night i heard a leopard
sing as beautifully as a bird,
he pined for his lover
cuz he knew that above her
were
all the grinning trees
with razor sharp teeth,
all the dancing bees
who've used up their stings,
all the wincing whale sharks
with much more bite than bark,
all the angry chickens' tusks
would overturn her bus.
& they would both be crushed.

but death is not a mystery,
just our only certainty.
so from the quicksand in which i was stuck,
i yelled at the leopard to "SHUT THE FUCK UP!"

We drove back around to the calmer part of Victoria Nile, where several National Park employees lounged in the shade, waiting for the next ferry. There was a large, worn globe by the water. I traced the path I had made across the African continent with my finger, proud and amazed at what I had done in such a short period of time.

From across the river, which wasn't very wide (but wide enough not to swim across), we could see Paraa Safari Lodge, where we would be staying. It looked like a POW camp. Finally a small, roofless ferry arrived, and several cars and our bus drove onto the platform. The rest of us walked onto the flat ferry and took the five-minute ride across the river.

Then it was back on the bus and a short drive to Paraa, which was actually the most posh lodge I'd yet seen in Africa. Everything was so expensive. The place had a monopoly on the national park; it was the only place with Internet access. Unless you were camping, there were few other places to stay when visiting the park.

The rooms were exquisite. I shared one with Father Odo. We had a porch that overlooked the River Nile and there was a large, clean, delectable pool with a swim-up bar called the White Nile Bar, which also overlooked the river. We could hear the hippos groaning, and the food was always so delicious. The lodge (really a hotel) also had wonderful old decorations such as an old typewriter, record player, luggage, and paintings of Livingstone and Baker and other famous nineteenth-century travelers of Africa.

Sharing a room with Father Odo gave me an opportunity to ask him a burning question.

"Father, before you became a priest, did you ever...have any sexual experiences?"

To his credit he took the question seriously.

"Oh yes, of course," he replied.

"Don't you miss it?"

"Yes, definitely, but I have a higher calling."

"I don't know, man. I don't think I could do it. You know, that's one of the biggest problems I have with the Catholic Church: the whole repression of sex thing. Priests not being allowed to marry, sex only being allowed inside marriage between a man and a woman, homosexuality being a sin, the list goes on. I mean, to me, human sexuality is the most beautiful, natural thing. In fact it's critical to maintain mental, emotional, and even spiritual health."

"Haha, I like having these discussions with you, Justin," he said, avoiding answering the question. We headed out to meet up with the girls for dinner.

. . . .

THE NEXT DAY, WE woke up early again to go on a safari through the national park. We saw all kinds of animals: a congress of baboons, a harras of cobs, a tower of giraffes, an obstinacy of buffalos, a bloat of hippos, a herd of antelope, and I finally saw some elephants! Everything you could think of except rhinos, unfortunately. These animals were completely wild, and had an incredible landscape to roam. There were birds resting on top of buffalos and hippos.

Whenever we would see an animal we wanted to take a picture of, the girls would say, "Look, it's posing for us!" and I would roll my eyes. Or every goddamn time we saw a warthog, they would call it Pumba. Their reference to real-life Africa was a fucking Disney movie. They even sang "The Circle of Life" a couple times. When we got off the bus to see some hippos up close, a bird flew in and landed on one of its backs. The bird spread its wings out to cool off. Again: "Aw, it's posing for us." Then: "Okay, bird, do another pose. It's getting a little old."

Back at Paraa, we went swimming. It was wonderful to see a few of the girls in their bikinis, just wonderful. *Twenty-year-olds may be daft, but they've got great bodies.* I swam up to the White Nile pool bar and ordered a drink. Father Odo was scared of swimming, so a couple girls and I tried to help him out. He clung to the side of the pool and very slowly walked along the underwater ledge that led into the deep end, gripping the edge like his life depended on it. We sat in the water at the bar and drank Nile Specials and cocktails, which were outrageously expensive.

After lunch, it was time for our cruise up the river. Sister Paula, Father Odo, and I got on one small cruise jalopy, and all of the girls got on the other one.

We had a knowledgeable tour guide who operated the boat and had a rifle at the ready. The river was *full* of crocodiles and hippopotami, which mostly avoided the boat because of its engine, but easily could have flipped us over if they tried. If any of us fell into the water, we'd be done for. We saw hundreds of hippos, elephants, baboons, birds, eagles, crocodiles, and a lone buffalo (who, according to the guide, was kicked out of his herd because he lost a battle, making him the most dangerous animal in the area), all living together, right next to each other, in and around the river. Our guide told us that each family of hippos had their own space, often very close to another family's, and if they crossed territories, it would be war. Often, the fathers killed their sons early on to avoid future battles for dominance. He said one hippo bite could cut a crocodile in half, which he had personally seen. Every day he sees something new out there.

With green jungle on either side of the river, a few patches of grazing pastures, and a long, dirt wall weathered by water and time, we went as far up the river to Murchison Falls as the current would let us, where a small rock island conveniently rested in the middle of the river. We got out and took pictures.

As the story goes, Samuel Baker, the first white European traveler to discover Murchison Falls, and his wife, Florence, were canoeing up the river when a hippo overturned their canoe. They swam to what they thought were logs but turned out to be crocodiles. Another canoe that was traveling with them rescued the couple. Baker named the falls after the then-president of the Royal Geographic Society, who never visited the falls or Uganda.

· · · · · · ·

At dinner that night, some of the hostility between the girls and me boiled to the surface. We had finished eating and I had asked the last pair of student teachers if I could take two minutes to interview them about what they were teaching in the villages. Before we left for Murchison Falls, I had made three announcements that I needed to interview two more pairs of student teachers. As I interviewed the second to last pair, the last two I needed left dinner and went to bed. I took it as an insult because I was sure they had heard me. When I asked them after dinner the night of the cruise on the Nile, one of them said in an annoying tone, "Does it have to be tonight?"

I was getting very frustrated. *Yes, it does have to be tonight, or it's not going to happen.* I wanted the information to be fresh in their minds.

"It's really for your benefit," I said. "I can easily write the article without your quotes if you don't want to be interviewed."

She looked shocked that I said that. One of the girls said, "Justin, you're so serious. We're just joking."

"Okay, fine, but I asked three times the other day to get these interviews out of the way, and these two snuck off to bed," I explained.

They claimed they never heard my announcements, which I knew was bullshit.

"I mean, if I seem irritable, that's partly why," I continued. Now the remaining girls, about five, were all listening in. I knew it.

"It's just, sometimes you come off as condescending, not irritable," said the older one. "Like you're somehow better because you've been in Africa longer than us."

"What are you talking about? What do my travels through Africa have to do with the article I'm writing about you? It's just that I have so much information and quotes and material that it's for her benefit if she wants to be quoted in the paper."

"Ohh..."

That seemed to calm the tension down a bit, and the two followed me inside to a quieter place, where I took up a whole five minutes of their precious time.

I decided later not to even write the damn article about them. *Who cares?*

Later that night we celebrated one of the girls' twenty-first birthday, but she was being a little brat about it. Several of us stayed up to party with her, but she acted like we were keeping her up against her will.

I know you're tired, but it's your twenty-first birthday in Africa. Go hard. Rage, for fuck's sake. What don't you understand about that?

I bought her a cocktail and she took two sips and then scampered off to bed without thanking me. I shook my head in disbelief and finished the drink out on the grass in the warm night air by the River Nile by myself, listening to hippos saying goodnight to each other.

....

ANOTHER EARLY RISE, ANOTHER shitty, bumpy, exhausting, long ride to Kampala. I swallowed too many Valium in preparation for the long haul. We stopped in Garden City, a famous shopping center. I rushed to Barclays, one of the two banks that accepted my debit card, and went inside to a teller to take out the 1,300,000 Ugandan shillings (520 dollars) I owed Elizabeth for the Murchison Falls trip. The teller asked for my passport, which was still on the bus. I ran all the way back but the bus was locked and the driver nowhere to be found. A couple guys said they thought they saw him walk off in a certain direction, so I ran over there and saw the Kampala Golf Course. I wanted to take pictures of it for one of my best friends back home who loved golf. The problem was, I had to jump over a large brick aqueduct to a small landing by a fence on the other side to get a couple good snaps. I had my slippers on, and I was a little loopy from the pills, but I thought I could make it. Holding my safari hat containing my wallet, camera, cigarettes, and lighter, I attempted to leap across. My right foot slipped and I fell hard on my left side against the slanted brick wall, then fell into the pit. The items in my hat went flying. There was a small stream of water at the bottom, covered by a broken piece of wood.

I couldn't move for a couple minutes because the pain was so intense. I wasn't sure what had happened exactly, it all occurred so fast. I was screaming in pain. On the top of the side I was trying to reach there was a piece of 2x4 with a couple rusty nails jutting up out of it. I wasn't sure if the deep cuts in my left elbow came from them or from the bricks. There was also a large bump sticking out of the side of my left leg, which hurt immensely. I also noticed a layer of skin had ripped off the side of my left pinky toe.

I grabbed my camera and other items out of the trickling stream and put them back in the hat. The batteries had fallen out into the stream. I grabbed them and dried them off. The lens of my camera was twisted, so I tried drying everything and turned the camera on. It worked, and the lens fixed itself when I used the zoom. I took a couple pictures of the golf course, but not very good ones. When I turned my camera off, the lens would retract, but the cover wouldn't close. Other than that it was fine. *Man, I put my cameras through the fucking ringer in Africa.*

I hobbled back to the bus, where I found the driver. He unlocked the bus and I grabbed my passport. I ran back to Barclays, but they told me that I was not allowed to take out that much money. I ran over to Stanbic Bank, where I had to wait in a queue, but they told me the same thing. I had enough in my account, but I could only take out 250,000 Ugandan shillings a day from the ATM.

I used the toilet and hobbled back to where the bus used to be parked, but it was gone. Elizabeth found me and said the girls went to a shopping center, and that we would take a taxi. On the way there, I explained what happened, and she became irate.

"If I knew you couldn't get the money, I would have said, 'No, you can't go to Murchison Falls!'" she yelled at me. "You could have at least tried to get two-fifty out of the Mityana ATM several days before the trip. I've been spending all my money and now I'm inconvenienced!"

She kept talking over me as I tried to explain.

"You're not listening to me," I said.

"Yes I am! You could have—"

"No, you're not! I told you already that I tried to go to the ATM every single day for a week before the trip, but the ATM was either out of cash or the power was out. If I had known the banks here were going to do this to me, I would have said no, too. I don't want to inconvenience you. Look, I'm in Mityana for a few more weeks. I can send you the money or bring it to you or—"

"No, I have trusted people before, and they let me down."

What pissed me off was that she was a millionaire. She just organized the trips to Murchison Falls, and charged 520 dollars per person, which I'm sure was way more than if someone just did it themselves. I gave her the 250,000 I was able to take out that day, and told her I would borrow the money from one of the Americans.

We got to the market and I went up to Sister Paula, explained the situation, and she lent me the 400 dollars I needed. I gave it to Elizabeth and said, "Sorted?"

"Yes, sorted," she said, much calmer now, but I was still pissed that this millionaire made me go ask a fucking nun for 400 dollars. My money was quickly running out.

I sat in terrible pain as the girls continued shopping. Eventually we got back on the bus and drove to Mityana. The oldest girl sprayed painful disinfectant on my wounds and applied Band-Aids and gauze, and made a sling for my left arm because it was too painful to bend either way.

No wonder these girls didn't like me. I was a fucking mess.

I went to Baanabakintu to rest.

. . . .

THE NEXT DAY, I took a very painful shower and went to a health clinic halfway up the road from Baanabakintu. A female doctor looked at my wounds, but she didn't give me any information I didn't already know. She applied a brown disinfectant to them and I asked for a sling for my arm.

"No," she said sternly. "Because you don't have a fracture. You must exercise your arm."

"If you don't give me one, I'm going to make my own," I replied.

She relented, on the condition that the next day I start stretching my arm. She gave me antibiotics but no painkillers. It cost me 10,000 Ugandan shillings. And then I really wanted to get high.

I met up with Adam, who said he had some dope for me, at his home. He lived with his wife (I guess they worked things out) and his son in one room in a concrete building that was subsidized by the government. Lots of people lived in the adjacent rooms; they were like tenements. Narrow, muddy alleys connected them all, and it was easy to get lost. It was essentially a maze. Around the corner from Adam's place, next to a random pile of cinderblocks, several guys sat on benches under a tarp, drank heavily all day, and played chess. They were always there.

We brought the dope to a woman who Adam said worked as a baby nurse at the hospital. She lived near Adam in the muddy-floored tenements off the main road.

I wanted this more than anything, but I knew something wasn't right. The dope looked like dirt when we cooked it up. I wasn't even sure any of it was really heroin.

Well, can't know if you don't try, I told myself.

The baby nurse was drunk as shit as she loaded up the fattest syringe I'd ever seen and plunged it into a vein in my hand. The instant she started pushing in the plunger I screamed out in pain and yelled at her to stop. Her body was swaying from intoxication, but I don't think she missed the vein. I think the problem was that it wasn't heroin, it was dirt. A huge welt formed on my hand. I had her try a vein on my foot. Same thing. *So fucking stupid.*

You can go anywhere in the world, but you can't get away from yourself. I learned that the hard way in Uganda. I left America and came to Uganda to escape the pervasive shittiness of heroin, but it had followed me. I was able to avoid it for a couple months, busying myself with traveling across and surviving Africa. But once I got comfortable and anxious, the desperation set in. I hadn't yet dealt with the issues I was running away from. They came back with a vengeance.

Adam said he would ask the guy he got the dirt dope from for my money back. I walked away from the nurse's tenement building dejected and depressed.

· · · · · · ·

THE NEXT TIME I was at Enro Hotel, Sister Paula wanted to have a conversation with me in private about the money I borrowed from her.

"I just want to make sure I'm not being had," she said.

"I assure you that I have the money to pay you back," I replied. "I tried my hardest to get the money before we left for Murchison Falls. I didn't know the banks in Kampala wouldn't let me take out that much. The money is there, I just need to take it out in small installments over the course of this week. I promise I will get it to you."

"Thank you for your honesty," she said. "I wasn't sure if you were using me, but I can see now that you were just desperate. I needed to hear all that."

We made a plan for me to pay her back, then she let me go. I walked over to the pool table. I made friends with a Pakistani guy at Enro, who was amazing at billiards. He and a couple others owned a construction plant nearby. We drank and played doubles with his Pakistani friend and his Ugandan girlfriend. When it was my shot for the eight ball, the cue ball got stuck, so the girlfriend picked up the eight ball, and I went ape shit.

"What the fuck are you doing?!" I yelled.

"The cue ball is stuck, there are no coins, and they have no key," she drunkenly replied.

"Who the fuck picks up the eight ball on the last shot? We could have figured something out. That's fucking bullshit," I kept saying.

The Pakistani guy came over to me and whispered, "She's crazy, bro, she's crazy. Why don't you go home and get some rest? We can play again tomorrow."

He was right; it was late and we were all wasted. My behavior became more and more erratic the further I slipped back into my addict mentality. I'd get fucked up and belligerent, and turn into someone I'm not. It took me years and a good woman to finally see that for myself.

. . . .

THE NEXT DAY I felt fucking horrible. It was a Saturday: Youth Fair Day at Baanabakintu Cathedral. A couple thousand people attended, including the American girls. They were leaving Mityana that afternoon, and Africa the next day. I slept until 1:00 p.m., then forced myself to take a boda-boda to Stanbic Bank to get money for Sister Paula.

When I got back I saw a couple of the American girls flirting with a few African guys, even the ones who had boyfriends back home. Now it was making sense.

We took a group photo, I hugged all of them goodbye, and even the ones who were the rudest to me thanked me profusely for my help throughout their trip, and I felt a little better about the situation. I actually felt bad for them.

At the time, I found them extremely annoying. I wasn't yet patient enough to explain to them the things they didn't get. I wanted them to see what I saw. It was right there in front of them, but they couldn't see it. I was irritated by their ignorance, but I didn't do anything about it. My irritation only affected me, though. They were in their own worlds; what did they care if I let myself be overcome with annoyance? I was in my own world, too: I certainly wasn't humble enough to recognize that this fact transferred to every other area of my life. No one cared that I was a drug addict, that I was depressed, and lost, and lonely. I had no right being those things in the fucking first place. It was all in my head.

After saying goodbye to Father Odo, the girls walked up the road and took a bus to Entebbe, where they would be spending the night and catching an early morning flight.

Mityana was mine again.

. . . .

MY BODY WAS STILL so sore the next morning, so I asked Father Odo to drive me up the road to a petrol station, where I bought ten copies of *Sunday Vision*, the Sunday version of *New Vision*, the biggest newspaper in Uganda. My feature story about my travels from Cape Town to Kampala was the feature story in the Sunday magazine insert. It was official: I was an internationally published journalist. *That's not nothing. Maybe I can still turn this thing around.*

BEDRIDDEN

I WENT TO MORE PHARMACIES and clinics and hospitals and health centers there, (for various reasons, more than I'd care to admit). A whooping cough, headaches, something like the flu, muscle pains, loss of appetite, back pains, bed sores, scrapes and cuts and bruises from falls, my hand and foot nearly needing amputation from that shitty dirt dope, all within a couple weeks. I thought perhaps Africa would be the end of me. I seemed to be improving, but who's to say. My focus shifted to my Foreign Service Officer test that Saturday in Kampala, which I began to study rigorously for.

I needed to get my Internet adaptor renewed, so I borrowed one of the priest's computers to study. On his desktop he had several files about injaculation: basically, how to orgasm without ejaculating semen. I was reminded of Father Odo saying he missed sex.

They've got to be so frustrated. Man, why do that to yourself? For what?

• • • • • • • •

A ROOSTER HUNG AROUND right outside my bedroom window, waking me up way too early every single day. It reminded me of the roosters back at Riverlodge, in Cape Town. That day, I went searching for it in the morning mist and found it right under my window. I brought out my Maasai club, but it ran off. If I had cornered it, I would have bashed its head into the fucking ground.

········

I STILL FELT HORRIBLE, and I was bored as shit, so I went wandering a little further outside my circle on the Baanabakintu property. I smoked a cigarette near the priests' graveyard, contemplating their stories, their perspectives, their dreams, and if they ever found happiness.

Baanabakintu's mentally ill, incomprehensible orator of idioglossia rhetoric that he probably didn't even understand, walked to his porch-like post that had a wooden door that led to nothing. His tone was angrier than usual. I think he was mad that I was smoking so close to the graveyard, because I knew he usually hung around there. I also heard the word mzungu a couple times, I think. He grabbed a large wooden cane, more of a stick, and pounded the door three times. Then he started to walk away, and I tried to stare at him to get him to look at me. When he thought I wasn't looking, he glanced over in my direction, and I could see his face through the Y-shaped trunks of a tree. The entire time he was "talking," (or making noises, at a high volume) like he wanted everyone to hear him, though by his demeanor it seemed like he wanted everyone to leave him alone. He was not approachable by anyone except a couple of the nuns who lived on the property and went up the road to get him food and water and whatnot. He looked like he hadn't showered in years, let alone gone shopping for new clothes. We stared at each other for a few seconds through the tree, about thirty yards away from each other. I brought the cigarette to my lips and he quickly turned away and walked off.

I was waiting to meet up with Adam. He said he had found a doctor who could hook up morphine injections. I decided to smoke a joint in the cow pasture next to Baanabakintu while I waited. There was a man going back and forth from a building to an open-air wooden structure where the cows would eventually go to feed once the man was done replenishing the troughs. Meanwhile, the cows grazed in an open, grass pasture, with a single, large tree that also had a Y-shape at head level. The pasture was a large rectangle surrounded by barbed wire and sharp vines. The only (sensible) way in and out was through the feeding structure. Once the man left, I walked over and squeezed myself through the horizontal wooden gate, going slow as to not cut my face on the protruding barbed wire that extended from the fence. I walked into the pasture to find five cows. They were busy mooing and chewing grass. I found a small hill where I could sit in the shade of the lone tree, and lit my joint. After a couple puffs, the largest cow started mooing angrily and walking rather quickly towards me. I stood up and put the tree between us. The cow jammed his head into the Y part of the tree; he was pissed. The other cows started moving now, a smaller one to my right. I quickly looked around for any means of escape if they started charging at me, but there was barbed wire everywhere. I looked around the ground and saw a large stick, close enough for me to grab if I had to start swinging it at these animals in self-defense. The whole time I was still smoking my joint. The large cow had a hard time getting his head out of the Y, but once he did, he started moving around the tree towards me. I circled the tree as well, making sure it was always between us. Then, all of a sudden, all the cows moved to the wooden structure, the feeding trough, the proper entrance...and exit.

Shit. Now how do I get out of here?

I ran north, away from them, to a barbed fence covered in sharp vines. I threw my water bottle over the fence, as well as my slippers, and managed to use a rather unstable post of bamboo as a step up to a small, circular top of a wooden post. I gained my balance on it on my left foot and jumped about five feet down onto the other side. I landed next to a gorgeous, enormous mushroom. The underside looked like fish gills, all perfectly aligned. The top was white but had small bumps like morning dew covering the surface. In the middle a rusty yellow half-sphere with tiny black spots had pushed its way up. Father Odo told me later that the cows were enraged by my smoking, and that they would have killed me.

Where is Adam?

. . . .

WALKING BACK, I HEARD a singing, dancing, and drumming troupe practicing on the steps of the community center just next to Baanabakintu Cathedral. I grabbed a drum from the rectory sitting room and walked out there. Several girls danced, a few guys drummed, and about twenty older ladies sang. They were so happy to see me join them. An older, white man watched from a distance and took some pictures. Eventually, he walked over to me and struck up a conversation.

This guy must have been in his late sixties or early seventies, but he was in the middle of a two-year project to dismantle and sell his dentistry office and work as a dentist in a facility on the Baanabakintu property, in a building where the nuns stayed inside all day, every day and had taken a lifelong vow of silence.

His name was Peter. He was German, but I thought he had some kind of UK accent, and he looked British. He told me about the Pentecostal mass that was conducted the night before. There were five or six women screaming and wailing at the top of their lungs, running around the cathedral. I had heard it that night, and almost went to see what was going on, but I didn't. I wish I had. They sounded like they had just found out all their kids had been burned alive for no reason whatsoever. Peter said the priests couldn't control the women, and there was one that was particularly hysterical. I asked Peter if they were mentally ill, and he said no, it was just mass hysteria. The priest kept saying, "In the name of the Lord Jesus Christ, calm these women," for about twenty minutes. His prayers for help received no answer. They usually don't. Eventually, after about half-an-hour of this, the main one who was running around and screaming had to be dragged out of the cathedral and lay on the brick ground outside, where she twisted and turned and continued screaming bloody murder.

"Never for a second think your life holds no more mystery," Peter told me.

He was right. I mean, the guy was about seventy, and there he was, selling his established business in Germany to try his profession in Uganda, something he'd worked on for a couple years, and would continue working on for another couple, I'm sure. Life does not end at thirty, or, in my case, twenty-six.

"Never give in," he said. "It's never too late to be happy."

FULL
CIRCLE

ALL WEEK, DOZENS OF people were flocking to Baanabakintu Cathedral, sleeping on the grass, meandering about, some of them walking around inside the rectory. With the priests gone most of the day and me sick in bed from some kind of flu or depression or drug sickness or whatever the fuck it was most days, I wondered who the hell these people were. I had never seen them before. I came to learn that once a year, about a million people from all over Uganda, neighboring countries, and indeed the world, as far as the United States, made a pilgrimage to a place further east than Kampala called Namugongo for an enormous mass. Most were Catholic, celebrating the lives of the thirty-odd Ugandan martyrs who were all murdered in different ways in different parts of the Buganda kingdom on the same day in 1886.

All of these people walked to Namugongo, with the Mass taking place on the last Sunday, so they visited each cathedral where a saint was murdered by the kabaka at the time, who was an ancestor of the current kabaka whom the people now adored. The former king thought the Ugandan missionaries were taking too much of his power away through Christianity, so he had them killed.

Through power outages, rain, you name it, those people kept coming and going, sleeping in the grass and attending mass. Apparently Namugongo was quite a sight to see with so many people jam-packed into one area for an outdoor mass. I wanted to go, but my only means to get there was Father Odo, who didn't want to go. He said it wasn't worth the hassle, but later that night he told me he would take me if I really wanted to. We stayed up late watching old boxing matches that took place in Boise, Idaho in 1996, in the lounge room of the rectory. One of the fights featured Floyd Mayweather.

Father Odo said we would have to wake up at 3:30 a.m. and be on the road by 4:00 a.m. It was already 12:30 a.m., and we were both tired. He said there was a Ssingo soccer match later the next day at Ssaza Playground, which I really wanted to see, but that we wouldn't be able to make it to both because he would have to perform a mass if he went to Namugongo.

"Why can't we just go as pilgrims?" I asked. "Why do you have to get vested up?"

"What's my name?" he said.

"...Edward," I mockingly replied, which was his real name.

He laughed and pointed at me.

"Haha, don't avoid my question! Edward is my old name. I'm a priest; I would have to do a mass. So you have to make a decision. If you want to go, set your alarm and wake me up at 3:30."

"Okay."

"By the way, when are you going to visit St. Noa High School to talk to them about teaching there?" he asked.

I had completely forgotten.

"I can go on Monday, I guess," I said, because it was a Saturday.

Since he was tired and didn't want to go to Namugongo, I decided not to set my alarm and let him, and me, get our sleep, even though it was rumored that President Museveni was going to be there. As much as I didn't like the guy and thought he was becoming a dictator, it would have been interesting to see him. Anyway, when I woke up at 7:00 a.m., Father Odo was gone. A fellow priest told me he'd gone to Namugongo.

• • • • • • •

I DON'T KNOW HOW Adam found Doctor Wagabo, the round, constantly smirking doctor with painkiller connections. The first time I met him, he didn't even ask me why I needed morphine. He didn't ask about my symptoms or what my pain level was. He just outright agreed to get it for me. Perhaps it was the cash in my hand.

Dr. Wagabo told me that he could get Pethidine, which was similar to morphine and the strongest painkiller used in Uganda. He had to travel to Kampala to get the stuff from his connection at the main hospital there, just for me.

Adam and I showed up at the doctor's clinic on a boda-boda at the specified time, careful not to tell anyone what was going on because everyone involved could get in huge trouble. Sitting in the small clinic, Adam and I made small talk and read the newspaper. I showed him my article. Then Dr. Wagabo's nurse, who introduced herself as Jumana, led us around the counter. The other customers glanced curiously at me but said nothing as we walked to the back room. It was filthy, but it was private. I had a view of a clothesline out the back door as I took my shoes and socks off, Adam tied me off, and Jumana prepared my shot. She used a butterfly syringe, which was much smaller than the needles I had previously seen in Uganda and ensured that the shot wouldn't miss the vein once the needle was in. The Pethidine, a clear liquid, came in small glass bottles that Jumana had to break open. After using the plunger to push the clear liquid through the butterfly setup and into my veins, I leaned back so my head was lower than my heart, and Adam held me while the chemical opiate rush enveloped my body and mind. Then it was right outside for a cigarette.

Adam never tried the Pethidine. He was just helping me out of friendship, but he wasn't worried about me. He truly accepted things as they were.

One day, after this routine, Adam and I were sitting in the outdoor, grass courtyard of the main Mityana hospital when we saw a few people wheeling away a dead woman on a stretcher in the direction of that dreaded mortuary. I shuddered. She had just given birth and died during labor. The baby was fine.

I saw a woman crying in the grass who was sick with AIDS and TB. Adam explained that she had slept in the grass there the night before because her man ran off and left her there, not having enough money to pay for her treatment. I went over and gave her 20,000 shillings so she could get something to eat and pay the doctors for some treatment. She was too sick to say thanks, but that's not why I did it. Anyway, Adam said she was happy. The doctors were amazed at my generosity, and agreed to treat her.

We saw her the next day, and she was crying because the doctors said she would be dead by the end of the year. Adam tried to console her in Luganda: "You still have time on this earth. Do not give up hope."

"I know," the twenty-year-old girl replied, "but I also know that I will be suffering the whole time I'm alive, and I don't know where I'm going once I die."

The next time she saw me she asked for more money.

. . . .

"LAST NIGHT, A WOMAN was accused of using witchcraft to kill a child," Adam told me as we walked to meet his friend. "The villagers were very mad. They wanted to burn her alive! The cops rescued her by either taking her away from the ignorant, crazy mob, or arresting her, I'm not sure which. Either way she and her family were kicked out of the village."

We hired a boda-boda from his friend and went into town to do our errands. Then he took me to a big, bumpy grass field and taught me how to drive the boda-boda. I was a natural. I didn't fall once. I even drove Adam on the main road. All the other drivers were so impressed that I learned so much on my first day. Adam and I planned on renting another boda-boda one day soon and having me drive us to Lake Wamala for some beers and a picnic.

On the day I was scheduled to take my Foreign Service Officer Test (FSOT), I took a minibus by myself to Kampala and then a boda-boda to the US Embassy, which was heavily guarded and gated. No stopping, parking, or photography was allowed in front. I went up to the front window and explained that I was there to take my FSOT to become a diplomat, and that I had an appointment. The Ugandan guard asked me the name of the person expecting me. I told him they didn't give me a name, just to show up with my passport. He looked it over for about half an hour and made tons of phone calls. I hadn't taken any pills or received a shot of Pethidine that day, but as I was waiting I wished I had, even though I knew I had to be clear-headed for this.

Finally, the guard got ahold of the right person. It was next to impossible to get into that place. I heard that even someone whose appendix had burst was forced to wait outside like me for an hour because she didn't have an appointment or someone inside waiting for her. I thought it was supposed to be a safe-haven for Americans. If I got hired and transferred here, that would be my first order of business.

I was led through the compound to a room lined with books. One of the three FSOs who administered the test brought me a delicious sandwich from a shop down the road from the embassy. Four other people took the test with me. Two had taken it during the morning slot.

The test was very difficult. It was composed of three sections: general knowledge, language comprehension, and two essays. They told me I would get my results in three to five weeks. By that time I would be back home in the States. If you fail the written test you can retake it only once a year. About 20,000 Americans take the written test every year, and only 3,000 pass. I found out, when I got home, that I was among those 3,000. I had to submit six personal narrative essays online. After an evaluation of my essays, if I was to move on to the next stage, they would schedule me for an intensive oral interview in Washington, D.C. within a year. Unfortunately, this was not to be. I found out a month or so after getting back to the States that I didn't pass the second round. I was still proud of myself for having passed the written test, especially under duress. Most people try several times before they get past that stage of the process, or so the FSOs told me in Kampala.

I didn't experience any withdrawals in Kampala, but as soon as I got back I was high again.

· · · · · · · ·

SINCE FATHER ODO WENT to Namugongo and ditched me, I went to the Ssingo soccer match at Ssaza Playground with Noah and Adam, who had never officially met before I introduced them that day. They had seen each other around town before but never really spoken at length. Adam had to pay for his ticket and stand behind the fence, while Noah and I went through to the journalist section. I sat next to the newly-elected head coach on the field right by the out-of-bounds line.

To my right sat Noah, and to my left was the coach, and then the rest of the players, including the newly-elected manager. At the Ssingo general meeting that Noah and I had attended a couple weeks before, the stakeholders had kicked out the old guard and elected new leadership after we left. Their gambit paid off. Ssingo played so much better this time. There weren't any new players, but it was like watching a completely different team than the one that played the game the kabaka attended. What the coach had done was switch their positions around, which worked beautifully. Their passes much more precise, their headers dead on, their energy revived, Ssingo won 5-0.

· · · · · · · ·

The last time I saw Charlotte, she had left her sweater with me. I thought it was a ploy to make sure I hung out with her again, and said so during one of the many arguments we had.

"You could give the sweater to Noah to give to me and I wouldn't care," she told me, which I knew was bullshit. She thought she was in love with me. She once sent me a text message that read, "Love is seeing people look at us and wonder what can make two people so happy."

But we weren't happy. At least, I wasn't. I didn't think we could help each other.

Though, if I hadn't been wrapped up in my own bullshit, I would have known how to let her off a little easier. As it was, I gave Noah the sweater to give to her, then Adam and I went to Dr. Wagabo to get high.

I was full-blown addicted again.

I never saw Charlotte again after that. Later, I heard she became a born-again Christian.

That night, I joined Father Odo and Mary, who was in town on a break from school, at Enro Hotel to see Afrigo Band perform, an ensemble band of about ten rotating musicians and dancers. There were 500 or more people there to see the concert, and they seemed to be enjoying this show much more than the last one we attended at Ssaza. Before the show, the three of us ate dinner inside Enro alongside the musicians and dancers. As Father Odo put it, we were "rubbing shoulders" with them, like VIPs. I spoke to one of the reggae singers about music.

During the show, I went to the front of the crowd to take pictures, and saw one fat, drunk Ugandan dancing slowly by himself. I decided to join him, and since there was a bright light shining at the stage, everybody could see me. They all started cheering when they saw me dancing. In Luganda, one of the singers said into the mic, "Even the mzungu is on the floor! Get up here and dance!" Dozens of people finally got the courage to join me and the other man. We danced the night away to beautiful Ugandan reggae music. Afterward, several people thanked me for dancing.

"I was just having fun," I replied.

"Yes, but you made them so happy," replied Mary. "And they're so interested in you because they've seen you around town, they've seen you with the kabaka on the soccer field, they've seen you with the group of American girls, they've seen you drive a boda-boda, they've seen your article in *Sunday Vision*. They say to themselves, 'Who is this mzungu?' And you have such a beautiful dance. You just let the music take your body where it wants to go, and it sticks to the beat."

· · · · · · ·

THE DAY AFTER THE show, a Monday, I finally went to St. Noa High School for the first time. I sat down with the headmaster and made a program and schedule for me to teach English, reading, writing, literacy, etc., to all four senior classes for the remainder of my time in Uganda. I started that day with classes Senior 4 and then Senior 3 (high school seniors and juniors). I was amazed at how important they thought the ability to read and write in English was, and how eager they were to learn it. I taught them the difference between a fiction and nonfiction story, and had them pick one and write a story for me. I then read their stories in my room at Baanabakintu and when I returned to their next class we went over them. We also talked about what they were struggling with. They all agreed that it was difficult to read English and understand it, so I put together a curriculum to try to help them with that. I showed them my *Sunday Vision* article to illustrate the importance of reading and writing English. They were very respectful and did what I asked for the most part. It was very hard, but it was also pretty fun. It gave me some purpose.

I had brought some books, including an illustrated dictionary, which I had dragged all the way across Africa for this very reason, to donate to the school. Nearly every day, I rode my bike to the school to teach at least one class, usually more. Some grades were easier than others. The school was on the nicer side as far as schools went in Uganda, though there were still things like holes in the walls between classrooms. During lunchtime, I joined the students and ate the crappy gray porridge with them that they were served every day. The teachers didn't have electricity at home, so during lunch and break times they all took advantage of the daylight and corrected papers in the teachers lounge, a cement room with one long, wooden table.

LIFE IS EXPENSIVE/
DEATH IS UNFAIR

"**Y**OU ARE ONE CRAZY, stubborn, spoiled mzungu," Jumana said one day as she was preparing my shot of Pethidine.

"Yeah, I guess so," I said, tying off my foot. It was useless trying to find a vein in my hands or arms. "Have you ever met anyone like me?"

"No, definitely not."

We had developed a special relationship, one where she knew the score and just laughed about it, but totally enabled it.

Adam and I rented a boda-boda from one of his friends. We loaded up on beer and sandwiches. I started up the boda-boda with Adam behind me, and I took us on a forty-five minute drive all the way to the shores of Lake Wamala, a large, swampy, muddy lake with a few small islands in the middle. We hired a man and his boy to take us in a blue canoe to an island called Bagwe. It was literally so cut off from the rest of the world that the only way to get there was an hour-long trip using paddles in a small canoe. A handful of people lived on the jungle island, which had no sand and no beaches, making it hard to find a landing spot among the reeds.

It was clear that the people who lived on the island didn't have much going for them, as the island had some of the most severe poverty I'd ever seen anywhere. Food, water, and booze was delivered to them via canoe and they spent all the money they made from their small plantations and fishing on alcohol. Every day, they woke up and started drinking and they didn't stop until they passed out. The entire island was like that: mud huts dotting the twelve-acre plot of land, separated by ten minute hikes through the bush. There were no roads. No speedboats. There was tourism, or so they said, and we did see what used to be a resort, but it was run-down and decrepit.

It was beautiful, though. It looked untouched. There were thousands of strange butterflies that swarmed around us all the time. The four of us (the father and son who paddled our canoe plus Adam and myself) walked through the jungle and passed by about eight very simple homes. There was no commercialization, advertisements, markets, water, electricity...no development whatsoever except their small farms, mud hut houses, and the unfinished or abandoned resort (I couldn't tell which, but probably the latter).

We smoked a joint there and relaxed, then walked back, about a twenty minute hike. A couple of random island dogs walked with us. First, we stopped to rest with some island residents under a large tree. I could see the madness of isolation in their eyes and their behavior. One woman kept talking drunkenly to me in Luganda. I told her I didn't speak Luganda and couldn't understand what she was saying, but she kept on with it, even after Adam explained to her. She was basically asking me for money for alcohol.

The four of us got back in the canoe, and although it was smooth sailing on the way to the island, it was a rough ride on the way back. Very windy and choppy, big waves splashing into the boat. The wind was blowing against us. The father and son let Adam and I paddle for a while. We finally reached the main "port," a muddy beach lined with old canoes.

I drove us back to Mityana on the boda-boda with no problems. It was liberating and refreshing to grip the handlebars and floor the fucker up and down the hilly road, the wind blowing in my hair. Back in Mityana, we stopped at an Internet café, and when we tried to get going on the boda-boda again, I started the engine, switched the gear, we started to go, and then a truck came out of nowhere and barreled right at us. I reflexively turned to the right, and Adam quickly jumped off the back and grabbed the seat and tried to pull the boda-boda back, which made me panic and lose my balance. My hand hit the accelerator instead of the brake, I fell off onto Adam behind me as the boda-boda crashed into the back of a parked car in front of me. It all happened in an instant, and I didn't have time to think.

Four men slowly stepped out of the car.

Fuck. That ain't good.

Several Ugandans got involved, yelling back and forth at each other and jabbing their fingers in my direction. Adam spoke with them in Luganda, then turned to me.

"Fuck, Chapman..." he said. "They want forty thousand shillings for the damage. What are we going to do?"

Forty thousand shillings was about fifteen dollars.

"Oh, that's fine, I've got that in my wallet," I said.

"Oh, wait, no," he said. "I meant four hundred thousand."

That made more sense: it was about 150 dollars.

"Oh...well, shit. Okay, well, tell them okay."

"Where are you going to get that much money?" he asked.

"I don't know."

It was the rest of my budget. I had the money, but I couldn't take it all out at once. Adam told them I would have to pay them in installments. They thought I looked like a bank, but they were taking everything I had in my account. They knew they could rip me off and I couldn't do anything about it because they could've gone to the police—I wasn't supposed to be driving a boda-boda. I should have called Noah. He could have rescued me. But I didn't want him to know I had crashed a boda-boda into a parked car. I didn't want any police involvement, but as Noah explained much later, when I finally told him and it was too late, he had connections, and it could have cost me 60,000 shillings to bribe one of the cops he knew, and less than 100,000 for the repairs. So I could have paid sixty dollars instead of 160.

I never was good at math.

I didn't have enough money to pay the full 400-large, so I paid the car owner 220,000 and said I'd have the rest the next morning. They said as collateral they were going to keep the boda-boda, which also had damage, until I paid them back. Meanwhile, the owner of the boda-boda kept calling Adam, asking for it back and wanting money for us renting it in the first place.

Adam had to ask his friend if we could keep it overnight, which he agreed to, but the next day Adam had to tell him the truth in person. Well, the half-truth. He took the blame for me and said he was the one driving, not me, and that I was just helping Adam out with the money because Adam was broke.

I was also broke. I only had access to 150,000 (sixty dollars), so I had to borrow 50,000 from Father Odo and ask my dad via email to put another 200 dollars in my account, in order to pay the full 400,000 plus 110,000 to fix the boda-boda.

As we walked along the road, dirty and dejected, Adam said, "If there's a God, he is not serious, man. He doesn't give a fuck about us."

. . . .

I TAUGHT AT THE high school again the next day. I had the lower grades write stories this time. I also had them read from the different books that I had hauled across Africa, mostly Dr. Seuss. They loved Dr. Seuss. After lunch I sat in on their student leadership election, in which the entire school gathered in one room and the teachers passed out paper ballots for each of the twelve positions. I added my name to the list of candidates on the chalkboard as a joke to challenge the other two running for Head Prefect, or school president. Everyone laughed, including the teachers and vice principal, who smiled and erased my name.

I started seeing things I didn't expect. The students there would get hit on the ass by a teacher with a large stick if they spoke in a language other than English, for instance.

I was to be paid 150,000 shillings for my *Sunday Vision* story. More than I expected. Noah was in Kampala and he went to great lengths to get that money and bring it back to me that day. I wasn't supposed to get paid for work under the terms of my tourist visa. Noah had New Vision put the money in his account as extra payment for one of his stories, then withdrew the money and gave it to me. I put aside 50,000 to pay Father Odo back, and in the morning I couldn't find it. I searched everywhere but it was gone. I couldn't see one of the priests coming into my room and stealing from me. Perhaps it was one of the cleaning or cooking girls. They seemed to have taken a dislike to me after they caught me sneaking Charlotte out of the rectory that one morning.

I went with Adam down to Stanbic bank to get another fifty out for Father Odo. There was a guard standing outside the ATMs 24/7, an assault rifle slung over his shoulder.

"Can I hold your gun?" I asked him.

"No."

I asked him again, dangling the possibility of money in front of him, and after some consideration he agreed to bring Adam and me around the corner and through a door to an empty, roofless alleyway. He closed the door behind us and emptied the gun of any ammunition. Then he handed me the rifle. Adam took pictures of me holding the gun in various poses. The guard never asked for the money, which was fine with me as I was nearly broke.

· · · · · · · ·

WHEN I WOKE, I learned that a young, thirty-eight-year-old priest named Father Andy had died in a car crash the previous night. Everyone was in mourning. Men delivered piles of tree trunks to make a large fire outside the cathedral as the body-viewing mass commenced, which I attended. It was a very somber event. Women wept and wailed uncontrollably. At the end of the mass, I walked up with the others, dipped my fingers in the holy water, and touched the dead priest's forehead, paying my respects. His face was the only part of him showing, though his jaw was covered with cloth.

I read in the paper that every two hours, a Ugandan dies. Apparently, Father Odo just happened to be driving down the main road to Kampala when two boys flagged him down. It was 11:00 p.m. There had been an accident. Father Odo recognized the car as the local parish's car, but usually the mzungu priest drove it, so he went down into the ditch and found Father Andy still alive, trapped in the smashed car. Father Odo always carried his anointing oils with him in his car, and blessed Father Andy in his last few minutes of life. Father Odo cried as he told me and the Baanabakintu priests the story. A boy was to receive his First Communion that Sunday, and usually Father Andy performed those, but the catechist schedule read that the mzungu priest, Father Paul, would perform the Holy Communion, because, "Father Andy will be traveling that day. He will not be around."

I attended the night mass as well, and sat outside with Father Odo before he went inside the church.

"It will be okay," I told him. "You did the right thing."

"Thank you," he said tearfully. He was still shaken up, still in shock. He was hurting, and scared. "Watching Father Andy die, I was reminded of the story of your first visit to the mortuary after the kabaka's convoy."

The images of that poor boy's blood and brains spilled all over the stained concrete mortuary floor flooded my mind, and I held Father Odo in my track-marked arms. As far as I could tell, the priests never caught on to my addict behavior.

"Why is Uganda plagued with so much death?" Father Odo cried out to the heavens.

The government's laziness in regards to filling the large trenches on the sides of the main roads had claimed another victim. I had fallen into those trenches a couple times walking home from Enro Hotel in the dark, and earned a few scrapes and bruises. This guy lost his life.

When Father Odo finally went into the church, I sat on the brick steps outside the enormous, wooden doors, just getting a glimpse inside. It was a glimpse of a world that was familiar, because I was raised Catholic and because I'd been in Uganda for a couple months; but it was also a glimpse of a world that was so strange, and unfamiliar, and foreign, because it was the exact opposite. I was so far removed from the Catholic Church at that point that even me attending mass for the first time made the priests take notice. My presence in church made them think something must be really fucked up here.

I sat out by the fire and drank Bond 7 Ugandan whiskey from my flask. I took a swig and poured one on the ground for the fallen priest (Noah said they also did that in Uganda). *Rest in peace, homie. Our flags fly at half-mast tonight.*

And in the day, about 3,000 people came from all around the region to Baanabakintu Cathedral for Father Andy's funeral, including the one and only Cardinal in Uganda. He wore a long, ivory white, frilly frock with twenty buttons from his neck to his toes. A long necklace with a large crucifix hung around his neck and a small, bright red yarmulke topped his bald scalp.

I approached him after the funeral on his way to the administration quarters and introduced myself, not bothering to cover my tracks. I figured this guy wouldn't know what they were, anyway. He was an elderly, soft spoken man, and very approachable. I told him who I was and how I traveled across Africa, and he seemed impressed. I was nervous about taking up too much of his time—he was an important man in Uganda—so I said it was nice to meet him and started to wander off. Apparently I left too soon. Father Odo told me later that the Cardinal wanted to continue speaking with me, but I had already started saying my goodbyes. I definitely would have talked to him longer.

The Cardinal led the mass. I had access inside and outside the cathedral, and could move freely at will. I had a knack for gaining unprecedented access to certain restricted areas and to high profile people, both in America and definitely in Africa.

I also met the Mayor of Mityana. We talked politics, and he was very impressed that I was a young politician. I sat next to him and one of the kabaka's officials inside the church. I was moved by Father Andy's colleague's speech, a mzungu priest who worshipped with Father Andy at the same parish. As a native English speaker, his eulogy was translated into Luganda. I was only disappointed by the ending, when the mzungu priest said that Father Adam loved Mother Mary and so whenever we feel grief, his advice was to remember that Mother Mary is with us, whatever the fuck that means.

I wanted from him something tangible. He couldn't provide that.

I had access to the roped-off procession route to the prepared grave. After the mass, about thirty priests, including Father Odo, the Cardinal, and Father Andy's relatives, led the coffin through throngs of people and reporters to the grave site. Moksa the photographer was there taking video of the funeral. The cardinal said some words, they lowered his coffin into the grave by hand, and one by one we all threw a handful of colorful flowers on top.

While this was going on, Noah was at Ssaza Playground, where the Local Government Association was having a big function which the Vice President of Uganda attended. I really wanted to go to that event, but by the time I got there they were wrapping up. I saw the vice president's convoy go by, led and followed by riot police, and I saw the vice president in his SUV. I delivered the tape that Moksa took of the burial to Noah.

Now, Noah was too scared to let me drive him on the boda-boda in town. He didn't trust me, and I hadn't even told him about the accident I had. Even with experienced drivers, he instructed them to slow down or avoid road hazards. He was very nervous about it, but he promised to let me drive him around the first field where I learned how to ride, though not around town. He and Adam and I went to Gaz Bar and had a drink. It began pouring rain; so heavy we couldn't leave. A wasted Ugandan showed up and began talking nonsense. He began to sing and dance for us, and actually entertained Noah, Adam, and I, and had us all laughing, forgetting our various sorrows for the moment, to focus on his.

He sang with energetic gusto, "Oh, I am so lonely, (indecipherable Luganda word). Oh, I'm feeling so lonely, (indecipherable Luganda word)." It's funny what becomes hilarious when all hope seems lost.

· · · · · · · ·

FATHER ODO AND I were watching a live soccer match on TV in the rectory lounge room when he asked me if I knew what African Justice is.

"No, what is it?" I asked.

"It's when you are penalized for something you didn't do, but the revenge doesn't come through."

The question came after the goalkeeper was going for the ball as a striker was preparing to shoot. In soccer, whenever a goalkeeper slides at or kicks at a striker's foot when he's trying to score, the keeper gets an automatic red card. But it wasn't the goalkeeper's intention to kick the striker's ankle, therefore he didn't deserve the red card. It was a bad call, but the other team got a free penalty kick anyway. However, the goalkeeper blocked the ball from going in.

"That," explained Father Odo, "is what we call African Justice."

· · · · · · · ·

IN UGANDA THERE ARE several clans, all named after animals found in the country. That night at dinner the priests asked me what clan I was part of, or wanted to be part of.

"Is there a tortoise clan?" I asked, because I have a pet tortoise.

"No."

"Okay, I will create my own clan," I said.

"Tortoise in Luganda is *nfudu* (pronounced nuh-FOO-doo)," Father Odo explained. "So you are creating the Nfudu Clan, of which you are the only member. So you have to have a new name now, like "Father Odo" instead of "Edward," my real name. How about *kafudu*? That means your clan is small."

The other priests chuckled.

"Did I ever tell you guys that I was ordained online as a reverend with the Universalist Life Church?" I said. "It accepts all faiths. I even have a certificate to prove it. So my new name, my Ugandan clan name, is Reverend Kafudu Chapman."

We all had a good laugh at that one. I told them about my pet tortoise Stockton, named after Hunter S. Thompson's middle name, and they suggested I go see the giant tortoises at the kabaka's palace in Entebbe. Thanks to Noah, I almost made it there. He knew the kabaka's press secretary, and we reached out to him for an interview with the king. But the kabaka was out of town, and I had to get on a plane back to the States before he'd be back. Noah said meeting the kabaka would have been the best thing that ever happened to him.

UNNECESSARY STRIFE

MY LAST COUPLE OF days in Africa were a whirlwind of activity, shoved in-between the morning and evening priorities of being injected with Pethidine, the morphine-like opiate. Each shot cost at least 40,000 shillings and kept getting more expensive, as I kept needing them to up the dosage. It began with half a bottle and grew to four full fucking bottles in one shot. Each time they thought I couldn't handle it, but I didn't care. I was also very quickly running out of money, but those concerns ceased existing as soon as Jumana released the tabs on the butterfly syringe and I fell back into Adam's sober, unconditionally loving arms.

Our situation with the boda-boda was bad. I kept trying to put it off until I left so I wouldn't have to deal with it. We owed the owner a lot of money, and each day he didn't have it he was losing money by not driving people around. Actually, he didn't own the bike; he was renting it, which meant he was getting shit from his boss.

Adam was working, so I followed the directions he gave me to meet up with him. I rode my bike on a path at the top of a deep-green valley. It was a beautiful view, but I was becoming increasingly distracted. When I got there, Adam was almost done helping load a truck with sandbags full of grain, or tea, or something. (I don't know. Doesn't matter.) He didn't get paid right away, though some of his coworkers did, and we were counting on that money. We had taken to pooling our resources.

We had to get to Jumana's living quarters in the hospital compound before 5:00 p.m., and since we no longer had access to a working boda-boda, we both had to ride my rental bike at the same time. He sat on the handle bars and I peddled. It must have been a sight for those Ugandans we passed to see, but it didn't matter. It had to be done.

It had been a sunny day, but as weather in Uganda is wont to do, that changed in an instant. Heavy rain began pouring down on us, so we pulled into a hallway that connected two roads between the Indian market and a small restaurant where we ordered chicken and chips. My vegetarianism had long since gone out the window by then. There wasn't much else to eat but chicken. We ate in silence, watching the dirt roads turn to mud. Afterwards, I lit a cigarette, and Adam went inside the restaurant to get a coke while I sat at the table in the hallway by the bike.

A large Ugandan man approached me and started chastising me for smoking.

"Hey! Here in Uganda we do not smoke," he said. "It is against the law. If you will please assist me in coming to the police station so I may charge you."

"Uh, no," I replied, more than a little confused as to what was happening. "If it's against the law, how was I able to buy these cigarettes legally next door at the Indian market?"

"I must take you to the police station," he repeated. Then he grabbed my arm and started reaching for the wallet in my pocket.

"Adam!" I called into the restaurant. "Adam, help!"

The man immediately let go and a big smile formed on his face.

"Haw haw," he guffawed. "I am only joking. It is okay. Haw haw. I joke hard."

He walked inside and started telling someone the "joke" he just pulled on the mzungu. But the way he gripped my arm and went for my wallet, I knew it was a ploy to get money from me. Adam came out, having not heard my cries for help. I told him what happened and he shook his head.

"Africans are mad," he said.

After about half an hour, the rain stopped as suddenly as it began, so we got back on the bike and continued towards the hospital. We arrived a little late and went to Jumana's room. She wasn't there. It was 5:10, but surely she wouldn't leave without giving me what I needed, would she? We went searching throughout the hospital, where she worked in the maternity ward. One nurse told us she wasn't around, and we were just about to run to Dr. Wagabo's clinic up the road when Adam decided the nurse was lying and charged into the room she was blocking, pushing her out of the way. I followed without looking at her. Jumana was inside with a patient.

"You're late," she smirked, shaking her head. "Wait outside while I finish up with this patient."

We sat down in chairs outside the door. I looked over at the row of beds in the ward, full of pregnant mothers waiting to give birth, all staring at me and Adam. Finally, Jumana exited the room and led us across the grass to the nurse bungalows. A sheet served as her door. We went inside and she prepared my shot. As Adam held my foot to pop up some veins and Jumana poked me with the butterfly syringe, I told them about my Nfudu clan. They got a kick out of it. I named them honorary members of the clan. As I was Kafudu, Adam became Adafudu. Each clan has main male and female members, Seka and Naka respectively, so Jumana became Nakafudu and we named Adam's son

Sekafudu. His real name was Prosper Favour. Naming kids after English words associated with good luck is common practice in central Africa. Dr. Wagabo we named Wafudu and Noah became Nofudu.

It was all very silly but entertaining. You had to keep it lighthearted when, as a white man, you were not-so-subtly manipulating the natives into enabling you to shoot synthetic morphine into your bloodstream twice a day for no good reason.

Jumana gave me a few bottles as a sort of parting gift, because she wouldn't be around the next day, my last full day in Africa. She and Wagabo wanted me to wire them money for the bottles when I returned home, but they didn't honestly expect me to do that. They were pleasantly surprised when I did. She gave the bottles to Adam along with a couple butterfly syringes and wished us well.

On the way home, Adam wanted to buy some weed, so I followed him past the dirt road where Wagabo's clinic was and down a grass hill to a stone wall. Adam pounded on the metal door and we heard a voice in Luganda tell us to go around the gate. We followed the wall to another opening and climbed through. A few naked kids were playing and running around, laundry was drying on ropes, and women stood in dark doorways watching us. We walked up to one of the doorways and Adam told me we had to wait for his connect. After a few minutes, a guy who had clearly just woken up came out with a handful of joints. His nappy dreads smelled like shit.

Adam and I smoked a joint as we walked towards his living quarters in the muddy tenements via an unpopulated and hidden path.

Adam decided to take a shower, which meant walking a few yards away from the door to his family's room and behind a cement wall to pour buckets of freezing cold water over himself. I told him I would catch up with him later.

I didn't want to go back to Baanabakintu Cathedral, so luckily I got a call from Noah. There was a protest going on down the road. He wanted me to meet him there. I rode my bike, and when I arrived, right near where I had just bought weed, there were a couple hundred Ugandans blocking the dirt road with trees they had knocked over. They were pissed because the government never fixed the shitty roads. Swarms of police came in and the situation reached a boiling point. I followed Noah and Moksa around everywhere, because I did not want to get caught in a violent clash. We were standing at the top of the road, which was the top of a steep hill. At the bottom of the road was a bridge, where the protestors had knocked down the trees. Lots of shouting was exchanged, and eventually the police moved the trees and debris themselves, and the protestors meekly and slowly started dissipating and disappearing. The roads remained shitty and unfixed. Nothing was solved.

I rode my bike to the Indian market to buy some mango juice and walked down the hallway to the Internet café. To my surprise, a gorgeous blonde girl was sitting at one of the computers.

"Another mzungu?" I said, sitting down at a computer next to her.

"Not mzungu, Mugandan!" she replied with an American accent.

"Seriously?" I thought for a split second that maybe there were native white Ugandans.

"No, I'm just kidding."

"Oh, I thought for a second you were for real because whenever Ugandans say, 'Hey mzungu!' I always reply, 'Hey Mugandan!' I didn't expect you to know to add the 'M' to 'Ugandan.'"

We made small talk, and I found out that she was staying on the same road as Baanabakintu Cathedral. However, she left abruptly without saying goodbye, just like that German chick

Alondra did at the Robben Island ferry back in Cape Town. Before the "Mugandan" girl's Internet timed out, I looked at what she had been writing. It was a Christian blog.

Oh, shit. Another fucking missionary. Goddammit. Why?

I decided to go by the bungalows where she and several other American missionaries were staying that night, anyway.

Before that, I met up with Noah and Adam at the bar across from Gaz, where we drank Nile Specials and talked. My departure was looming, but none of us were ready for me to leave. I wanted to extend my stay, but I knew if I did I would probably not survive much longer.

I got into a discussion with the woman who owned the nameless bar, which was one room missing its fourth wall, about Obama and gay marriage. People loved Obama in Africa, but they hated that he had just come out in support of the right for homosexuals to get married. Many people were homophobic in Uganda, which was fueled by extremist Christian missionaries, many of whom came from America.

"What do you think about it?" the woman asked me, referring to Obama's support of gay marriage.

"I think it's about damn time," I replied.

"Ah! That means you are a supporter of all those gays."

"Uh, yep. That's exactly what that means."

"But the Bible says it's wrong."

Ugh. If that's going to be someone's argument, that I must believe what they believe because some book written by early, uneducated human beings says so, there's no point in continuing to argue with them.

I owed her some money for beers, so I told the guys I would take a boda-boda down the road to the ATM and be back in fifteen minutes.

I hailed down a boda-boda and hopped on. Noah told the

driver he would pay him, and not to charge me. As we were driving, I asked if the driver had seen me driving around town.

"Yes, very nice job," he said.

"Would you mind if I drove your boda now?"

He pulled over and we switched places. It was tricky getting the thing to start, because it puttered out if I didn't release the hand clutch at the same slow pace that I pulled on the hand accelerator. I drove us down to the ATM and took money out. When we got back on, the boda-boda wouldn't start. The driver tried it himself and he couldn't do it, either. We had no idea what was wrong with it. We had to push it across the street to a garage where it would be repaired in the morning.

Meanwhile, we went around asking every boda-boda driver we could find if I could drive their boda-boda with them and the original driver as passengers. I'm sure they all recognized me or heard about me crashing one of the boda-bodas into a parked car, so they all said no. Eventually, we found someone who agreed. It was hard enough to drive a boda-boda by myself, harder still with one passenger, but two was pushing it. Especially at night.

By the time I pulled into Gaz Bar's dirt parking lot, at least forty-five minutes, if not more, had passed. I saw Noah and Adam emerge from the dark, nameless bar, livid. The three of us got off the motorbike as Noah and Adam started screaming at me and the original driver.

"What the fuck are you doing, Justin?" Noah yelled.

"What? It's fine."

"*No, it's not fine!* You said fifteen minutes. It's been almost an hour."

"We were worried," Adam said.

I tried to explain what happened but Noah couldn't and wouldn't listen. I wondered how pissed he'd be if he knew I'd crashed a boda into a parked car. I still hadn't told him yet. He began berating the original boda driver as the second driver got on his boda-boda and took off. Noah got into an argument with the driver for letting me drive at night and for taking too long.

Noah said he wasn't going to pay him. The driver became irate and tried to appeal to me for payment.

"Come on, Justin," the driver said. "You know what's right here."

Noah separated us and told me he would handle it. I sat down in the bar with Adam and told him why we took so long. Finally, the driver left and Noah rejoined us. After I told him what happened Noah calmed down a little, but was still pissed that I drove at night. I knew he was just worried about me and that he would feel personally responsible if anything happened to me.

"It's so dangerous," he said. "And you don't even know what you're doing."

"Look, everything's fine. No one got hurt. I'm a good driver."

He just shook his head. He was probably right. I was just being stubborn. If I had crashed, I didn't have the money to fix that situation.

Every day I threw the dice.

• • • • • • •

THE NEXT MORNING, AS I was walking my bike up the hill from Baanabakintu to the main road, the driver from the previous night was waiting for me where all the boda-boda drivers hung out.

"That man...is a bad man!" he said, referring to Noah.

"No, he was just worried about me, that's all," I replied. I paid him the 1,000 shillings (about forty cents).

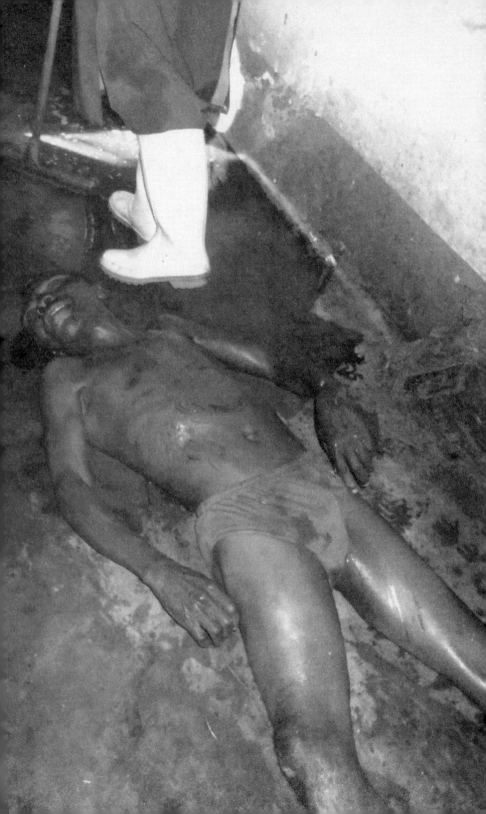

BLINDED BY
THE DARKNESS

As I HEADED TO Adam's place, I thought about the night before. After the kerfuffle outside Gaz, I stopped by the missionary compound on the way home. I knocked on the large, metal gate that protected the compound, and a good-looking Australian man named Jason, who was about thirty-five years old, opened the gate. I told him who I was and that I was staying just down the road with some priests. He turned out to be the head of a particular sect of crazy Christian missionaries that lived on the compound. He invited me into his home. I told him and his wife about my adventures in Africa. They had a newborn baby, Trinity (as in, The Holy). What was interesting, though, was that even though they knew the Catholic Baanabakintu Cathedral was just down the road, they never interacted with the priests I had been staying with, and didn't seem interested to begin doing so. The Catholic priests, when I told them about the missionaries later, also told me that they chose not to associate with the missionaries. It seemed the missionaries were part of a sort of radical sect of Christianity that Catholics wanted no part of. The Australian couple, who had been living there for two years, seemed rational enough, but they were insanely religious, which became clear when certain subjects came up. I tried not to let on that I thought they were full of shit.

Jason decided I should talk to an Indian couple that lived in one of the bungalows on his compound. He walked me over to the main house where they were hanging out with a group of twentysomething Americans, including the gorgeous blonde from the Internet café I had come here to see. She glanced at me once and then pretended like I wasn't there. Not even a hint of recognition.

What the fuck is this?

Jason introduced me to the Indian couple, then he joined the hot blonde in the other room. I heard him say something about "the sin of homosexuality." I wondered if it was in reference to me. I couldn't see any reason why it would be, but, then, I couldn't see any reason for any of this.

The Indian wife told me her story of living in a Hindu community in India. That community hated Christians, and so did she until she went off to university, where she changed her mind and converted. When she returned home, her mother and father cast her out and told the neighbors, who all chased after her and tried to kill her.

"While they were chasing me through a forest, just about to catch me, God made them all blind so I could get away," she said. She was completely serious, and I tried not to laugh in her face.

The husband had marijuana leaves tattooed on his arms. He used to do drugs. He told me he gave up that life, though, and met his wife in Uganda. They said they had decided to put faith to the test and be extremely devout and let God provide for them, without telling anyone what they were doing, for six whole months. Every day they read the Bible and prayed, and while food didn't come every day, it came enough. According to them, they would go weeks without food, and then a neighbor would bring them something before they starved to death. Then another few weeks without food, and just before they were about to give up, they woke up one morning to find hundreds of crickets only on their porch and nowhere else, which they feasted on for a couple days. Again, totally normal looking people, but broach the subject of religion and their insanity oozed out of them.

"We are lucky to have met Jason," said the Indian wife. "He has put a roof over our heads, praise God."

I wanted to say, *Sure, that's nice and all, but missionaries do way more harm than good in Africa by forcing their faith in a society where it doesn't make sense. It has clearly handicapped an already struggling people. I mean, just look at the evil homophobic fervor and hate that your religion has produced.* But I bit my tongue.

Before I left, Jason wanted to lead us all in prayer. He grabbed my hand and his wife's, who joined hands with the Indian couple.

"Praise be to God. We ask you, oh Lord, to look after your servant Justin as you have during his travels in Africa," Jason began, eyes shut tight. "As he prepares to move on to his next adventure, continue to reach out to him and show him that you are the Way..." and on and on he went. It was clear he was aware I thought their God was a fallacy. Still, I didn't tell him I thought what he was doing in Uganda was absolutely disgusting and morally reprehensible. That without his and other missionaries' homophobic and repressive influence, the people of Africa wouldn't be so confused and ashamed. That perhaps it was Christianity itself, mixed with centuries of colonization, that handicapped these people in the first place. That perhaps the native way of life was superior to modern civilization: simpler and somehow more human. But thanks to them, we'll never know.

I left the compound with my stomach all twisted in knots.

· · · · · · · ·

THE NEXT MORNING, AS I walked my bike up the hill to Adam's scheme, I shuddered, remembering the Indian woman's certainty that God had blinded people so she could escape, the tightness of Jason's grip as they prayed, and the look of total nonrecognition on the blonde girl's face when she saw me.

I bought some mango juice and veggie samosas at a small shop, then rode my bike the rest of the way, through the alleys of the tenements, past the drunkards playing chess. I needed a hit. My African chimera was rapidly culminating, and I wasn't ready. It would be a few more months before I got a handle on my addiction, resolved the issues that drove me to use in the first place, and committed to never using ever again.

After Adam helped me shoot the last of the Pethidine into my body and held me as it rushed to my head, washing away all that Jesus malarkey, I stepped outside to smoke a cigarette and got a call from Noah. There was another protest going on, this time at the Mityana Town Council office. I told Adam and we rode my bike together.

A group of young people were upset because they heard the local Mityana government had received some funds that were supposed to be spent on youth programs, but never were. Only a handful of people were protesting in front of the small building, but they were threatening to bring many more. Noah filmed the scene and Adam joined the protest.

"I am a youth, I must join the cause," he said matter-of-factly.

We were waiting for something to happen, so I walked past the three police officers that were stationed there to control any outburst or uprising to the bathroom, a small, concrete stall where the filthy latrine holes were. I pissed and lit a joint. I was only about thirty or forty yards from the police, and it was possible that if they caught me even Noah couldn't help me out of that jam, but luckily I got away with it because apparently they didn't smell it. When I got back, the town clerk, a round, mean-looking Ugandan woman, was calling us into her office to try to talk out the situation. Several of us were crammed inside her tiny office: Adam and a couple others representing the youth protestors, a few police officers and soldiers holding rifles, and present members of the media, including Noah, Moksa, and myself. Of course, I was the only white person in the room. Goes without saying.

They spoke in English, ostensibly for my benefit. The woman was so mad that the protestors had drawn media attention, and the attention of a mzungu, presumably, embarrassing everyone involved. She looked at me once, when I took a picture of her, a look of dyslogistic disbelief on her face, but never again after that. The discussion lasted nearly an hour, and she acknowledged that they had received some money from the federal government, but they didn't have enough to put it into all the areas they wanted. They asked the community what their budget priorities were, and received no response from the youth faction. They decided to divvy the money up and spend a certain amount each year on one thing. That year it was nurse funds; the next year it was going to be youth funds. Adam eventually apologized on behalf of the youth protestors.

• • • • • • •

WHEN ADAM AND I parted ways later that day, he gave me a note that he wrote: "*Hai bro Justin Kafudu, In fact you will take a long time to go away into my memories. Nothing I can say to you but I wish you success in every you do. Say hay to mum, dad & all my friends in US. I love them so much. May God bless & your family. Tell them that their in my hearts for ever. How ever much we struggled when am with you in Uganda. So never for get me in your life. Keep on texting to me and I will do the same. So Good bless you Justin in every thing you do."*

Tears rolled down my cheeks. Adam had shown me pure, unconditional love. I didn't have that back home in the States. Or, at least I thought I didn't.

. . . .

HAVING SAID GOODBYE TO Adam, I made plans to meet Noah for one last beer that night at Gaz. I was waiting for him there when he called me.

"Justin, there has been a boda accident down the road!" he said, eagerness in his voice.

There is a certain detachment from life and excitement about death that comes with being a journalist.

"I'm on my way to my house on a boda to pick up my camera," he continued.

He had to pass Gaz to get to his house, so I told him to stop on the way back to pick me up. We rode the boda-boda down the road, three of us including the driver sandwiched on the small motorbike. It was about 10:00 p.m. and there were no streetlights in Mityana. When we came to the scene, we knew something bad had happened. About thirty people were crowded around something on the ground, by the side of the road. We paid the boda-boda driver and walked through the crowd.

I looked down and saw a dead body, blood staining his shirt and brains leaking out his head. It looked eerily similar to the first dead body I saw during the kabaka's convoy and in the mortuary. Another young man.

We were told he was driving a boda-boda by himself when he was hit from behind by a car, which took off down the road. There were pieces of his boda all over the street, but not the bike itself.

"People who knew him took the damaged boda off the road, because most drivers do not get their bodas registered and are driving around illegally," Noah whispered to me. "If the boda was still here when the police arrived they would confiscate it. The boda is probably very near us, somewhere here in the dark."

I looked around. Everywhere it was pitch black. Noah started taking pictures of the body so I followed suit. We were the only ones who did so. The crowd knew we were journalists. They told Noah in Luganda that someone had witnessed the accident and seen the car that hit this young man, and they were going to find the driver and kill him.

The police commander, a fat, expressionless man, showed up with two officers in a pickup truck. He didn't say a word, and his behavior indicated that this was more than routine. The two officers slipped on plastic gloves, lifted the body, and threw it into the bed of the truck.

They took off into the night and the crowd dispersed. I watched the locals and myself disappear in the darkness.

EPILOGUE:
THE PAST ≠ THE FUTURE

I WAS A HEROIN ADDICT, off and on, for nearly ten years. This book chronicles a time when my addiction largely controlled my behavior and decisions.

People do drugs for a variety of reasons, the main (and most overlooked) being the simple fact that they make you feel really good. If they didn't alter one's consciousness to the point of experiencing something that can't be experienced otherwise, people wouldn't do them. This is important to remember when blaming drug addiction on an addict's weakness, lack of will or self-control, worthlessness or hopelessness, moral ineptitude, or simply labeling it some kind of vague disease and calling it a day.

Today, I am years clean, with a commitment to myself and those I love that I will never try to destroy myself with drugs ever again. Much has changed in terms of who I am, what I want, and how I view myself, life, and the world since I had the experiences chronicled in this book. The Justin writing this epilogue is not the same Justin who traveled Africa. That was another lifetime. Today I love life. I love my life, and I love myself. I don't regret the path I took. I regret the people I hurt who loved me, but I'm proud of myself for "going there and coming back," as my dad put

t. I quit heroin, one of the most powerfully addictive substances on the planet, by myself, forever. (If you think that's impossible, I invite you to not critique what you don't understand, and worry about yourself before you judge others). I learned quite a bit about myself in the process. I learned what I'm capable of: anything. I learned that I am not powerless over my own choices. And I discovered what is truly important to me in this existence.

If you are suffering the pangs of addiction, make it a priority to reevaluate and deeply reflect on why you started using, why you continue to use, and what you stand to gain by overcoming your addiction forever. Figure out what is missing in your life—mentally, emotionally, psychologically, as well as tangibly—and immediately chart a path toward obtaining whatever that is. All it takes is a shift in perspective. Empower yourself into believing that you are capable of controlling the decisions you make. If you think it's hopeless, it will be. Reach out to those who love you. Strengthen your support network. Do not be afraid or embarrassed to ask for help. Addiction does not define the real you, so don't let people put you in a box. I don't.

The past does not equal the future. Who you were yesterday does not define who you are today, and who you can be tomorrow. Your life is entirely yours to create. The possibilities are limitless.

ACKNOWLEDGEMENTS

MANY THANKS ARE DUE to many people for helping make this book a reality.

First and foremost, thank you Tyson Cornell, Alice Marsh-Elmer, Julia Callahan, and everyone at Rare Bird for taking a chance on a new, unpublished author. I am proud to join the ranks of your authors.

Seth Fischer, without you this book wouldn't be the amazing book it is today. Thank you for your advice, your patience, and your trust in me. You knew what I was trying to say and helped me say it. Thanks for helping me bring out my voice.

Mom and Dad, thank you and I'm sorry for all the worry I put you through. I love you and Galvin and Kelsey and the rest of our big clan so much. Thanks for always being there for me, for always seeing greatness in me even when I didn't.

Thank you Gramps for all your support. You were there for me in one of the hardest times of my life.

Mercedes, thank you for your help in making this book happen and your beautiful work on me. I wouldn't be who I am today without you. I love you.

Irvine Welsh, thank you for your incredible compliment. Your books taught me to be fearless in my writing, which has been the most important lesson of all.

Jerry Stahl, thank you for your advice, your books, your leadership, and for connecting me with Rare Bird. You showed me that happiness was possible for people with our past.

Everyone who worried about me while I was in Africa, thank you, you're why I came back.

Thank you Luke and Alex, your friendship got me through it. Thank you Father Kizito and everyone else throughout Africa who took me in and took care of me. Your kindness will never be forgotten.

Thank you Tom and Dorothy for giving me a reason to go to Africa in the first place. Art Aids Art continues to be an inspiration and sheer proof that individuals can make a difference.

Sid and Nancy, many thanks for your coaching and support.

Thank you Jay, Tori, Dan, Kevin, Joe, André, Tim, Gillian, Derek, Solveig, Corien, Byron, Wendy, Rachael, Roanne, Stacy, David, Shai, Jim, and everyone else who helped me become the traveler and writer I am today.

And special thanks to the People of Africa. You taught me how to appreciate life in ways I never knew existed.